UNASHAMED ANGLICANISM

UNASHAMED
ANGLICANISM

Stephen Sykes

DARTON·LONGMAN+TODD

FOR KEITH AND JEAN
FRIENDS

First published in 1995 by
Darton, Longman and Todd Ltd
1 Spencer Court
140–142 Wandsworth High Street
London SW18 4JJ

ISBN 0–232–52103–4

A catalogue record for this book is available
from the British Library

Phototypeset in 10/13pt Bembo by Intype, London
Printed and bound in Great Britain by
Page Bros, Norwich

Contents

Acknowledgements

The first publication of the essays collected in this volume is given below. Where publication was in several countries, the British publisher is listed here, or the first publisher if the essay has not been published in Britain.

Introduction:
Newly published.

Part I: DRAWING FROM OUR ROOTS

1. 'Baptisme doth Represente unto us Oure Profession'
   Margot Johnson (ed.), *Cranmer, a Living Influence for 500 Years: a Collection of Essays by Writers Associated With Durham* (Durham, Turnstone Ventures, 1990), pp. 122–143.
2. Cranmer on the Open Heart
   D. S. Armentrout (ed.), *The Sacred History* (Mass., Cowley Publications, 1990), pp. 1–18.
3. 'Love Bade Me Welcome'
   Newly published.
4. The Fundamentals of Christianity
   Stephen Sykes and John Booty (eds.), *The Study of Anglicanism* (London, SPCK, 1989), pp. 231–245.
5. Richard Hooker and the Ordination of Women to the Priesthood
   J. M. Soskice (ed.), *After Eve* (London, Collins, 1990), pp. 118–137.

Part II: THE ANGLICAN DOCTRINE OF THE CHURCH

6. Anglicanism and the Anglican Doctrine of the Church
   J. Robert Wright (ed.), *Quadrilateral at One Hundred* (Anglican Theological Review, 1988), pp. 156–177.

7. Foundations of an Anglican Ecclesiology

   Living the Mystery (London, Darton, Longman and Todd, 1994), pp. 28–48.

8. Authority in the Anglican Communion

   Anglican Primates' Meeting, Washington USA, April 1981, *Four Documents on Authority in the Anglican Communion* (London, Anglican Consultative Council, 1981), pp. 1–17.

9. Authority in the Church of England

   Robert Jeffery (ed.), *By What Authority?* (London, Mowbray, 1987), pp. 7–25.

10. Episcopé and Power in the Church

   Bruce D. Marshall (ed.), *Theology and Dialogue, Essays in Conversation with George Lindbeck* (Notre Dame, Indiana, Notre Dame Press, 1990), pp. 191–212.

Part III: ANGLICAN DIRECTIONS

11. An Anglican Theology of Evangelism

   Sewanee Theological Review 34.4 (1991), 11–18, with material added from the version published in *Theology* (November/December 1991), pp. 405–414.

12. The Genius of Anglicanism

   G. Rowell (ed.), *The English Religious Tradition and the Genius of Anglicanism* (Wantage, Ikon, 1992), pp. 227–241.

Introduction

To announce that one is not ashamed of Anglicanism is perhaps to invite a certain gentle ridicule. After all, St Paul was not ashamed of the Gospel (Rom. 1:16). Have we got to the point where theologians have a greater concern for nice denominational distinctions than for the very faith itself?

The relationship between biblical faith and the life of a modern Christian denomination is by no means simple. It would be convenient, of course, if it were possible to say that whereas all Christians are agreed about the biblical fundamentals, the different denominations are in disagreement only about extra details or peripheral matters. But a moment's thought reveals that this is not the case. The disagreements between denominations are about the interpretation of the Bible itself. Does the Bible require us to believe that Jesus himself founded a Church equipped with the means for deciding all future faith questions with complete certitude? Does the biblical doctrine of justification by faith relativise each and every attempt to create an institutional or structural means for governing the Church? Does the Bible require or forbid baptism of infants? Can the credal formulations of the later Church be imposed as a criterion of the right interpretation of the biblical writings? Does Scripture determine the place of women in the church? None of these is a minor detail or a peripheral matter, and the denominations differ on how to resolve them.

The Anglican Communion is one family or federation of Provinces within the One, Holy, Catholic and Apostolic Church. The Provinces of the Anglican Communion are legally autonomous, but morally interdependent. They are internally complex and comprehensive – but not uniquely so. Most Christian denominations can rightly claim a measure of comprehensiveness, including the most overtly centralised, the Roman Catholic Church. Most Christian denominations also experience internal struggles and consequent problems concerning the delineation of their unity and identity, for reasons which will shortly be explained. It is precisely out of these struggles that the urgent question arises of a twofold coherence, with the Gospel itself on the one hand and with brothers and sisters of the same public allegiance on the other. All Churches develop a more or less loose way of promoting their own coherence. Let us call that a 'language'. The 'language' of Anglicans includes not just the circulation of specific concepts (drawn from their authorised documents), but also the tone and colouring given to all internal communication by the way Anglicans structure themselves in a hierarchy and synods. People who in later life become Anglicans, having been members of another denomination, find themselves in effect learning a new language. They have to become fluent in Anglican. Exactly the same is true of new members of the Orthodox Churches, of Roman Catholics, of Baptists, of Methodists, of Lutherans, or of Presbyterians. Each denomination has a system of communication which its members absorb, sometimes quite unconsciously, and which enables them to communicate with speed and fluency inside their own churches. Certain words and phrases are sometimes key indicators of belonging. Attitudes to office-bearers and skills in decoding official pronouncements are developed. None of this is any way disgraceful or a cause of shame. Indeed it is simply inevitable in any large-scale denomination.

But what is the relationship between such 'languages' and the Gospel, the other side of the coherence question? The metaphor of language does not entirely help at this point. It is not the case that 'the Gospel' is another language. The relationship between what St Paul meant by 'the Gospel' in Romans and the 'language' of Anglicanism, or of any other denomination, has to be explained in another way. We are obliged to focus on the rise of institutions as conveyers, vehicles or means for sustaining the proclamation of the Gospel. Modern sociology has developed the concept of the 'routinisation of charisma' (Max Weber) to interpret what happens when a movement initiated by a 'charismatic leader' (in the secular sense of the word 'charismatic') has to provide for its continuance after the leader's departure.[1] There are problems of stable leadership and of finance to solve. The movement's charismatic potential has to be conveyed through organised, regular channels. Routines replace immediate inspiration; and on Weber's own analysis, the process is already at work in St Paul's own churches. In these there is evidence of considerable concern over who the real leaders are, in St Paul's absence, and whether, and how, any leader is to be paid.

All this is a long way, of course, from a modern denomination (let alone the Church of England with its Church Commissioners, investment portfolio, Pensions Board and Boards of Finance). But it is obvious enough that the early Church's growth in size imposed organisational problems, notably the preservation of unity; and in due course the building of its own churches exacerbated questions of finance and authority. A modern denomination has the task of proclamation and of reasonable organisational efficiency; or rather it must aim at the kind of efficiency which serves the ends of the Gospel which it professes. There has to be an instantiation or embodiment of the Gospel in the institutional reality of a particular denomination, the Churches of the Anglican Communion included.

In the collected volume entitled *The Study of Anglicanism* (which Professor John Booty and I edited in 1989), the longest chapter was devoted to an account of 'the Gospel in Anglicanism'. This was a deliberate indication of the fact that we, the editors, held that the most important matter for interpretation within the phenomenon of Anglicanism was how it proclaims the Gospel. Yet the challenge to any denomination is not merely to preach the Gospel in words, but to live and exemplify the Gospel in its structures and disciplines. Every part of the life of the Church, the totality of the system of communication by which it promotes its own coherence and effectiveness, ought to stand for a facet of the Gospel. There should not be a sharp division between what a Church teaches and how it manages its institutional arrangements. A denomination is bound to teach a theology of the Church, and that theology has necessarily to refer to its own institutional being as Church. The truth about the Church has to be done as well as spoken. The Pauline sentence, 'I am not ashamed of the Gospel', therefore, implies taking seriously the question of whether one is ashamed of being an Anglican.

One of the essays in this collection is specifically devoted to recent Anglican reticence on this matter ('Anglicanism and the Anglican Doctrine of the Church', pp. 101–121 below). A prominent tradition of major Anglican interpreters has advanced the idea that 'Anglicans have no special doctrines of their own'. At best this proposition could only be half true. Against it I argue that Anglicans are obliged to teach that the Church to which they belong has the authority to determine what constitutes a sufficient statement of the apostolic faith, and to decide controversies about the faith. And since it manifestly does so in a way which is different from other denominations, it professes implicitly a doctrine of the Church which is special to itself. In my view Anglicans have the responsibility of articulating that doctrine, so that it may be studied by others and subjected to criticism and correction. The normal Christian quest for the truth must apply to Anglican claims, explicit and implicit. Not to be ashamed of Anglicanism would mean the exposure of the explicit and implicit claims Anglicans make about themselves as part of the One, Holy, Catholic and Apostolic Church.

These claims are, however, relatively modest compared with those of the Roman Catholic or Orthodox Churches; and the ecumenical movement has set all denominational claims in a new perspective. So it is important to press the question whether concern for Anglicanism might not represent a 'neo-confessional backlash' against the kind of indifference to internal denominational coherence which passionate concern for the unity of the Churches engenders. Anglicans were, in the early years of this century, prominent in promoting Christian unity. Is late twentieth-century 'unashamed Anglicanism' unashamedly content to promote and reinforce a distinct identity?

The plain answer to this question is an emphatic negative. At no stage in its history has Anglicanism presented itself as the purest form of the Christian faith. The words of Arthur Michael Ramsey are classic on this point: 'it [the Anglican Church] is sent not to commend itself as "the best type of Christianity", but by its very brokenness to point to the universal Church wherein all have died.'[2] All forms of Anglicanism can at best be a contribution to the Church Catholic, and in themselves only provisional. Nothing is right merely because it is Anglican.

At the same time Anglicans have no business tolerating something which is wrong and Anglican. They have a duty to reform and reshape what is wrong. And the fact that something is a feature of Anglicanism compels Anglicans to ask whether or not it is commendable. As a result the defence of something which is plainly Anglican is not itself surprising or even disgraceful. Moreover, the very fact that Anglicans have learnt lessons of tolerance during their turbulent history may itself be worth commending. It is a marked feature of English culture, and the whole of international Anglicanism has been influenced by it. Demanded by Baptists, Congregationalists and Quakers in the seventeenth century, toleration was partially conceded in the Act of Toleration of 1689. Though the point of the Act was to unite English Protestants against Roman Catholicism, specifically in the person of the deposed sovereign James II, it nonetheless gradually taught the English people that disagreement about religious doctrines did not entail either civil disorder or religious indifferentism. Moreover there were, from the seventeenth century, those who argued that religious freedom of conscience corresponded to, and was required by, the voluntary nature of Christian belief.

The twentieth-century history of this tradition has seen some notable landmarks. The provision of the Butler Education Act of 1944 for undenominational Christian religious education in Welsh and English state schools has been celebrated by the Anglican historian, Norman Sykes (no relation), in *The English Religious Tradition* (1955) as an example of 'the English [sic] genius for compromise'. Religious broadcasting on the BBC is another example of how different religious traditions can co-operate within a framework of religious toleration. The explicit affirmation of freedom of conscience as the foundation and pre-condition of Christian belief, given in the Second Vatican Council's Declaration on Religious Liberty, greatly strengthened the central Christian consensus on this matter. It might indeed have been a moment when Anglicanism emerged as vindicated by history. The Roman Catholic Church moderated the excessive papalism of the Counter Reformation and qualified the centralising tendencies of the First Vatican Council. It endorsed the long-established Anglican traditions of lay Bible study and the use of the vernacular in the liturgy.

What could have developed at this stage was a strong ecumenical consensus. Instead Anglicanism began to betray some serious internal tensions. Whereas the thirty-year process of Anglican-Roman Catholic ecumenical discussion was launched in 1966, simultaneously Anglicanism, especially in England, began to demonstrate the symptoms of a failure of nerve about its own identity. Did the Church really believe in the central doctrines of the Christian faith as traditionally taught, the

Holy Trinity, the incarnation, the atoning work of Christ? Or was there now to be a greater comprehensiveness to embrace a radically 'non-supernatural' interpretation of belief? From Bishop John Robinson's *Honest to God* (1963), to the non-Trinitarian theologies of Professors Wiles and Lampe (1976 and 1977), the publicised doubts of Bishop Jenkins and the post-modernism of Don Cupitt, the theological agenda for Anglicanism appeared to throw into question its very participation in the development of a central ecumenical consensus.

It must be acknowledged, of course, that the last twenty years of theological history have brought about new alignments in all the Churches. In addition to a continuing, and strong, traditional trinitarian incarnationism, every Christian denomination, except the Orthodox Churches, has developed radical wings of the kind mentioned in relation to the Church of England. These were the years in which Professor Hans Küng developed his own moderately radical programme, and was denied official use of the term 'Catholic' to describe his theological lectures and publications. Other Roman Catholic theologians in Europe and the Americas have been disciplined in the same process. Radical alliances across the denominations have briefly flourished. Alarmingly authoritarian traits have appeared in high places. Nor must one fail to mention a third force, which is likewise interdenominational: the charismatic movement. Though broadly supportive of traditional theology, charismatics often have a very different attitude to the Church's structures and to theological scholarship. Characteristically they too have very little investment in specifically denominational differences.

But working to loosen the sense of identity was a far more deeply-laid trait in Anglicanism. This was, strangely enough, the ambivalent role of the Oxford Movement itself, as it lost touch with its own historic origins. On the one hand the very term 'Anglicanism' was a coinage of the Oxford Movement, perhaps even of the Anglican Newman himself who used it in an essay of 1838.[3] From the first, the account given of this Anglicanism had a more than descriptive function. It involved the recognition of a 'classic' epoch, that of the seventeenth-century Caroline divines, whose self-understanding (it was asserted) might be taken as normative. The theory of Anglicanism has been a constant preoccupation of successors to the Tractarians.[4]

On the other hand this same tradition has played a major role in weakening Anglicanism's claim to a consistent identity, by throwing into doubt its status as a confession. A characteristic of each of the major Churches of the European Reformation was its production of a 'confession', as a public statement of theological identity and as a foundation charter for the life of the Church. Although at an early stage the Church of England produced its own Articles (later to be known as the Thirty-nine Articles), and although these were extensively modelled upon the Lutheran Confessio Augustana of 1530, at no stage in the life of the Church of England have these Articles had the exclusive status of the confessions of the Lutheran or Calvinist Churches. The impact of the nineteenth-century Oxford Movement was further to weaken the status of the Articles, without providing any clear substitute.[5] Tractarian writers produced catenae of quotations from the Caroline divines to support high-church doctrines. But it was soon recognised that these were selective, and that many major Anglican divines could be quoted in an altogether different sense. Some Tractarians openly denigrated the actions, theology, and confessional and liturgical productions of the sixteenth-century English reformers. The movement to separate international Anglicanism from its sixteenth-century 'confessional' basis in Articles, Book of Common Prayer and Ordinal can be traced through the Lambeth Conferences from 1867 to 1968, when a hastily constructed motion encouraging member Churches not even to print the Articles in their prayer books was passed with few abstentions.[6] (The author remembers a conversation with Arthur Michael Ramsey, who presided at the Conference as Archbishop, in which he expressed regret at the speed of this action.)

Provided one realises that the Articles, Prayer Book and Ordinal were only 'confessional' in a rather specific and different way, it is not unfair to regard these nineteenth-century and twentieth-century developments as a history of 'deconfessionalisation'. Out of it came the shibboleth that 'Anglicans have no special doctrines of their own', which was intended to emphasise the strongly patristic formation of Anglicanism: what Anglicans confess (so it was said) is the faith of undivided Christendom of the earliest (five or six) centuries. It was a serious matter, therefore, when two leading Anglican patristic scholars, Maurice Wiles and Geoffrey Lampe, Regius Professors in both Oxford and Cambridge, publicly argued against trinitarian incarnationalism.[7] What then did Anglicans believe? Were there no limits to

Anglican toleration? Was the long-honoured tradition of comprehen-siveness now to include a 'liberalism', 'modernism' or 'radicalism' (the labels were various and imprecise) which denied or held in doubt the doctrines of the Trinity and incarnation, and even of the classical doctrine of God? Suddenly, at a moment when the central Anglican tradition ought to have been celebrating its ecumenical and inter-national coming of age, it was plunged into an anxious and self-absorbed debate about its own identity.[8] *The Integrity of Anglicanism*, which I published in 1978, attempted to deal with the question of liberalism and comprehensiveness. It was written on the basis of the English Anglican agenda, but reviews elsewhere indicated that it had relevance to other situations within the Anglican communion.

But in truth there were two aspects to the agenda for Anglicanism, not one. 'Liberalism', which was a convenient label for a variety of concerns – historical relativism, anti-hierarchicalism, pluralism, and, in due course, post-modernism – was an international phenomenon, bearing upon every Christian denomination. So also was the second major challenge, that of liberation theology, though at first international Anglicanism was less overtly involved in liberation struggles than was, for example, the Roman Catholic Church. In part the reason for this was the Anglican Church's weakness in Latin America, where in the late 1970s, the impact of liberation theology was first felt.

But the criticism levelled at the theology of the academy for its lack of involvement in activity on behalf of the poor manifestly applied to 'classic Anglicanism'. Implicitly the theology applied to the political and social condition of Africa, where Anglicanism was both numeri-cally strong and institutionally identified with colonialism.

In due course the feminist version of liberation theology was bound to challenge the priestly patriarchalism of Western catholicism. Here the North American feminist movement made and still makes the running. Among the topics which are deeply affected by feminism (which embraces a wide variety of procedures, demands and proposals) are the doctrines of God, the Holy Trinity, the incarnation, the atoning work of Christ, priesthood, and Eucharist. Some Anglicans at least, making common cause with forms of more radical feminism, obliterate virtually all signs of traditional denominational identity in their search for authentic liberation.

How then do matters fare for Anglicanism? On the face of it, it is in crisis, having been redefined in the nineteenth century as possessing no distinctive traits, and then in the later twentieth century having its allegedly normative patristic identity subjected to devastating internal and external body-blows. But all is not what it seems. None of these important challenges has actually been an unqualified success. There is an elusive but real corporate identity which persists, by no means unchastened or unchanged, but discernibly and in actuality. As a concrete example one may take the survival of the Chicago-Lambeth Quadrilateral of 1888, the list of four features of the practice of the Church, a kind of hierarchy of usage,[9] advanced as a basis for ecumenism.

> That, in the opinion of this Conference, the following Articles supply a basis on which approach may be by God's blessing made towards Home Reunion:
>
> (a) The Holy Scriptures of the Old and New Testaments, as 'containing all things necessary to salvation,' and as being the rule and ultimate standard of faith.
>
> (b) The Apostles' Creed, as the Baptismal Symbol; and the Nicene Creed, as the sufficient statement of the Christian faith.
>
> (c) The two Sacraments ordained by Christ Himself — Baptism and the Supper of the Lord — ministered with unfailing use of Christ's words of Institution, and of the elements ordained by Him.
>
> (d) The Historic Episcopate, locally adapted in the methods of its administration to the varying needs of the nations and peoples called of God into the Unity of His Church.

As the 1988 Lambeth Conference indicated, there is still considerable agreement that these articles remain a central Anglican contribution to ecumenism.[10] Of importance, of course, is the explicit trinitarian content of the Nicene Creed. The challenge to trinitarian incarnation in modern theology, mounted from a variety of sources, has not resulted in abandonment of the status of the doctrine in the Church's public confessions. On the contrary, contemporary theology shows every sign of a return to a renewed and deepened grasp on the doctrine of the Holy Trinity, even within certain strands of feminism.[11]

Neither is there any apparent weakening in the grasp of Anglicans upon the implications of the episcopal office for its life and unity, difficult though the abandonment of the male-only tradition is and will be. Again, on the contrary, the signs are that ecumenical questioning is forcing Anglicanism to a deeper articulation of its grounds for persisting with the episcopate, within the context of the apostolic character of the Church as a whole and not in opposition to it, or in isolation from it.[12] The long tradition of the bishop-in-synod evidently has a future, not just a past.

Perhaps most obvious of all is the persistence of international Anglicanism with its inheritance of Scripture-in-liturgy, that is of using the common worship of the Church as the educational matrix for the reading and the teaching of the Scriptures. Of course, there is a loosening of the ties of the ancient Prayer Books. Alarmists have greatly exaggerated the implications of this, and have underestimated the implications of the international and ecumenical liturgical movement of the twentieth century in providing stability and coherence to the numerous revisions of, or alternatives to, the standard Books of Common Prayer. What in effect has happened is that in place of clones or translations of the 1662 *Book of Common Prayer*, the provinces of the Anglican communion have produced a range of liturgical books with a common family resemblance. This has occurred not without anxiety, or controversy, as a Resolution of the Lambeth Conference of 1988 indicated.[13] But 'family resemblance' does not require that each member of the series should possess every one of a list of essential features. It survives the occasional eccentric production. But the Anglican Provinces all evidently believe that the Church of Jesus Christ must be one in lifting up heart and hands in the common praise of its Lord and Saviour, when it meets together 'to render thanks for the great benefits it has received at his hands'.

Not to be ashamed of Anglicanism means, therefore, to offer one's fellow Christians the experience of living the Christian faith within this tradition. Occasionally one glimpses aspects of other traditions of which one is inclined to be critical; so there always is a danger of self-satisfaction about any such offering. Provided one does not stand in the centre of the temple and loudly thank God that one is not like other denominations, Orthodox, Roman Catholics, Lutherans, Calvinists, Methodists or even like this Baptist, there is nothing lost within the fellowship of the One Church in the deployment of a modest argument in favour of certain traditions. If these traditions have shown what Newman once called 'chronic vigour' (a feature he denied to Anglicanism, having recently become a Roman Catholic), then there is good reason to explore their basis and potential.

Each one of the essays which follow were written rather more out of surprise and gratitude than out of defensiveness. They begin with five explorations of the Anglican inheritance of faith, specifically in relation to the sacraments and the ministry. Careless, one-line dismissals of the past are one of the diseases of our culture, and reformers are always prone to simplify their task by constructing and then pulling down figures of straw. On closer examination, however, the classic documents and writers of the Anglican past, including the Books of Common Prayer and the works of Thomas Cranmer, Richard Hooker and George Herbert, contain a truly inspiring richness of theological insight. The modern reception of this tradition need be no uncritical celebration of it. The essay on the 'Fundamentals of Christianity' attempts to draw lessons from the failure of that theological device to resolve with economy and precision a very complex problem of theological method.

The second section argues that Anglicans must openly state their doctrine of the Church, and offers a preliminary sketch of ways in which that doctrine can be explicated. The currently important questions of authority and *episcope* can only be approached within the context of an ecclesiology. I readily acknowledge that much more work needs to be done in this area. But we need not berate ourselves unduly for our failings, as though they were unique to Anglicanism. Dogmatic ecclesiology is in systematic disarray in the Churches as a whole. The peculiar urgency for Anglicans is that their insistence on the retention and commendation of episcopacy immediately tumbles them into the heart of an ecclesiological argument. Experience shows how wide is the range of issues which must then be considered, not least the urgent question of a theology of power.

Finally, I offer two contemporary pieces which put, so to speak, the Anglican tradition to work. In *Renewal of Anglicanism*, Dr Alister McGrath mildly remarks on the absence of 'evangelism' from the index of *The Study of Anglicanism* (1988).[14] Despite the fact that that book contains whole chapters on 'The Newer Dioceses of the Anglican Communion', where startling church growth has taken place, and on

'Anglicans and Mission', the criticism has a point. Classic Anglicanism saw its task largely in terms of the deepening and disciplining of the lives of the already baptised. Anglicans engaged in missionary and evangelising thought and activity have drawn more directly on the Scriptures themselves for their theologies of evangelism. But then both classic and modern Anglicanism have always insisted on the normativity of Scripture. My essay on evangelism attempts to show that there can be a biblical approach to evangelising which rests on the Anglican tradition of liturgical praise, rather than on dubious nineteenth-century and twentieth-century models.

Finally, the exigencies of a particular course of lectures in celebration of the bicentenary of John Keble extracted from me an essay on the 'genius' of Anglicanism. It is an earlier use of the term 'genius', to refer neutrally to the characteristic temper of mind, which was intended. From the eighteenth century onwards 'genius' came to mean an extraordinary, even divinely inspired capacity for original creation. Though I would not hesitate to affirm that God has work for Anglicans to do, self-satisfaction ill becomes us. That family of Churches which constitutes the Anglican family is undoubtedly growing more disparate, and like other denominations has some difficulty in preserving its coherence. Its contribution to the kingdom of God can only be described as modest. Its failings and weaknesses are all too clear. But they are not, I judge, mortal; and the journalistically circulated rumour of the demise of the Anglican Communion is greatly exaggerated.

Anglicans have the blessed freedom of enjoying the beneficial fruits of all the major traditions of Christian faith. They may study the early Christian writers, and go to school with the medieval philosophers. Luther and Calvin, Zinzendorf and Schleiermacher, Newman and Barth, can be their conversation partners. They may thank God for Karl Rahner and Henri de Lubac, Vladimir Lossky and Georges Florovsky. Provided they recognise contradiction when it occurs, and do not fail to appreciate the depth of other traditions, their own tradition can be an astonishing joy and liberation, a finding that their feet have been set in a very large room indeed. In that sense I have come unashamedly to love the Anglican inheritance of faith, and I long to assist the realisation of its potential among the Churches of God's rich and diverse economy.

NOTES

1. 'Routinisation' is an attempt to translate a German noun *Veralltaglichung*. See M. Weber, *The Theory of Social and Economic Organization* (NY, 1964); for commentary, F. N. Eisenstadt, *Max Weber on Charisma and Institution Building* (Chicago, 1968) and M. Hill, *A Sociology of Religion* (London, 1973) ch. 7.

2. A. M. Ramsey, *The Gospel and the Catholic Church* (London, 1936), p. 220.

3. See P. Avis 'What is "Anglicanism"?' in S. Sykes and J. Booty (eds.), *The Study of Anglicanism* (London, 1988), p. 407.

4. See P. E. More and F. L. Cross, *Anglicanism: The Thought and Practice of the Church of England, Illustrated from the Religious Literature of the Seventeenth Century* (London, 1962).

5. This has been skilfully expounded by Paul Avis in his wide-ranging survey, *Anglicanism and the Christian Church* (Edinburgh, 1989), esp. Part Three.

6. Resolution 43, The Lambeth Conference 1968 (London, 1968), pp. 40f; see also Addendum, 'The Thirty-Nine Articles and the Anglican Tradition', pp. 82f.

7. See their contributions to A Report by the Doctrine Commission of the Church of England, *Christian Believing* (London, 1976).

8. An important work which analyses this crisis is William S. Sachs, *The Transformation of Anglicanism: From State Church to Global Communion* (Cambridge, 1993). It does, however, overemphasise the negative aspect of the situation, for lack of comparative material relating to other denominations.

9. Argued in S. W. Sykes, 'Episcopacy, Communion and Collegiality', in *Anvil* 5, 2 (1988), pp. 101–12.

10. See Resolution 18, The Lambeth Conference 1988, *The Truth Shall Make You Free* (London, 1988), pp. 216f, and 'Ecumenical Relations', paras 54–6, pp. 136f.

11. See, for example, C. M. La Cugna, *God for Us: The Trinity and Christian Life* (San Francisco, 1991).

12. Notable evidence lies in the international Anglican-Lutheran dialogue, especially *The Niagara Report* (1987), *Toward Full Communion and Concordat of Agreement* (1991) and *Together in Mission and Ministry* (Porvoo Common Statement) (1993).

13. Resolution 18, pp. 216–7, asking for an Anglican Advisory Body on Prayer Books of the Anglican Communion.

14. Alister McGrath, *The Renewal of Anglicanism* (London, 1993), p. 25.

PART I

DRAWING
FROM OUR ROOTS

1

'BAPTISME DOTH REPRESENTE UNTO US OURE PROFESSION'

Modern hermeneutical theory should alert us to the fact there is a diversity of ways in which a liturgical text can be 'read' and that the 'reader' should himself or herself become the subject of careful reflection. This is especially the case when one considers that a significant number of those who 'read', for example a baptismal liturgy, have themselves been performers of the ritual drama to which it points. It alters one's relation to a text when one has been involved to that degree; and the liturgy of baptism is, or should be, nothing if not self-involving for all participants, as we shall see.

It is, perhaps, a difficulty with this line of argument that the text which we shall consider, that of the 1552 *Book of Common Prayer*, is liturgically obsolete, having been replaced first by the lightly revised but standard text of 1662, and secondly by the widely used revision of 1928 (An Alternative Order of the Ministration of Publick Baptism of Infants). None the less we shall assume first that, because Cranmer's 1552 text was substantially retained in later revisions, it can be read from the standpoint of a participant; and, secondly, that such a reading should focus on structures, dramatic actions, rhythms and repetitions, as well as upon overt doctrinal context.

Anglicans, of course, have a further motive for taking seriously the text of 1662. The Church of England declares in its canon law that its doctrines may be found in particular in its Articles, Prayer Book and Ordinal.[1] It is true that a later Canon qualifies this by speaking of those sixteenth-century and seventeenth-century documents in the past tense as 'this inheritance of faith'; but even here it demands, from those who make the Declaration of Assent, loyalty to that inheritance as an example of how God has guided the Church in the past.[2] This is to

3

726 PUBLIC BAPTISM

SOURCES

1549

PUBLIKE BAPTISME

⚭ Non plures quam vnus vir & vna mulier debent accedere ad suscipiendum paruulum de sacro fonte . . . nisi alia fuerit consuetudo approbata : tunc tamen vltra tres amplius ad hoc nullatenus recipiantur.

H parentes infantium Pastoribus Ecclesiarum id maturius significare, & ab iis Baptismum . . . infantibus suis petere humiliter debent. . .

⚭ In primis deferatur infans ad valuas ecclesie :

When there are children to be Baptised vpon the Sonday, or holy daye, the parentes shall geue knowledge ouer nyght or in the mornyng, afore the beginning of Mattyns to the curate. And then the Godfathers, Godmothers, and people, with the children, muste be ready at the churche doore, either immediatly afore the last Canticle at Mattens, or els immediatly afore the last Canticle at Euensong, as the Curate by his discrecion shal appoynte. And then

& inquirat sacerdos ab obstetrice vtrum sit infans masculus an femina. Deinde si infans fuerit baptizatus domi :

standing there, the pryeste shall aske whether the chyldren bee Baptysed or no. If they aunswere .No. Then shall the prieste saye thus.

H Lieben freunde in Christo, wir hören alle tag auss Gottes wort . . . Das wir von Adam her alle sampt in sünden empfangen vund geboren werden . . .

S. Jo. iii 5

DEare beloued, forasmuche as al men be conceyued and borne in sinne, and that no man borne in synne, can enter into the kingdom of God (except he be regenerate, and borne a newe of water, and the holy gost) I beseche you to cal vpon God the father through our Lord Iesus Christ, that of his bounteouse mercy he wil graūt to these childrē that thing whiche by nature they cannot haue, that is to saye, they maye be Baptised with the holy ghost, and receyued into Christes holy churche, and bee made lyuely membres of the same.

Necessary doctrine f. Q iv. : made againe the liuely membres of Christis mysticall body.

L Last vns beten.

Almechtiger Ewiger Gott der du hast durch die sindflutt, nach deynem gestrengen gericht, die vngleubige welt verdampt, vnd den gleubigen Noe selb acht, nach deyner grosssen barmhertzigkeyt, erhalten. Vnnd den verstockten Pharao mit allen seynen ym rotten mer ersewfft, vnd deyn volck Israel trockenn durch hin gefuret, damit dis bad deyner heyligen tauffe zukunfftig bezeychnet, vnd durch die tauffe deyns liebes kindes vnsers herren Ihesu Christi den Iordan vnd alle wasser zur seyligen sindfluth vnd reychlicher abwasschung der sun-

Then the priest shall saye.

Let vs praye.

ALmyghtie and euerlasting God, whiche of thy iustice didest destroy by floudes of water the whole worlde for sinne, excepte .viii. persons, whome of thy mercye (the same tyme) thou dydest saue in the Arke : And when thou dydest drowne in the reade sea wicked King Pharao with all his armie, yet (at the same time) thou didest lead thy people the children of Israel safely through the middes therof : whereby thou diddest figure the washing of thy holy baptisme : & by the baptisme of thy welbeloued sōne Iesus Christ, thou

Figure I: From F. E. Brightman, *The English Rite* (London, 1915) II, pp. 726f.

1552

PUBLIQUE BAPTISME.

¶ When there are chyldren to be Baptysed vpon the Sonday, or holy day, the Parentes shal geue knowledge ouernyght, or in the morning, afore the beginning of *Morning prayer* to the Curate. And then the Godfathers, Godmothers, and people, with the children, muste be ready at the *Fonte*, eyther immediatly *after* the laste *Lesson* at *Morninge prayer*, or els immediatlye *after* the laste *Lesson* at Eueni*nge* prayer, as the Curate by his discrecion shal appoynte. And then

stã ding there, the Priest shal aske whether the chyldren be Baptysed or no. If they answere, no. Then shall the Priest saye thus.

DEare*ly* beloued, for asmuche as all men be conceyued and borne in synne, & that *oure Sauiour Christe sayeth*, no*ne* can entre into the Kyngdome of God (excepte he be regenerate, and borne a new of water and the holye Ghoste:) I beseche you to call vpon God the Father, throughe our Lorde Iesus Christe, that of hys bounteous mercye, he wyll graunt to these chyldren, that thyng which by nature they cannot haue,

that they maye be Baptysed with *water and* the holy ghost, and receyued into Christes holye churche, and be made lyuelye membres of thesame.

Then the Priest shal saye.
℣ Let vs praye.

ALmightie & euerlastinge God, which

of thy *great* mercy diddest saue *Noe & his familie* in the Arke, *from perishing by water* : & *also*

dyddest safely leade the chyldren of Israel, thy people through the redde Sea : figuri*ng* *t*hereby thy holy Baptisme, & by the Baptisme of thy welbeloued sonne Iesus Christe,

1661

¶ [8]And note, that there shall be for every male child to be baptized, two Godfathers, and one Godmother : and for every female, one Godfather and two Godmothers.

¶ When there are children to be baptized, the parents shall give knowledge **thereof** over night, or in the morning **before** the beginning of *morning prayer*, to the Curate. And then the Godfathers **and** Godmothers and **the** people, with the children, must be ready at the *Font*, either immediatly *after* the last *Lesson* at *morning prayer*, or els immediatly *after* the last *Lesson* at eveni*ng* *Prayer*, as the Curate by his discretion shall appoynt. And the Priest **coming to the Font (which is then to be filled with pure Water) and** standing there shall **say,** [8]Hath this childe been already* baptised, or No? Jf they answer, no : then shall the Priest **proceed as followeth**

Dear*ly* beloved, forasmuch as all men **are** conceived and born in sin, and that *our Saviour Christ sayth*, no*ne* can enter into the Kingdom of God except he be regenerate, and born anew of water and [4]*of* the holy Ghost : I beseech you to call vpon God the Father, through our Lord Iesus Christ, that of his bounteous mercy he will grant to this Child that thing which by nature **he** cannot have,

that **he** may be baptized with *water, and* the holy Ghost, and received into Christs holy Church, and be made **a** lively member of the same

¶ Then [4]shall the Priest * say.
Let vs pray.

Almighty and everlasting God, who[8]

of thy *great* mercy didst save *Noah*[6] *and his family* in the Arke *from perishing by water*, and *alsoe*

didst safely lead the children of Israel thy people through **the** red Sea, figuri*ng* *t*hereby thy holy baptism ; and by the baptism of thy welbeloved son Iesus Christ **in the river Iordan**

II : S

St. Mark. [*Portions not found in Matthew or Luke.*]	St. Mark. [*Complete.*]
	I. 1–8
1 The beginning of the gospel of Jesus Christ, the Son of God. 2 Even...	1 The beginning of the gospel of Jesus Christ, [1] the Son of God. 2 Even as it is written [2] in **Isaiah the prophet,**
Behold,. I send my messenger before thy face, Who shall prepare thy way. (*But the words* "Behold, I send my messenger before thy face, who shall prepare thy way" *are found in Matthew xi.* 10 *and Luke vii.* 27).	Behold, I send my messenger before thy face, Who shall prepare thy way ; 3 **The voice of one crying in the wilderness,** **Make ye ready the way of the Lord,** **Make his paths straight ;**
4 ...came, who baptized [?]...and...	4 **John** came, who baptized **in the wilderness** and **preached** the **baptism** [?] of **repentance** unto remission of sins.
5 And...all (they of Jerusalem)...	5 And there **went out** unto him **all the country** of Judæa, and all they of Jerusalem ; and they were **baptized of him** in the river Jordan, confessing their sins.
6 And...was...and did eat (Gr. *eating*)...	6 And John was clothed with camel's hair, and *had* a leathern girdle about his loins, and did eat locusts and wild honey.
7 And he preached,...stoop down and (Gr. *stooping down*)...	7 And he preached, saying, There **cometh** after me **he that is mightier than I,** the latchet of **whose shoes I am not** [3] **worthy** to stoop down and unloose.
8 ...but [? ?]...	8 **I baptized you** [4] with **water ;** but **he shall baptize you** [4] **with the** [5] **Holy Ghost.**
	[1] Some ancient authorities omit *the Son of God.* [2] Some ancient authorities read *in the prophets.* [3] Gr. *sufficient.* [4] Or, *in.* [5] Or, *Holy Spirit :* and so throughout this book.
Mark i. 8, W. & H. omit the Greek preposition in both cases.	

Synopticon, pages 1–2.]

Figure II: From E. A. Abbott and W. G. Rushbrooke, *The Common Tradition of the Synoptic Gospels* (London, 1884) in the Text of the Revised Version.

St. Matthew. [*Passages parallel to Mark.*]	St. Luke. [*Passages parallel to Mark.*]
	III. 1-4, 7, 15-17.
	1 Now in the fifteenth year of the reign of Tiberius Cæsar, Pontius Pilate being governor of Judæa, and Herod being tetrarch of Galilee, and his brother Philip tetrarch of the region of Ituræa and Trachonitis, and Lysanias tetrarch of Abilene,
	2 In the high-priesthood of Annas and Caiaphas, the word of God came unto **John** the son of Zacharias **in the wilderness.**
III. 1-6, 11-12.	
1 And in those days cometh **John** the **Baptist**[?]**, preaching in the wilderness** of Judæa, saying,	3 And he came into **all the region** round about Jordan, **preaching** the **baptism** [?] of **repentance** unto remission of sins ;
2 **Repent** ye : for the kingdom of heaven is at hand.	4 As it is written in the book of the words of **Isaiah the prophet,**
3 For this is he that was spoken of [1] by **Isaiah the prophet,** saying, **The voice of one crying in the wilderness, Make ye ready the way of the Lord, Make his paths straight.**	**The voice of one crying in the wilderness, Make ye ready the way of the Lord, Make his paths straight.**
4 Now John himself had his raiment of camel's hair, and a leathern girdle about his loins ; and his food was locusts and wild honey.	7 He said therefore to the multitudes that **went out** to be **baptized of him,** Ye offspring of vipers, who warned you to flee from the wrath to come ?
5 Then **went out** unto him Jerusalem, and **all** [?] Judæa, and all [?] **the region** round about Jordan ;	
6 And they were **baptized of him** in the river Jordan, confessing their sins.	15 And as the people were in expectation, and all men reasoned in their hearts concerning John, whether haply he were the Christ ;
	16 John answered, saying unto them all, **I** indeed **baptize you** with **water;** but there **cometh he that is mightier than I,** the latchet **of whose shoes I am not** [1] **worthy** to unloose : **he shall baptize you** [2] with **the Holy Ghost** and *with* fire :
11 **I** indeed **baptize you** [2] with **water** unto repentance : but **he that cometh** after me is **mightier than I, whose shoes I am not** [3] **worthy** to bear : **he shall baptize you** [2] with **the Holy Ghost** and *with* fire :	
12 Whose fan is in his hand, and he will throughly cleanse his threshing-floor ; and he will gather his wheat into the garner, but the chaff he will burn up with unquenchable fire.	17 Whose fan is in his hand, throughly to cleanse his threshing-floor, and to gather the wheat into his garner ; but the chaff he will burn up with unquenchable fire.
[1] Or, *through.* [2] Or, *in.* [3] Gr. *sufficient.*	[1] Gr. *sufficient.* [2] Or, *in.*

speak only of the Church of England, and by no means all the Provinces of the Anglican Communion treat the Articles, Prayer Book and Ordinal of the Church of England as the chief exemplar of their own doctrinal stance.[3] Even so, the Archbishop of Canterbury is bound by the Canon Law of the Church of England and, as the personal focus of communion in the Anglican Communion, supplies an authoritative norm for the belief of the whole. Attention to the 'inheritance' of the *Book of Common Prayer* is, therefore, an integral element (to put it no higher) in the theological formation of all Anglicans.

We have spoken of the doctrine contained in the *Book of Common Prayer*. But is this not in tension with our earlier emphasis on structures, dramatic actions, rhythms and repetitions? It has to be admitted that Anglican history has been scarred by an exclusive emphasis on the doctrinal use of the Prayer Book. In the specific case of baptism, for example, one need only recall the bitter controversies of the later nineteenth century relating to baptismal regeneration, or those of the twentieth century concerning the gift of the Holy Spirit in baptism and in Confirmation. Christian liturgical texts have doctrinal content and can be studied as repositories of doctrine. It is also correct to regard them as of outstanding importance in the discharge of the teaching office of the Church, in the sense that if they inculcate false doctrine the damage they can inflict is exceptionally serious. But it is a failure of some consequence when liturgical texts are examined as though they were simply a collection of dogmatic declarations or confessional state-ments put into the mouths, alternately, of priest and people. Of course it is true that liturgies have often been made the vehicles of theological instruction, especially in the Reformation and Counter Reformation, and it is a matter of delicate judgement to perceive when the boundary between appropriate doctrinal content and intrusive theological propa-ganda has been crossed. For all that, it remains the case that 'reading' the text of the ministration of baptism involves being responsive to what is conveyed to the participant by its structure, dramatic actions, rhythms and repetitions as well as by its overt doctrines.

It has to be said that such a 'reading' is not encouraged by the hitherto dominant source-critical method practised by generations of liturgical scholars, and reflected in many contemporary text-books.[4] Just as in the study of the synoptic gospels, students were indirectly encouraged to treat the text as a pastiche of elements drawn from earlier sources, so, in relation to the Prayer Book, extensive enquiry was mounted into Cranmer's sources, and elaborate discussion was undertaken of the supposed motives behind changes of wording as between 1549, 1552 and 1661. Figure I, taken from the work of a major Prayer Book scholar, illustrates the point. Here, arranged in the three right-hand columns, are the texts of 1549, 1552 and 1661, with verbal alterations carefully indicated by the use of different kinds of type. In the left-hand column, a series of supposed sources are printed in Latin, German or English, enabling the student to make quick and accurate comparisons of a strictly limited character. Figure II illustrates the same method in its application to the synoptic gospels.[5] What neither example of this method enables the student to do with any ease is to detect the difference and similarities which arise from a reading of a text as a whole, or from the perception of internal rhythms created by stress or repetition.

This is not to denigrate the achievement of source-criticism, since we have independent evidence that many of the verbal changes introduced in 1552 or in 1662 were the consequence of argument and were plainly deliberate. But the method presupposed a highly misleading paradigm of the 'scientific' or 'objective' study of the text. It was as assiduously practised on Shakespeare as upon the Bible and Prayer Book. But, as a Shakespearean scholar was to put it, it was a little like the enterprise of savouring a rissole by watching the meat and onion pass through the mincer;[6] and in due course, at least in biblical studies and more widely in literary theory, first redaction-criticism and later reader-response theories began to provide less sterile perspectives.

It remains the case, of course, that there are historical questions to put to our evidence. Cranmer's own theology of baptism may be studied from the brief and fragmentary treatment it receives at his hands in the course of his other, major controversies.[7] It is historical enquiry which alone can assure us that the two Edwardine Prayer Books were substantially his own work.[8] Cranmer's relationship with, but independent judgement upon, German Church orders can only be evaluated from detailed knowledge of their contents, and it is highly pertinent to the changes introduced in 1552 to have considered in detail Martin Bucer's *Censura* on the 1549 Prayer Book, whether or not it was produced at Cranmer's invitation.[9] None the less it remains the case that source-criticism, with its historicist bias, remains but one of the tasks of an interpreter. Cranmer's liturgies invite a response from participators or potential participators who understand his work as worship. Ratcliff's judgement that Cranmer was 'the master, or rather the creator of English liturgical style, because he had apprehended the nature of worship'[10] – typically made at the end of a historical treatment of his work – will be the presupposition of what follows. Given that he understood worship (and here it is not necessary to suppose that he understood it *better* than any of his contemporaries, Catholic or Protestant), we shall ask what was the character he gave to the Church's dramatic act of baptising infants as Christian worship.

The Structure of the Service

The basic pattern of the service, which was conceived by Cranmer as a kind of self-contained sacramental event within the pattern of Matins or Evensong, is extremely simple (see Figure III). It comprises two main elements, those of Word and Sacrament, prefaced and followed by brief transitional statements and prayers. Between the reading of the Gospel (from Mark 10), and the actual baptism of the child, are a set of promises made by the godparents in the name of the child, which constitute a kind of hinge in the service on which entry into the grace of baptism turns. These promises are the human response to God's promises declared in the Gospel. The whole service, therefore, has the form of a covenant between God and the child, initiated from God's side.

The prefatory material with which the rite begins contains a simple question whether the child has already been baptised, a brief declaration of the necessity of baptism and two general intercessions for the child (the so-called 'flood' prayer, and the 'promise' prayer). This introduction serves two ends. It achieves, prior to the reading of the Gospel, a focusing of the congregation's attention upon the child; but it does so, secondly, in relation to two themes of major importance, those of God's mercy ('which of thy great mercy diddest save Noe and his familie in the Arke') and of his reception of the children ('Receiue them (O lord) as thou hast promysed'). Because structure is composed not just of sequences, but of significant repetitions, it is as well for us to look closely at certain recurring words.

'Reception' has already been used in the rubric at the head of the service to describe the purpose of baptism ('The receyuinge of them that be newely Baptysed into the noumbre of Christes Churche'). It is now used in each of the elements of the introductory material ('receyued into Christes holye churche', 'receyued into the Arke of Christes Church', 'maye receyue remission of theyr sinnes', and 'Receiue them (O lord)'). But its most striking use occurs in the Gospel and exhortation on the Gospel. Here Christ's action of taking the children into his arms and blessing them is used as an analogy for baptism.

> Doubt not ye therefore, but earnestly beleue, that he wyl
> lykewise fauourably receyue these present infantes, that
> he wil embrase them wyth the armes of hys mercye, that
> he wyll geue vnto them the blessynge of eternall
> lyfe, and make them partakers of hys euerlasting kingdom.

The emotionally powerful image of the child being embraced in the arms of Jesus' mercy forms the affective heart of this liturgy. The word 'receive' significantly continues to echo at regular intervals throughout the rest of the service, in the address to the godparents, at the blessing of the water, in the priest's declaration after baptism (note: 'We receyue this childe'), and finally at the prayer of thanksgiving ('to receyue hym for thy owne childe by adopcion').

Excluding the rubric, there are in all no less than ten uses of the word 'receive' in this liturgy. This, we should note, compares with four uses in the *Alternative Service Book's* Baptism of Children. Cranmer's liturgy we might well conclude was, by reason of its structure, drama, and repetitions, a liturgy proclaiming Christ's reception of little children. When the priest at the height of the drama takes the child into his arms he is doing what Christ himself did. The congregation witnesses Christ's own embrace. The sacrament is God's own act ('thy holy Baptisme', in both the flood and promise prayers). Thus the theology, Gospel reading, drama and repetitions cohere in the word 'receive' and hence the poignancy and appropriateness of the declaration 'we receyue this childe into the congregacion of Christe's flocke'. However, in the *Alternative Service Book*, Mark 10 is, after centuries of usage, dropped as the Gospel, an omission justified by the observation that the passage does not refer to baptism at all.[11] This is pedantry of the first

11

PREFATORY MATERIAL

Question

invitation to prayer
flood prayer
promise prayer

THE WORD

Mark 10, Exhortation, Prayer

address to parents about promises
demands to renounce sin, believe gospel, desire baptism
'grant' prayers

THE SACRAMENT

water prayer, baptism, signing, Lord's Prayer

POSTLUDE

prayer of thanksgiving
exhortation to godparents
extempore instruction

Figure III: The Structure of the Service

order. We already know from the text of the liturgy that the Church
has been commanded to baptise. The justification for baptising infants
lies not in any direct precedent of Christ's, but in the quality of his
response to little children, conveyed by the phrase 'embrace with the
arms of his mercy'.

The central block of the service contains Word (Gospel reading and
exposition) and Sacrament, both embodying a mutual promising or
covenant. Again the structure is undergirded by another highly significant repetition, this time of the word 'promise'. The second of the two
opening prayers for the child repeats the word twice, making the text,
'aske & you shal have, seke & you shal fynd' central to its invocation,
as though daring the participants in the rite to disbelieve. The exhortation on the Gospel reinforces this with reference to the avoidance of
doubt, to earnest belief and to being persuaded. After a brief prayer,
the priest turns to the godparents with a positive battery of references
to promise:

> Ye haue heard also that our Lord Iesus Christ hath promysed in
> hys Gospel, to graunte all these thinges that ye haue prayed for:
> which promise he for his parte wyll moste surely kepe & per-
> forme. Wherfore after thys promyse made by Christ, these inf-
> antes must also faithfully for theyr parte promise by you that be
> their suerties . . .

Why is so much emphasis laid upon the promise of the Gospel?
The historical reason has doubtless much to do with the promissory
emphasis of Luther's sacramental theology;[12] but in Cranmer's baptismal
liturgy the theme of promise amounts to a structural element, not just
a doctrinal allusion.

The permeation of the theme of promise throughout the service
suggests that the life of the participant is itself being structured by the
liturgy. Quite apart from what may feature in this particular liturgy, we
could observe from the standpoint of Christian doctrine that baptism,
as the sacrament of initiation into the Church, might well be expected
to express a sense of the totality of the Christian's life within the
Church; or, putting it another way, that, as the sacramental incorporation into Christ, baptism might well be expected to elicit the complete
sense of fellowship with him. As it is, Cranmer makes absolutely
unambiguous what he hopes that baptism will achieve for all adult

participants. In the opening rubric, he states that the point of public baptisms at main services is that 'euery man present may be put in remembraunce of hys owne profession made to God in hys Baptisme'; hence, of course, the use of an English liturgy. Furthermore the concluding exhortation to godparents offers an explicit explanation of the content of this remembrance to the following effect:

> rememberynge always that Baptisme doeth represente vnto vs oure profession, whiche is to folowe the example of our sauiour Christ, & to be made like vnto him: that as he dyed and rose agayne for vs, so shoulde we whiche are baptysed, dye from synne, and ryse agayne vnto righteousnesse, continually mortyfyinge all oure euyll and corrupte affections, and daylye procedinge in all vertue and godlines of lyuynge.

This comprehensive summary of the Christian life constitutes the structure of the liturgy from first to last, and is reinforced by constant repetition at every stage.

The Christian 'profession' entails a journey 'in Christ', which begins with a dying to sin. This in itself presupposes that humanity apart from Christ is in a state of sin, the information appropriately conveyed by the words with which the liturgy begins ('Dearely beloued, for asmuche as all men be conceyued and borne in synne'). This scriptural reference (Ps. 51:5, Coverdale's translation) Cranmer evidently preferred to the idea that unbaptised infants amounted to persons possessed by demons, who must be exorcised. Bucer had argued in the *Censura* that though baptismal exorcism was an ancient custom, it diminished the stature of the Gospel exorcisms.[13] Cranmer appears to have agreed with this, and the demonology of his service is muted and apotropaic.

Delivery from sin through the atoning death of Christ brings the Christian into the company of those undertaking the journey of sanctification, a constant further dying to sin and growth in obedience and godliness. The final state is that of enjoyment of the kingdom and eternal life. Thus deliverance from sin, sanctification and entry into the kingdom constitutes a comprehensive summary of life 'in Christ'. Because the self-same promises of the Gospel accompany the Christian throughout his or her entire life, baptism is a reminder of the Christian profession, a structure and framework for the whole of Christian living.

It is not, therefore, accidental that in the pivotal address to the godparents before they make their promises, what is entailed in Christ's reception of and blessing of children is spelt out as follows:

> to release them of theyr synnes [1662 adds, to sanctify him with the Holy Ghost], to geue them the kingdom of heaven, and euerlasting lyfe.

This pattern is constantly reiterated, often with only two of the three elements being mentioned. For example, as we have seen, the first words of the service refer to being born in sin; this is immediately followed by a reference to being born anew of water and the Holy Ghost and thereby entering the kingdom. The 'flood' prayer which follows contains a similar sequence, washing, sanctification and final entry into everlasting life. The next, 'promise' prayer refers both to washing and entry into the eternal kingdom. The thanksgiving after baptism contains another comprehensive brief summary of the Christian life, speaking of being buried with Christ in his death, of the utter abolition of the whole body of sin, followed by final inheritance of the everlasting kingdom.

The sense that baptism comprehends and accompanies the whole of a Christian life is caught in George Herbert's poem, entitled 'Holy Baptisme I'. Using the traditional image invoked in the prayer before baptism, that the baptismal waters are one with the water which flowed from the side of Christ, Herbert writes:

> O blessed streams! either ye do prevent
> And stop our sinnes from growing thick and wide,
> Or else give tears to drown them, as they grow.
> In you Redemption measures all my time,
> And spreads the plaister equall to the crime.
> You taught the Book of Life my name, that so
> What ever future sinnes should me miscall,
> Your first acquaintance might discredit all.

The efficacy of the baptismal water, like the Christian name entered into the register, accompany the believer throughout his or her life; so that 'your first acquaintance' – that is the introduction and mutual naming of a merciful, promising God to the child as his adoptive heir –

is sufficient to discredit whatever shameful names subsequent sinning might seem to justify. In baptism, redemption measures and accompanies the entire life-span of the believer.

The final thing to observe about the structure of the service is its open-endedness. Indeed it hardly ends at all. A rubric instructs the Minister to command extempore that the children be brought to the bishop for confirmation at the proper time. The 1549 rubric, instructing the congregation to depart in the name of the Lord, was omitted in 1552. It is wholly appropriate that there should be no formal closure, because the liturgy itself opens out on to the daily service of the church, the life of growth in all virtue and godliness of living. Naturally enough, the congregation's hope and expectation that the infant will grow physically and mentally becomes the implicit metaphor for Christian life ('that al thinges belonginge to the spirite, may liue & growe in them'). There is reference to increased 'power and strength', to manhood and warfare, and to the anticipated learning of which the infant is shortly expected to be capable. The simultaneous address to the assembled adults of these evocations of the basic metaphor of growth becomes explicit in the prayer after the Gospel:

> We geve thee humble thankes, that thou haste vouchsafed to call vs to knowledge of thy grace & fayth in thee, encrease this knowledge, & confirme this faythe in vs euermore.

In other words, this liturgy is characterised by a structure and a pattern of repetitions expressive of the way in which a Christian becomes involved in the divine plan, and the consequence of having done so. The structure focuses the drama upon the child, deploying the powerful thought of divine tenderness towards small children, but at the same time addresses adult participants through the metaphor of growth to maturity. It deliberately sets out to remind all present of the fundamental character of their own baptism, and to reinforce and encourage Christians in the profession of their faith.

The Drama and Symbols of Baptism

In his liturgical work Cranmer intended above all else to be faithful to Scripture, and the Scriptures lack any explicit description of the rituals of early Christian baptism. The general aim of simplification imbibed from the continental Reformation inclined him against a plethora of dramatic or symbolic rituals, even when these were capable of perfectly acceptable evangelical interpretation. Bucer was of the opinion that proper teaching about the use of these rituals was a distraction from the main aim of a simple instruction in the faith, at least for the time of pastoral emergency in which he lived. He seems not to have considered the possibility that the symbols might be capable of speaking for themselves without extensive verbal interpretation, or that they had arisen from meditation upon the Scriptures.[14] At all events Cranmer's liturgy represents in itself a dramatic reduction of ritual actions, as compared with the medieval Sarum rite.

But it is not devoid of drama, nor is its language symbolically impoverished. The liturgy contains no less than ten images of baptism, namely, washing, drowning or rescuing from being drowned (as in the cases of Noah or the children of Israel at the Red Sea), deliverance from wrath and condemnation, reception into (the ark of) the Church, being embraced by Christ, becoming a living limb or member of the body, being born again, burial and resurrection with Christ, the imagery of the sacrificial blood and water from the side of Christ, being grafted into Christ, and being adopted as a child of Christ. Ample use has, therefore, been made of the rich possibilities provided by the Scriptures for the interpretation of baptism.

The rituals themselves are simply those of baptising by dipping the child into the water (presuming a certain measure of undress), or, in the case of certified weakness, sprinkling it with water, and signing it with the sign of the cross. By 1552 the drama of exorcism ('the priest lokyng vpon the children', 1549) has been abandoned, as has the ceremonial blessing (with use of the sign of the cross) of the water. In 1661 the latter was to be partially restored by the insertion into the prayer before baptism of the words 'Sanctifie this Water to the mystical washing away of sin', an inclusion which incidentally reinforced the threefold pattern of deliverance from sin, sanctification and entry into the kingdom.

But even the ritually low-keyed version of 1552 is not without verbally reinforced drama. As we have argued, the centre or hinge of the service is the point at which the covenant is made. Here, at the moment when godparents make their promises as sureties for the child, Cranmer has placed a series of ejaculatory prayers, each beginning with

17

the word 'grant'. In 1549 these were added to the blessing of the font and were eight in number. By 1552 they had been reduced to four. Their origin may have been in part from the *Missale Mixtum*, a Spanish book edited in 1500 by Cardinal Ximenes, and the *Missale Gallicanum vetus*.[15] It was Cranmer's genius, however, to pick from the texts the major dramatic themes of burial of the old Adam and resurrection of the new, of death to the flesh and life in the spirit, and of warfare and triumph over the devil, the world and the flesh; and to heighten their impact with repetition of the word 'grant'. It may not be too much to say that the effect was calculated to compensate for the loss of the drama of exorcism, and to substitute a sense of radical movement from an old to a new condition, a major feature of rites of passage.

But it would be inappropriate at this point not to comment on the losses entailed in Cranmer's 1552 efforts at simplification. If we inspect the rituals from the perspective provided by the anthropological theory of *rites de passage*,[16] what is most strikingly absent is the sense of the separation of the baptisand from the structures of society. In the Sarum rite this is amply provided for by the order for the making of a catechumen, with its very extensive and elaborate preliminary rituals. The exorcism and administration of salt to make the candidate hungry for spiritual food, the separate rituals for male and female children, and the adjuration and exorcism of the devil, are all conceived of as forms of preparation so that the candidate may be ready to approach baptism and fit to receive its grace. They separate the child from its natural community for adoption within the new covenant.

In Cranmer's first revision of Sarum in 1549, the first half of the baptismal order was, according to the rubric, to be conducted at the church door. This has the consequence that the opening prayer, signing with the cross, exorcism, proclamation of the Gospel and profession of the creed could all be regarded as preparation (and thus separation) before arrival at the font. But so attenuated a residue of the rite of separation had, plainly, lost its *raison d'être*, and it fell victim to Bucer's reductive observation that the practice amounted simply to a sign of the fact that children are conceived and born in sin.[17] Since, he argues, that is admitted in so many words in the text and 'since a multitude of signs does not become a new people', nothing would be lost by having the entire baptism at the font. Cranmer concurred with this reasoning in 1552; but we in our day may beg to disagree. In a

18

secularised culture there is everything to be said for a solemn rite of separation, a reminder to both parents and godparents that their renunciations may have costly consequences in their daily lives. Discussion of the retention of exorcism in such a context presents specialised and complex problems, into which it is impossible to enter here.

Baptism and the Lord's Supper

It remains to ask what connection Cranmer envisaged or established between his two liturgies, of Holy Baptism and Holy Communion. Irrespective of what we may actually find to be the case, the question is forced on us by our observation of the pattern which baptism places upon the living of the Christian life. We are bound to enquire whether the Order for the Eucharist is consistent with this pattern, whether it reflects and embodies the same fundamental convictions about the character of the covenant between God and humankind.

On the connection between baptism and Holy Communion Cranmer himself occasionally commented in his eucharistic writings. For example, in the 1550 *Defence of the True and Catholic Doctrine of the Sacrament*, he relates baptism and Eucharist as different modes of the one, divine action; 'Our Saviour Christ is both the first beginner of our spiritual life (who first begetteth us into God his Father), and also afterwards he is our lively food and spiritual life.'[18] Again, subsequently, Cranmer discusses a passage from Hilary's *De Trinitate* which, he asserts, makes no distinction between the believer's union with Christ in baptism and in the Eucharist. Both affirm Christ's 'natural' presence in us, a oneness of the believer with Christ and of Christ with the believer, which can only be spoken of as a spiritual union.[19] The purpose of the argument is to overthrow the case from tradition for transubstantiation, which he understands to be the doctrine of a real and corporal presence of Christ in the bread of the sacrament. But, replied Cranmer, if we truly partake of Christ at baptism we do so without any miraculous change of the water. The indwelling of Christ in the believer as a result of baptism is both true and 'natural'. But because it is a mutual indwelling, involving the believer in being in Christ, as Christ is in him or her, it should not be spoken of as corporal but as spiritual.

Though the confusion of the terminology is considerable, Cranmer's intention is perfectly plain. It is to focus attention on the covenantal aspect of the eucharistic rite. Just as in baptism Christ meets the believer through his or her response to his promise, so, through faith in the promise, precisely the same encounter is to take place at the Eucharist. The 'presence' is neither greater nor less in one case or in the other. The most striking evidence, therefore, that baptism and Eucharist are conceived on the basis of the same ground-plan, lies in the renewal of the mutual promising which, as we have seen, is the hinge between word and sacrament in the baptismal rite. We should not, therefore, be surprised to find the same movement in the order for Holy Communion, articulated in an absolution which directly refers to the same comprehensive summary of life in Christ as found expression in Holy Baptism. The absolution recalls that the God of mercy has promised forgiveness of sins to all who turn to him with repentance and true faith. Such a God will pardon and forgive sins, will confirm and strengthen in all goodness, and will bring the believer to everlasting life. These are his sure promises, and in the light of them the believer may be lifted up in heart and mind to feast with Christ at his table in the heavens.[20]

But 'everyone of us must be guests and not gazers'.[21] This fundamental affirmation of the *Homily of the Worthy Receiving and Reverent Esteeming of the Body and Blood of Christ* is pertinent to the issue of growth in understanding which we have seen to be an important metaphor through which adult participators in the baptismal liturgy are addressed. Infants are to be brought to a state of comprehension of what it is that the Eucharist recalls, so that they may feast at the Lord's Table with understanding. Like the passover feast, partakers must be instructed in the cause and end of the Eucharist; otherwise there can be no true memorial of the death of Christ. Because that death accomplished a complete atonement for sin, the remembrance of it entails both a serious calling to mind and a thorough repentance of our own sins. The Eucharist is the 'nourishment and augmentation' of what was begun in baptism because in it, adults lay hold of forgiveness. Forgiveness, both forgiving and being forgiven, is the means by which Christians are to grow into an ever more complete union with Christ; 'that we may euermore dwell in hym, and he in us'.

It is for this reason that so profound – even terrifying – an emphasis is placed upon 'worthy reception'. The Exhortations in Cranmer's

1552 eucharistic rite place believers in a double bind. They will be punished if they fail to examine themselves before receiving the Eucharist; they will also be punished if they fail to come to the Eucharist. 'Worthy reception' of the Eucharist is, however, merely identical with what the Article XXVII 'of Baptism' refers to as right reception. Because there is a continuing requirement deriving from participation in baptism, baptism and Eucharist are inseparable from each other. Those who receive baptism rightly are those who have come to understand for themselves the terms of the new covenant in the blood of Christ. The incompleteness of the rite of infant baptism points forward, therefore, to a true partaking of the spiritual food of the most precious Body and Blood of Christ, to lively membership of the mystical body of Christ and to the promise of the inheritance of his everlasting kingdom.

Our review of the text of Cranmer's liturgy of Public Baptism has revealed a depth and subtlety of content and structure which it might be tempting to contrast with the 'alternative' service. It is, however, sufficient to add that that service is, indeed, alternative, and that the norm of its interpretation remains the *Book of Common Prayer*. Precisely because baptisms are public rituals it remains possible for parishes to recapture the substance of what Cranmer achieved, even whilst using the modern text. Instruction, choices of readings and hymns, and the organisation of processions give parishes the opportunity to establish those patterns and resonances so important to the liturgy of 1552. It is to be hoped that future revisers of the alternative services will be less dominated by the historical and source-critical school of liturgiology, and will lay securer hold upon the texts as worship.

NOTES

1. Canon *A5* of the Church of England reads thus: 'The doctrine of the Church of England is grounded in the holy Scriptures, and in such teachings of the ancient Fathers and Councils of the Church as are agreeable to the said Scriptures. In particular such doctrine is to be found in the Thirty-nine Articles of Religion, the Book of Common Prayer and the Ordinal.'
2. Canon C15, Of the Declaration of Assent.
3. See P. H. E. Thomas, 'A Family Affair: The Pattern of Constitutional

Authority in the Anglican Communion' in *Authority in the Anglican Communion*, ed. Stephen W. Sykes (Toronto, 1987), pp. 119–43.

4. To a very large extent the pattern was set by Francis Proctor's *History of the Book of Common Prayer* (London, 1855), a work revised and rewritten by W. H. Frere in 1901, and published in successive impressions until 1961. There was a dogmatic motive reinforcing the trend towards historical and source-critical treatment of the *Book of Common Prayer*, in that Anglican writers influenced by the Oxford Movement greatly preferred the 1549 Prayer Book Eucharist to that of 1552, and had an apologetic interest in demonstrating the continuity of Anglican forms with earlier Catholic models. Most liturgical scholars have been Anglo-Catholics.

5. The tradition of printing the text of the gospels in parallel columns goes back beyond the early critical work of Griesbach (1745–1812) on the synoptic problem, to the ancient tradition of gospel harmonies. The extract from Abbott and Rushbrooke illustrates well how theory-laden these apparently objective comparisons actually are. I am grateful to Dr Peter Head, of St Edmund's College, Cambridge, for his observations on this point.

6. 'Analysis of the creative act is fascinating in its own right; but it tends to present great art as a rissole one learns to savour by watching meat and onion through the mincer', D. L. Frost, *The School of Shakespeare* (Cambridge, 1968), p. 23.

7. See G. W. Bromily, *Thomas Cranmer, Theologian* (London, 1956), ch. V.

8. E. C. Ratcliff, 'The Liturgical Work of Archbishop Cranmer' in E. C. Ratcliff, *Liturgical Studies*, ed. A. H. Couratin and D. H. Tripp (London, 1976), pp. 184–202.

9. Or that of Bishop Goodrich of Ely, as seems probable: see C. Hopf, *Martin Bucer and the English Reformation* (Oxford, 1947) and E. C. Whitaker, *Martin Bucer and the Book of Common Prayer*, Alcuin Club Collections 55 (Great Wakering, 1974).

10. Ratcliff, p. 199.

11. R. C. D. Jasper and P. F. Bradshaw, *A Companion to the Alternative Service Book* (London, 1986), p. 350.

12. See especially Luther's treatise, *The Babylonian Captivity of the Church* (1520), and *The Large Catechism* (1529).

13. J. D. C. Fisher, *Christian Initiation: The Reformation Period*, Alcuin Club Collections 51 (London, 1970), pp. 101f.

14. *The Rationale of Ceremonial*, produced in England sometime between 1540 and 1543, had provided an explanation of the baptismal rituals of the Sarum manual in terms undoubtedly uncongenial to Cranmer at the time.

15. Fisher, op. cit., p. 151.

16. Classically formulated by A. Van Gennep in 1908, in a subsequently translated work, *The Rites of Passage* (London, 1960).

17. Fisher, op. cit., p. 98.

18. *The Work of Thomas Cranmer*, ed. G. E. Duffield (Appleford, 1964), p. 69. The passage is from Book I, ch. X.

19. ibid., p. 175. The passage is from III, ch. XV.

20. See Peter Brook's suggestive discussion of what he calls 'the *sursum corda* approach to the heavenly Christ', in *Thomas Cranmer's Doctrine of the Eucharist* (London, 1965), pp. 101f.
21. *The Two Books of Homilies* (Oxford, 1859), p. 439. The Homily in question, from the second collection of 1563, is generally ascribed to Bishop John Jewel.

2

CRANMER ON THE OPEN HEART

That Thomas Cranmer at some times sounds like a rationalist, and at other times a mystic, is a feature of his theology on which John Booty has wisely commented in his discussion of the background to the Books of Common Prayer from 1549 to 1559.

> [Cranmer's] common-sense reasonableness is qualified by that right-reason to which the humanists and Richard Hooker referred, reason with qualities of heart and soul, conscience as well as mind, the moral law of reason. Which is to say that when Cranmer is most rational, exercising common sense most avidly, he insists upon Christ's bodily absence, but when he is most devotional, when rationality is most qualified by right reason, he speaks of mutual indwelling.[1]

The purpose of this contribution to the celebration of John Booty's most fruitful combination of the virtues of the scholar and of the mystic is to examine Cranmer's attempted balance between the mind and heart. We shall do so by investigating his deployment of the metaphor of the heart both in his liturgical work and in his theology. It will be argued that we have to take seriously the physicality of the metaphor and the way in which it is deployed so as to create space and distance for the idea of a journey or pilgrimage of the heart. I will show how the eucharistic liturgies of the 1549 and 1552 Prayer Books embody a doctrine of ascension in heart, and need to be taken seriously as rituals. The essay implicitly challenges the common assumption that Protestantism is properly described as anti-ritualistic, a designation in which it has uncritically colluded. Scholars have too readily accepted at face value the qualitative difference Protestants have proposed between the external and internal phenomena of faith, between the monuments of a physical landscape and the interior topography of the heart. Nothing, in my opinion, is more important to the contemporary relations between Catholics and Protestants of all kinds than that they cease to think and speak as though the theology of the matter could be developed on the basis of so inadequate a description.

The Open Heart

> Almightie God, unto whom all hartes bee open,
> and all desyres knowen
>   and from whom no secretes are hid:
> Clense the thoughtes of our hartes
>   by the inspiracion of thy holy spirite:
> That we may perfectly loue thee
>   and worthely magnifie thy holy name.[2]

The Collect for Purity, which Cranmer placed at the opening of the reformed service he called 'The Supper of the Lorde and the Holy Communion, commonly called the masse', is, we remind ourselves at once, part of the Latin Catholic tradition. We do Thomas Cranmer's reputation no service if we strive to trace all his liturgical insights and activities to the new, or allegedly new, doctrinal initiatives of the sixteenth century. It is common biblical, patristic, and catholic thought that the heart is open to God, its desires are known by him, and none of its secrets are hidden. So the priests who had said this opening collect of the mass *ad postulandam gratiam Spiritus Sancti*, had reminded themselves since the days of Alcuin.[3] As a vesting prayer in the Sarum rite it had achieved still greater currency. And it was already available in English by the mid-fourteenth century to readers of *The Cloud of Unknowing*, the prologue to which began with the intercession,

> God, unto whom all hearts be open, and
> unto whom all will speaketh
> and unto whom no privy thing is hid:
> I beseech thee so for to cleanse the intent
> of mine heart with the unspeakable gift

of thy grace,
that I may perfectly love thee and worthily
praise thee. Amen.[4]

But if there is nothing doctrinally new in the content of this prayer, nonetheless we may speak of a certain development of its use. In the mass it was a priestly prayer, and even the vernacular *Cloud of Unknowing* was fierce in its warning that the book was only to be used by contemplatives. *The Book of Common Prayer* gives the prayer an extended currency, in a new and common context, as part of the ritual process of a whole Christian community.

But what is this open heart? At this stage we should take a moment to remind ourselves that much of the biblical use of the word 'heart' turns upon the physicality of the metaphor. It is true, of course, that what went on in and between the internal organs of the body was obscure to the ancient Hebrews. But they knew perfectly well that emotions like sorrow or joy were felt physically. They reasoned, correctly, that there must be links between perceptions, cognitions and the viscera; and if they were wrong physiologically to locate the seat of the transactions in the heart, rather than in the brain, their instinct to speak physically was not mistaken.[5]

There are more than 700 uses in the Old Testament alone of the Hebrew words for 'heart', faithfully reduplicated in Greek and Latin translations. And so they pour into the European languages a huge stock of mixed metaphors, with hearts that are stony or of flesh, circumcised or uncircumcised, and in every permutation of elation or depression, divided, hardened, trembling, smitten, lifted up, upright, double, hot, like wax, broken, fixed, fat as grease, pure, withered, poured out like water, and so forth.

As Professor Derek Brewer has pointed out, Chaucer has both relayed into English and expanded the imagery of the heart. In *Troilus and Cresside* alone,

The heart is on fire, is the eye of the breast, frequently dear, ready to burst, the source of thought, is playing, felt to weep, soft enough for thoughts to sink into, is warm or cold, gay, torn out, exchanged with another, capable of bleeding, is dancing,

26

laughing, could be of stone, personifies a dear or sweet person, is able to be steered, shut in by sorrow, seeming to die, capable of being opened, weeps bloody tears, can be deeply engraved, floats in joy, contains the beloved, is gnawed by woe, can speak to oneself, can be stern and cruel, contain a weeping spirit, can be burnt to a powder, is the memory, has a visage to be turned up to God, and so forth.[6]

Now the transactions of God with the human heart assume peculiar importance, once we have noted its inclusion of what we commonly refer to as the emotions. To speak of the 'heart' seems to imply both the 'affective processing' of communicative input and the viscerally experienced consequences of that processing. This is how religious ideas get into the guts. The physiology of the linkages may one day be clarified, and we shall all have to become what William James derided as 'medical materialists'. But at the very least the fact that we cannot inspect the heart's transactions has lent powerful, common-sense support to the religious tradition which insists that the heart has its secrets. Without any commitment to the correlative thesis about the value of introspection, we can see how such a tradition would want to affirm that God alone can construe the human heart.[7] Who I am, *qua* human being and particular individual, what I amount to in any belief-worthy scheme of things, is by no means easy to interpret from my knowledge of human history or from a review of my past actions or speech. The heart has its secrets, therefore, because human meaning is obscure, both in general and in particular. In so far as I may realise that I am myself capable of a variety of behaviours, I may come to see my own meaning as doubtful or uncertain; and my heart, I will say, is deep or even divided.

Through extension of the same perceptions arises the phenomenon of self-deception, again a philosophical puzzle of enormous complexity.[8] When I realise how it is possible for a person systematically to misconstrue the moral quality of his or her own behaviour or intentions, my heart, I will say, is deceitful above all things and desperately wicked (Jer. 17:9).

The biblical story of David and the prophet Nathan will become a paradigm of how monstrous past behaviour (in this case, David's) can be reconstructed in a narrative (in Nathan's parable of the poor man's ewe lamb) in such a way as to confront the sinner with an undeceived perspective on his or her behaviour.[9]

> Create in me a clean heart, O God;
> and renew a right spirit within me
> (Ps. 51:10; *et spiritum rectum*
> *nova in visceribus meis*, Vulgate)

becomes the paradigm prayer of desire for deliverance from the heart's deceitful potential.

The Topography of the Heart

We are now in a position to explore some of the ramifications of Cranmer's view of the heart, and the natural place to begin is with his understanding of faith. In the so-called Annotations on the King's Book, Cranmer distinguishes between what he calls a general faith which is, broadly speaking, propositional, and 'pure Christian faith' which only 'those that truly belong to Christ' can have.[10] The contrast is biblical; drawn to interpret the human meaning of people who honour God with mouth and lips, but whose heart is far from him (Isa. 29:13; cited of the Pharisees by Jesus, Mark 7:6). True faith is not only in the mouth, but engraven in the heart (compare Prov. 3:3; 7:3; Jer. 31:33; the translation of the Great Bible of 1540, for which Cranmer supplied the preface, is in all these cases substantially that of the Authorised Version) and expressed in acts and deeds.

> If the profession of our faith of the remission of our own sins enter within us into the deepness of our hearts, then it must needs kindle a warm fire of love in our hearts towards God, and towards all other for the love of God.[11]

This, says Cranmer, is 'the very right, pure, perfect, lively, Christian, hearty, and justifying "faith, which worketh by love", as St Paul saith,' and cites the Vulgate of Acts 15:9, 'fide Deus purificans corda' ('God justifying hearts by faith'). The later homily on faith, commonly attributed to Cranmer, deals, in its third part, specifically with self-deception in the matter of faith, the only remedy for which, he states, is to set aside self-flattery and 'look upon our works, and so judge of our faith, what it is'. He is, moreover, plainly conscious of the possibility of illusion in the kind of description of faith which he has given; the antidote is for such a person to perceive 'by the trade of his life that he unfeignedly hath the right knowledge of God, a lively faith, a steadfast hope, a true and unfeigned love and fear of God'. The phrase 'unfeigned love,' we note, is biblical (2 Cor. 6:6, 'by love unfeigned'; 1 Pet. 1:22, 'unto unfeigned love of the brethren').

The metaphorical range of the language of the heart is already considerable, as one would expect, but we note in particular how faith in the remission of sins is to enter into 'the deepness of our hearts'. Again the phrase is biblical. The enemies of Psalm 64 'imagine wickedness and practice it: that they keep secret among themselves, every man in the deep of his heart.' It is, therefore, in the deepness of our hearts that the warm fired love must be kindled. The 'fire of love' is not a biblical phrase, but one familiar to English readers from the *Incendium Amoris* of the fourteenth-century mystic, Richard Rolle, whose psalter was so beloved of the Lollards. Probably from Rolle are the following lines of a lyrical meditation on the passion of Christ:

> Ihesu receive my heart
> and to thy love me bring
> all my desire thou art,
> (but) I covet thy coming.
> Thou make me clean of sin
> and let me never twin [forsake thee],
> kindle me fire within
> that I thy love may win,
> and see thy face, Ihesu, in
> joy that never shall blin [cease].[12]

Two comments are pertinent at this stage. The first is that under the spatial metaphor of depth, Cranmer is obviously engaging with the phenomenon of human deviousness, the residual ambiguity which attaches to protestations of assent and declarations of intent. Second, the metaphor of the heart guarantees that he is doing so under the condition that the desired-for reduplication of speech and intention in action, deed and truth, can be vitally assisted by the 'warmth' of love. Now warmth, together with the other ways of referring to love or desire, is physically locable in the viscera (to put it no more precisely). The idea that Cranmer has embraced a standard body-mind dualism, dissociating religion from all contact with physicality, cannot be sustained despite the patent influence of Erasmian neo-Platonism.[13] The heart is simply not reducible to the mind. 'That it may please thee to geue us an hearte to loue and dreade thee, and diligently to lyue after thy commandments,' prays Cranmer in his litany.[14] References to 'pouring' are similarly physical in basis, and with St Augustine's identification of the Spirit with love comes the possibility seized upon in the Gelasian collect, translated for the 1549 *Book of Common Prayer* thus:

> God, whiche haste prepared to them that loue thee, suche good
> thynges as passe all mannes understanding:
> Poure into our hartes such loue toward thee.
> That we louing thee in al thinges, may obteine thy promises,
> whiche excede all that we canne desyre.[15]

The topography of the heart reveals it to be a place with caverns and recesses, which can be inspected, in which fires can be lit, into which and out of which liquids can be poured, and which can be made a certain kind of place. As George Herbert was going to say:

> within my heart I made
> Closets; and in them many a chest;
> And, like a master in my trade,
> In those chests, boxes; in each box, a till.[16]
> ('Confession')

Herbert's image is domestic, small scale and meticulous. But its point is the task of discovery which it sets the reader, who is invited to search for keys and modes of entry into spaces which are unexplored and potentially full of surprises.

Precisely the same relationship is established with the reader in a topography of larger scale, of heights, and depths, hospitable of the notion of pilgrimage. Here we are on familiar, Augustinian ground already explored by Erasmus in a notably neo-platonic vein.[17] Our homeland is in heaven – the reference is to 2 Corinthians 5:6–8 – and our hearts and wishes long for it, while our bodies are still connected with the earth. But for Cranmer the heart itself has secret depths, and hence derives the importance and great difficulty of self-examination prior to penitence. In due course we shall see how pivotal has become the liturgical instruction to 'lift up your hearts' in the ritual process of pilgrimage to the Lord's Table devised by Cranmer. But the start of the journey, the exploration of the depths of the heart, shows that the metaphorical process is full of hazard and demands the closest attention. The Prayer Books of 1549 and 1552 strongly emphasise to potential communicants that it is spiritually and physically dangerous to receive the sacrament unworthily. Repentance and restitution are needed beforehand, and a promise given to God ('from the botome of your hartes') that one's life will be amended.[18]

Thus we find again the metaphor of depth in a phrase which the New Oxford English Dictionary traces to the 1549 *Book of Common Prayer*, but which Cranmer readily uses in other contexts – for example, in his correspondence. One particular occurrence shows Cranmer's application of the phrase to his own self-scrutiny. In a letter of 12 May 1535 to Thomas Cromwell, replying to the somewhat mischievous complaint of the Bishop of Winchester that the ecclesiastical title 'Primate of all England' derogated from the royal supremacy, Cranmer protested:

I pray God never be merciful unto me at the general judgement, if I perceive in my heart that I set more by any title, name, or style that I write, than I do by the paring of an apple, further than it shall be to the setting forth of God's word and will. Yet I will not utterly excuse me herein; for God must be judge, who knoweth the bottom of my heart, and so do not I myself; but I speak for so much as I do feel in my heart; for many evil affections lie lurking there, and will not lightly be espied.[19]

But all is not what it seems with this now-familiar phrase, 'the bottom of the heart', which Professor Brewer has pointed out to me in Chaucer. So taken with it is Cranmer that he attributes it, wrongly, to Scripture in the first of the sentences in the 1552 Morning Prayer, as part of the newly introduced penitential rite:

> At what time soever a synner doeth
> repente hym of hys synne from the bottome
> of hys heart; I wyl put all his wickedness
> oute of my remembraunce, sayth the Lorde.[20]

Neither the Vulgate nor any of the extant English translations of Ezekiel 18 justify this rendering, nor have I been able to trace it to any other liturgical source, Latin or Greek. As the Prayer Book connotations note, all these scriptural verses are chosen to illustrate and teach the evangelical doctrine of the completeness of divine forgiveness. In the provocatively Protestant notes printed in the margins of the first authorised English Bible, the so-called Matthew's Bible of 1537, the doctrine of forgiveness in Ezekiel 18 is highlighted for special comment. God's forgiveness is final and irrevocable, says the commentary, sharply dissenting from the 'sophisters' who teach the necessity of seven years' punishment in purgatory, tartly adding: 'If this is not to mock with God and his Holy Word, I wot not what is mockage.' The response of God to the sinner's radical repentance is an equally radical forgiveness. But in the end it is God, not the sinner, who sees into the murky depths where sins lie lurking, not easily espied.

So we uncover an ambivalence: an ecclesiastical demand for repentance from the bottom of the heart; and a theological and psychological perception that the knowledge of what lies in the depths is possible only to God. It is part of George Herbert's achievement to turn the ambivalence into a dramatic encounter – God 'struggling with a peevish heart' – a dialogue which continues throughout the pilgrimage to the banqueting table of love, cavilling continuing to the very moment of sitting down to eat.[21]

Cranmer on the Real Presence

We come, therefore, to reexamine the long-controversial substance of Cranmer's revision of the eucharistic liturgy, his recasting of the pilgrimage of the heart in the Supper of the Lord. On this subject John Booty has written with notable authority and insight, emphasising especially the communal element in the liturgical plans of Cranmer and his collaborators.[22] It is, indeed, a subject which calls for a combination of delicacy and frankness, as we enter a battleground which again shows disturbing signs of being assembled along confessional lines.[23] Attitudes towards the writings and activities of the leading reformers, continental as well as British, have a way of being predetermined by attitudes towards the Reformation itself, with passages and episodes being deployed merely as illustrations. It is probably unwise to underestimate the degree to which Cranmer's reputation has popularly suffered at the hands of nineteenth-century Anglo-Catholics anxious to dissociate Anglicanism from the sixteenth-century English Reformation.

Contemporary Anglicans, however, have no obligation to choose between the apologetic alternatives of Evangelical endorsement and Anglo-Catholic rejection of the Reformation. Nor should we fall into the error of attempting hypothetically to reconstruct what might have been reformed without the generation of violent anti-papalist polemic and the advancement of the doctrine of the godly prince. If a providential view of history is required of a Christian, as Sir Herbert Butterfield maintained, then it seems preferable to judge that neither Catholic nor Protestant would readily have conceded liberty of conscience to individual human beings without the discovery of the sheer impossibility of imposing conformity after hundreds of years of bloody and futile endeavour.[24] By this standard it is difficult to find many heroes among the major sixteenth-century protagonists, and it is not as a hero of reform that we seek to elucidate Cranmer's attitude to his Catholic inheritance.

When Cranmer emerged at the age of forty out of the relative obscurity of a fellowship in Jesus College, Cambridge, on to a national and European stage, he did so in a context already massively riven by conflict. The precarious balance achieved through centuries of strife between the rival bureaucracies of Church and empire was again disturbed by challenges of new potency to the exclusive powers and dignity of the priesthood. The printing press, though apparently a neutral medium for the spread of any form of propaganda, had given a decisive advantage to Protestantism with its emphasis on the lay reading of the Scriptures and on more democratic and national forms of worship. Protestants, in fact, allied themselves to a movement which the papacy, in its sweeping censorship decree of the Lateran Council of 1515, had already tried to control.[25] As Professor Elton has pointed out, the first national propaganda campaign to make full use of the Press in any European state was that of Thomas Cromwell on behalf of Henry VIII.[26] Cranmer comes into prominence at a time when the monarch, whose advisers were already drawing upon a long tradition of imperial theology, could plainly see the advantages in an Archbishop interested in probing to the full the possibility of independence of papal jurisdiction. By the same token, a Cambridge Scripture scholar could see the advantages in a monarch of humanist sympathies for advancing the cause of Church reform on scriptural lines.

By 1533 (the date of Cranmer's consecration as Archbishop) the Continental Reformation was already well into a routinised phase. Luther had been scalded by the insurrection of the German peasantry in 1524–26, out-radicalised at the Marburg Colloquy of 1529, and subjected to severe propositional formulation in the articles of the Augsburg Confession in 1530. Cranmer had every inducement to support the kind of reform which preserved such symbols of continuity as were, at least in his view, consistent with the supreme criterion of scriptural authority. But the humanist campaign against superstition in religion was never likely to satisfy Cranmer's instincts. In 1551 he was to write:

> What availeth it to take away beads, pardons, pilgrimages, and other such like popery so long as two chief roots remain unpulled up? . . . The very body of the tree, or rather the roots of the weeds, is the popish doctrine of transubstantiation, of the real presence of Christ's flesh and blood in the sacrament of the altar (as they call it), and of the sacrifice and oblation of Christ made by the priest, for the salvation of the quick and the dead.[27]

The words are painful to us, but apart from the pejorative adjective 'popish', they are very precise. They refer to these Catholic doctrines in the way in which their defenders spoke of them, and in the right order. For the orthodox doctrine of the sacrifice of the mass depended for its very orthodoxy upon the doctrine of the real presence. If it were not Christ's very flesh and blood which was sacrificed upon the altar in the mass, then the mass would be another sacrifice than the very sacrifice of Calvary. What we make of Cranmer theologically turns, therefore, upon his attitude to transubstantiation and the real presence.[28]

One should say, of course, 'attitude' or 'attitudes', because Cranmer plainly changed his mind on the subject, it may be more than once.

Here we are indebted to a brilliant treatment of the issue by Peter Brooks, who has liberated us from the generalising slogans of previous Reformation historiography. Cranmer's so-called 'Lutheran phase' and his subsequent 'Zwinglianism' dissolve in a more differentiated analysis of the relevant texts. There emerges a theologian, who was also a player on the political scene, responding over a period of some twenty years to a common stock of exegetical investigations and arguments in a somewhat independent way.[29] By the 1550s it had become apparent to a number of reformed theologians, most impressively Calvin among them, that in respect of the Eucharist or Lord's Supper 'there is not yet any published formula in which agreement has been framed, as would be expedient.'[30] We should note the words 'published formula' (*formulaire publié*), because both the inherited traditions of scholastic dispute and the needs and opportunities of printed apologetic required an easily communicable form of words in which to encapsulate a theological position. Protestant formulae there already were, and Cranmer entered the lists at a time when the air was thick with slogans. When it comes to the complex and controversial task of interpreting Cranmer's eucharistic beliefs, it seems to me that we are already in possession of all the historical information necessary to locate him within his sixteenth-century battleground. What we now lack, I suggest, is not information so much as a perspective; I should like to say, in particular, a perspective upon the doctrine of the presence of Christ.

One long-established perspective has, it seems to me, run into the most severe difficulties. This is the ecumenically well-intentioned view that what Cranmer objected to was not the Catholic theology of the mass *per se*, but rather the popular late medieval abuses by which it was surrounded. It was a standpoint attractive to certain kinds of post-Tractarian Anglicans, but evidence was already piling up against it when in 1960 Francis Clark administered the *coup de grace* in his book, *Eucharistic Sacrifice and the Reformation*.[31] Clark demonstrated with ample examples from later medieval and contemporary sources both that mature and standard Catholic theology was in plentiful supply in mid-century England, and that the Reformers themselves were well informed of its positions and arguments. The conclusion he invited his readers to draw was that it would be preferable to admit that the chief liturgical architect of Anglicanism held a view of the eucharistic presence utterly different from, and incompatible with, that of Catholic doctrine, than to attempt to save appearances.[32] Clark took some comfort from the support for this argument of certain Evangelical Anglicans, such as Stephen Neill, Philip Hughes, G. W. Bromiley and J. I. Packer, who praised his clear presentation of the differences. Indeed it is important to note how important and frequently the term 'clear' and its cognates occur in Clark's text. While Cranmer lay in prison Cardinal Pole wrote him a letter which, we are told, 'stated the issue clearly'. The letter formulated the dispute between Catholics and Cranmer in the following terms:

> We believe that, from the moment the priest has consecrated, the body and blood of Jesus Christ are really and veritably contained under the appearances of bread and wine. You on the contrary argue that, from the authority of Scripture and the words of Jesus Christ himself, the things there are only signs.[33]

But the brevity of this formulation, and its deployment of summary phraseology, such as 'really and veritably contained under the appearance of' and 'only signs', by no means guarantee its clarity. On the contrary, I would argue that a sound perspective on the arguments used to justify such formulae is only attainable on the condition that we do *not* hold them to be clear, that we assume them to conceal puzzles, and that, as a consequence, we take very great pains to describe the liturgical processes and doctrinal convictions to which they refer. Two such puzzles must now be given a brief account by way of support for this position.

Transubstantiation and Digestion

Cranmer argued at least from 1548 to the end of his life that the inherited doctrine of the real presence made no sense of the digestive process. He wants to know, bluntly, why the transubstantiated body should not be held to have quality and distinction of parts, and if so, how long it remains inside the body of the believer. The question has already been formulated by December 1548 at the House of Lords debate. Some say, he argues, that the body of Christ flies to heaven so that it may suffer no wrong; others that the body remains in the bread until it comes into the stomach, and then ascends, so that it may not suffer in being digested. Our faith, on the contrary, he affirms, 'is not to believe him to be in bread and wine, but that he is in heaven.'[34]

The same arguments recur in Cranmer's published controversy with Bishop Stephen Gardiner. Against Gardiner, who objected that to discuss transubstantiation in terms of the problem of digestion was unacceptably crude, Cranmer showed without difficulty that it had been seriously discussed in this way by reputable medieval authorities. Gardiner's reformulation of the Catholic position is an evasion of the issue, albeit a very welcome one:

> The catholic doctrine is, that by the holy communion in the sacrament we be joined to Christ really, because we receive in the holy supper the most precious substance of his glorious body, which is a flesh giving life. And that is not digested into our flesh, but worketh in us and attempereth by heavenly nurture our body and soul, being partakers of his passion, to be conformable to his will, and by such spiritual food to be made more spiritual.[35]

And to Cranmer's subsequent charge that to insist on the supposed real, true or substantial presence of Christ's body, but then to deny distinction of place, is a systematic confusion of the concept of body, Gardiner replied:

> That our senses be not privy to that presence, or to the manner of it, but by instruction of faith; and therefore we say Christ's body to be not locally present, not by manner of quantity but invisible, and in no sensible manner, but marvelously in a sacrament and mystery truly, and in such a spiritual manner as we cannot define and determine, and yet by faith we know his body present, the parts of which be in themselves distinct from one another, in their own substance, but not by circumscription of several places to be comprehended of our capacity.[36]

The pressure under which Gardiner twice resorts to saying that we know Christ to be present in such a spiritual manner as to be known only to faith, implies a refusal of the demand for an explanation. Not unnaturally Cranmer continued to press his original objection on two further occasions. In the astonishing scene which took place at his trial for heresy in Oxford, where Cranmer was invited to take part in a doctrinal disputation of John Harpsfield, Cranmer raised the question of how Christ's body is in the sacrament, whether with quantity and qualities, form, figure and similar properties. Foxe gives a vivid, though probably not unbiased account of the variety of opinions which this question elicited from the assembled theologians, in the course of which Cranmer pressed the issue of how long the transubstantiated body of Christ remained inside the body of the believer.[37] To the reiterated objection that these were inappropriate questions, he replied that they only became relevant on the assumption of a doctrine of 'real and veritable' presence, which Cranmer nicknames 'carnal'.

Finally, in a letter to Queen Mary after his trial, when Cranmer was put through the ordeal of waiting eighty days until the expiry of his purely theoretical right to appeal to the pope in person, he returned to the same theme. In Catholic doctrine, he says, Christ's body is divided in two, one body: the natural human body with members, form and proportions, being in the heavens; the other, having neither form, fashion or proportions, being in the sacrament.

> And such a body is in the sacrament, teach they, and entereth no farther than the form of bread goeth, nor tarrieth no longer than the form of bread is by natural heat in digesting . . . What comfort can be herein to any Christian man, to receive Christ's unshapen body, and it to enter no farther than the stomach, and to depart by and bye as soon as the bread is consumed?[38]

What are we to make of this apparently crude *reductio*? Is it to be dismissed as a piece of highly selective, phoney Protestant rationalism of nominalist origin?[39] The question is far from clear. Even if we were to take our sightings by St Thomas Aquinas's highly sophisticated account of transubstantiation, part of which Cranmer misquoted and misconstrued, we would still be in disputed territory. For despite the deployment of considerable philosophical resources, the change in the substance of the bread and wine is explicitly stated to have no parallel in the natural world, and amounts to a categorically unique miracle brought about by the power of God. The language used of this event cannot be said to clarify it; what it does rather is to apostrophise it.[40] It could be argued, further, that the very attempt to develop a precise vocabulary in order to speak of it confuses the issue by giving a specious air of technical clarity to what in the end cannot be illuminated except negatively. Of this negative illumination, Gardiner's replies to Cranmer are still instructive examples.

Eucharist and Ascension

The lack of clarity in this question can be further illustrated with reference to the assumption on which Cranmer relies – that Christ's body in heaven is his natural body. It was common Catholic teaching that Christ ascended, body and soul, into the heavens. But it was an idiosyncratic deduction, first advanced by a Dutch humanist and then developed by Johannes Oecolampadius, that for this reason there could not simultaneously be a natural body on earth, let alone a plurality of such bodies in the eucharistic sacrament.[41] This doctrine was vigorously expressed in the so-called 'Black Rubric', the declaration on kneeling to receive the sacrament affixed to the end of the 1552 rite.

> As concernynge the naturall body and blood of our sauiour Christ they are in heaven and not here. For it is agaynst the trueth of Christes true natural body, to be in more places then in one, at one tyme.[42]

An assertion of this kind depended, of course, on the assumption that the natural body of Christ occupied space in heaven. But some, at least, of Cranmer's supporters would have had no such convictions. Martin Bucer, for example, in an English writing of 1550, is plainly unhappy about proposals of that kind, arguing that Scripture knows of a non-local heaven, far above human conceptions. 'We place not Christ's body in heaven after the manner of the fourth book of Aristotle's Naturals.' And on the presence of Christ, whether in word or sacraments, he argues that it is not a presence of place, of senses, or of reason, but of faith, 'forasmuch as we are conveyed into heaven by faith, being placed in Christ.'[43]

With this later point Cranmer would have been in firm sympathy. Calling attention to the fact that it is a doctrine common to a number of reformed theologians, including Calvin himself in addition to Oecolampadius, Dr Brooks, in a happy phrase, has spoken of it as the *sursum corda* approach to the heavenly Christ. 'Lift up your hearts: We lift them to the Lord' is, of course, an integral part of the mass. Similarly traditional is the Gelasian Collect for Ascension Day, translated in Cranmer's 1549 Prayer Book as follows:

Graunte we beseche thee almightie God,
that like as we doe beleue thy onely-begotten Sonne our Lorde to haue ascended into the heauens:
So we may also in heart and mind thither ascend, and with him continually dwell.[44]

The Christian life is thus traditionally conceived under the metaphor of ascent, and it is this metaphor to which Cranmer turned so as to provide an interpretation of the nature of Christ's presence in the Eucharist. By faith, that is, in heart and mind, the believer ascends into the heavens, to feast there at Christ's table:

Being like eagles in his life, we should fly up into heaven in our hearts, where that Lamb is resident at the right hand of his Father, which taketh away the sins of the world.[45]

If we analyse the structure and movements of the 1549 Holy Communion we will note a remarkable ritual of separation immediately preceding the *sursum corda*. At this point the rubrics instruct those who are to be 'partakers' (a highly significant, and frequently used term) to gather in the choir of the church, while the others depart. The partakers, we should recall, are those who have already examined themselves in the presence of God, 'who sees all men's hearts', and have promised amendment of life from the bottom of their hearts. Physically separated from non-partakers they are thus ready for a liturgical text of separation, which conveys them into heaven – by faith – to 'laud and magnify' God's holy name with angels and archangels. The true significance of this liturgy is articulated at the point where the priest, having exchanged the peace with the congregation, expresses the common intention, 'Let us kepe a joyfull and holy feast with the Lorde.'[46]

The further revised liturgy of 1552 pivots, for all its modifications in detail, on precisely the same point, if anything further dramatising the elevation of heart and mind by preceding it with confession, absolution and declaration of the Gospel words of comfort. Thus the believer arrives in the heavens already shriven to make a classic act of ritual obeisance in the presence of God ('we doe not presume to come to this thy table'), and is immediately admitted to the 'Goddes borde', the table at which is recalled the meal on the night on which the Lord was betrayed.

What Cranmer was doing was giving textual, literary, and therefore ritual expression to the pilgrimage of the heart, 'flying up to heaven in our hearts'. We should particularly note that both of these liturgies conform to the pattern of the ritual process as described by the late anthropologist Victor Turner.[47] They are, moreover, rituals which, in the belief of the participants, are preceded and attended by miracles of divine agency, the very faith of the 'flying' believers being an act of the Holy Spirit and their consequent nourishment a mutual indwelling with Christ. To speak of Cranmer's Lord's Supper as anti-ritualistic or as a merely mental commemoration is absurdly inadequate. Furthermore we can be quite confident that Cranmer himself knew that what he was proposing was a ritual. Against those who sought to prevent kneeling to receive the sacrament, he wrote in 1552 with great spirit:

> They say that kneeling is not commanded in Scripture: and what is not commanded in Scripture is unlawful. There is the root of the errors of the sects! If that be true, take away the whole Book of Service; and let us have no more trouble in setting forth an order in religion, or indeed in common policy. If kneeling be not explicitly enjoined in Holy Scripture, neither is standing or sitting. Let them lie down on the ground, and eat their meat like Turks or Tartars.[48]

For Cranmer kneeling was the appropriate bodily corollary of the prayer of humble access, of not being worthy 'so much as to gather up the crommes under thy table', both word and deed being controlled by an overwhelming sense of coming into God's own presence, by his gracious and loving invitation.

But if we can be sure of the narrative outline of the pilgrimage, and of the visceral, bodily way in which the cognitive content of the pilgrimage is processed, the same cannot be said of the theology of the matter which remains inchoate and obscure behind its formulae. Cranmer's local presence in the heavens has, in the end of the day, to be as obscurely qualified as Gardiner's assertion of a real, veritable or substantial presence. Indeed, if we are to make progress at all in the

41

discussion of the subject in contemporary theology we must be clear that the notion of presence itself, especially the sense in which the transcendent can be said to impinge upon our experience, deserves a quality of attention which it rarely receives.[49]

The Power of the Priesthood

In what has preceded, a somewhat self-conscious attempt has been made to close the gap between Cranmer and Gardiner by drawing attention to obscurities in their respective formulae. But on one point the gap apparently refuses to close, namely about the role of the priest and the consequences of his intentions, words and actions. If there is nothing un-Catholic about Cranmer's *sursum corda* approach to the presence of Christ, nonetheless its exclusive use to preclude divine movement in the other direction, from heaven to the altar on earth, in virtue of the priest's faithful utterance of the words of consecration, was and remains problematic. The revolutionary character of what Cranmer was proposing is clear from the extensive use he made of the analogy of Christ's presence in the rite of baptism. As he was never tired of insisting, in baptism it is Catholic teaching that the baptised receive Christ himself, body and soul, humanity and divinity, to ever-lasting life, without benefit of any transubstantiation of the water. He even took the trouble to formulate the thought in an aphorism of stunning inelegance ('if the Holy Ghost be not inaquate, no more is Christ impanate').[50] It can hardly have escaped the notice of his opponents that baptism might be administered, of necessity, by layper-sons, notably, of course, by women.

It is not possible to deny that with the Reformation a shift takes place in Christian thinking about the 'power' of the priesthood. In answer to the Western rebels' demand that the mass should be cele-brated as before, by priest alone without communicants, Cranmer replied that priests speak and act in the names and persons of the congregation, 'for all the whole that is done should be the act of the people and pertain to the people, as well as to the priest.'[51] We hear an echo of the deployment of the Collect for Purity – a priest's vesting prayer in the Sarum rite – as a preparation of the whole congregation, priest included. Nonetheless, though in Cranmer's rituals priestly 'powers' have been reduced, they have not been eliminated; though the mystique of the priesthood has been diminished, it has not been abolished.

We note, for example, not least in the liturgy of public baptism, that the priest is given a role which precisely and dramatically represents that of Christ, receiving and embracing children in the arms of his mercy. Similarly, in the exhortation delivered to the people when they are found to be negligent in coming to the Holy Communion, the priest explicitly and in accordance with the known duties of priestly office summons the people to the feast 'in the name of God' and 'in Christ's behalf'.[52] Thus it is the priest's role, and not anyone else's, to initiate the action of celebrating the Lord's Supper in which the presence of Christ is enjoyed and the believer miraculously nourished.

Ascent – Descent

For all this, it may properly be asked whether there is not some cost involved in a liturgy of ascension, as compared with one which embodies the descent of divine condescension on to a public, local altar. Is there not in the former an implicit individualism which locks the believer's miraculous encounter with the ascended Christ into the apparently uninspectable privacy of the individual heart, rather than open it out to be visibly acknowledged and greeted by a communal act of reverence?

This is a powerful and important argument, and there are good reasons why, as Cranmer insisted, the miracle of holy communion should be marked with corporate and public rituals of respect. But in one particular the objection is seriously misconceived. The offer of Cranmer's liturgies was made to a whole community, indeed to a whole nation. It is an invitation to a pilgrimage to make common sense out of life by adopting a common pattern of affective processing. Religious rituals, including of course linguistic rituals, have the potential to pattern or structure human experience as a whole. Cranmer's liturgies amount to a map of the heart as *topos*, a map for pilgrimage from the depths to the heights. It is a pilgrimage with God, who is struggling with the heart, addressing comfortable words to it, pouring in the grace of his Holy Spirit to lift it up, melting it, remaking it, carving things upon it – the whole gamut of metaphor and metonymy, available in a public liturgy in the vernacular to influence, and perhaps decisively to shape, the linguistic habits and imagination of a whole culture. Such a presence of Christ is not conceived as cheap grace; it involves serious self-examination and repentance. It is not private to the individual, but involves public reconciliations and restitutions. It is not a disembodied mental process, but one linking mind and guts. (The use of the new religion, said a well-placed observer in 1553, 'is not yet printed in the stomachs of eleven of twelve parts of the realm'.)[53]

So it becomes impossible to take at its face value the belief of sixteenth-century Protestants that rituals and physical transactions were intrinsically a threat to the spiritual content of Christianity. The exigencies of arguing for the simplification of over-elaborate rituals, and of resisting what Mary Douglas has called the ritualisation of ritual,[54] made Protestants congenitally blind to their own ritual, including, of course, formulae of belief, characteristic phraseology and slogans, as well as rule-bound modes of ritual behaviour and arrangements of church furnishing. In due course the English Reformation, protected by its comparative conservatism from the reckless assumption that right belief made rituals unnecessary, was to receive a sociologically impressive apologia from Richard Hooker. But the foundation is already there in Cranmer, through his vision of a prayer book for the whole people, mapping, guiding and structuring their pilgrimage of communion with Christ.

From all that has been said it will come as no surprise that Cranmer interpreted his own final days in terms of the pilgrimage metaphor we have examined. When formally declared guilty of heresy, he appealed 'to the just judgement of the Almighty: trusting to be present with him in heaven; for whose presence in the altar I am thus condemned'.[55] He professed – and we may believe him – 'that the loss of his promotion grieved him not: he thanked God as heartily for that poor and afflicted state in which he then was, as ever he did for the times of his prosperity.'[56] The barbarous ceremony of ritual degradation (a 'rather Protestant Service [said the late Professor Gordon Rupp] since its object was to erase what on catholic principles might be supposed to be indelible'[57]) elicited from him the remark that 'it needed not; for that he had done with this gear long ago'.[58] With Christians since the days of St Paul, Cranmer unhesitatingly, in a letter from prison to Peter Martyr, applied to himself the inversion contained in the sentence, 'when I am weak, then am I strong.'[59] On the Christian map to be down is to be up. The liturgical pattern of pilgrimage, from the bottom of the heart to the height of the heavens, imprints itself in inverted form as the schema for the interpretation of suffering.

It may be that this is a way in which we can make intelligible to ourselves the mystery of the abjectness of his recantations, and his subsequent rejection of them. In the last and sixth of these texts, probably drafted for him, he professed himself to be not only a viler sinner than Saul in his days as a persecutor, and the thief on the cross (the latter, of course, though penitent, was crucified) 'but the most accursed of all whom the earth had ever borne'.[60] Could it be that the very act of self-vilification triggered in his mind a pattern to which he had given such effective liturgical shape? An open heart, even an especially devious one, which yet contains no secrets from God, is a place in which God himself is encountered. Precisely at this point the potentiality of inversion is at its most profound. Totally alone, treated without consistency of policy, confronting the certainty of death by burning, Cranmer returned to his liturgical pattern of meaning so as to make sense of his situation. His recantations cannot express the bottom of his heart. Below it and above it is another reality, and God is in it.

As one reads the story of Cranmer's behaviour on the day of his burning one cannot but be profoundly moved, whether one is convinced that he died for a good cause or for a bad one, or simply that all involved were deeply mistaken. It is of the death of this scholar–mystic that a magnanimous Catholic bystander wrote,

> His friends sorrowed for love; his enemies for pity; strangers for a common kind of humanity whereby we are bound one to another.[61]

NOTES

1. J. Booty (ed.), *The Book of Common Prayer, 1559*, Folger Library (Charlottesville, VA, 1976), p. 365.
2. All quotations from the 1549 and 1552 Prayer Books are taken from *The First and Second Prayer Books of Edward VI*, Everyman Library (London, 1910); in this case from 1549, ibid., p. 212.
3. This mass was sung before Cranmer's trial at Oxford. 'They had mass of the Holy Ghost solemnly sung in prick-song [plain-song with descant]

by the quier-men of Christ's church.' J. Foxe, *The Acts and Monuments of John Foxe*, 4th edn., rev. and ed. J. Pratt, Vol. VI (London, 1870), p. 441.

4. P. Hodgson, *The Cloud of Unknowing* (London, 1973), p. 180. See also S. Brook, *The Language of the Book of Common Prayer* (London, 1965), p. 76.

5. On heart in the Old Testament see art. 'Leb.', in G. J. Botterweck et al., eds., *Theologisches Wörterbuch zum Alten Testament*, IV (Stuttgart, 1984), pp. 413–51.

6. Derek Brewer in P. Boitani and J. Mann, eds., *The Cambridge Chaucer Companion* (Cambridge, 1986), p. 238.

7. The fact that God alone sees and tests the human heart is repeatedly affirmed in both Old and New Testaments (see 1 Sam. 16:7; Jer. 11:20; 17:9f; Luke 16:15; Rom. 8:27; 1 Thess. 2:4; Rev. 2:23) and gave rise to the term *kardiognostes*, knower of hearts, used in Acts 1:24; 15:8 and not found in secular Greek. It is generally held that the term 'introspection' appeared first in the second half of the seventeenth century. But the classic text describing how the mind reflects upon itself is Augustine's *de Trinitate* X, 13. In a recent work systematically critical of the theses of introspectionism, William Lyons has proposed that what is occurring when we claim to be introspecting is to refer to some already formed culturally inherited model of our inner cognitive and appetitive processes. This is fully consistent with the affirmation that God alone knows the human heart. See W. Lyons, *The Disappearance of Introspection* (Cambridge, 1986).

8. See *inter alia*, M. R. Haight, *A Study of Self-Deception* (Brighton and New Jersey, 1980); M. W. Martin (ed.), *Self-Deception and Self-Understanding* (Lawrence, 1985); and B. P. McLaughlin and A. O. Rorty, *Perspectives on Self-Deception* (Berkeley, 1988).

9. See D. M. MacKinnon's comment on 'the disturbing effect of parabolic discernment', in this case, *The Problem of Metaphysics* (Cambridge, 1974), pp. 91ff.

10. *Miscellaneous Writings and Letters of Thomas Cranmer*, ed. J. E. Cox, Parker Society (Cambridge, 1846), pp. 84ff.

11. ibid., p. 86. Cited hereafter as Cranmer, *Works* (PS) ii.

12. F. M. M. Comper, *The Life of Richard Rolle, Together with an Edition of his English* Lyrics (London, 1928), pp. 228–29.

13. In the course of a debate in the House of Lords in December 1548, Cranmer (according to the notes apparently taken at the time) argued that 'the spirit and the body are contrary.' Whether this can be taken as a general indication of Cranmer's neo-Platonism seems to me very doubtful, not least because the context, a discussion of Bishop Tunstall's use of the terms spirit and body, is very obscure. See F. A. Gaspuet and E. Bishop, *Edward VI and the Book of Common Prayer* (London, 1890), ch. XI and Appendix V.

14. 1552, *The First and Second Prayer Books*, p. 363.

15. 1549 (7th Sunday after Trinity), ibid., p. 146.

16. *The Works of George Herbert*, ed. F. E. Hutchinson (Oxford, 1941), p. 126.

17. See on the theme of *peregrinatio* in Erasmus, M. A. Screech, *Ecstasy and the*

Praise of Folly (London, 1980), pp. 152–58. I am grateful to Dr Eamon Duffy for drawing my attention to this reference.

18. 1549; Exhortation 'if . . . the people be negligent to come to the Communion,' *First and Second Prayer Books*, p. 217.

19. J. Strype, *Memorials of the Most Reverend Father in God, Thomas Cranmer*, 3 vols. (Oxford, 1848), Vol. I, p. 352.

20. 1552; An Order for Morning Prayer, *First and Second Prayer Books*, p. 347.

21. 'Sion', *The Works of George Herbert*, 106; and 'Love (III)', ibid., pp. 188f.

22. 'Communion and Commonwealth: The Book of Common Prayer', in J. E. Booty (ed.), *The Godly Kingdom of Tudor England* (Wilton, CT, 1981), pp. 139–216.

23. See the review of Reformation historiography in A. G. Dickens and J. Tonlin, *The Reformation in Historical Thought* (Oxford, 1985), and R. O'Day, *The Debate on the English Reformation* (London, 1986).

24. See H. Butterfield, *Christianity in European History* (London, 1952), p. 34.

25. Elizabeth Esenstein, *The Printing Press as an Agent of Change* (Cambridge, 1980), pp. 353f.

26. G. Elton, *Policy and Police* (Cambridge, 1972), pp. 206–7.

27. *Writings and Disputations of Thomas Cranmer . . . relative to the Sacrament of the Lord's Supper*, ed. J. E. Cox, Parker Society (Cambridge, 1844). Cited as Cranmer, *Works* (PS) i.

28. J. A. Mueller usefully observes that whereas Cranmer began by a denial of transubstantiation and from there passed to a denial of any corporal presence in the sacrament, Gardiner reversed the order, affirming the presence and from there arguing for transubstantiation, *Stephen Gardiner and the Tudor Reaction* (London, 1926), p. 211.

29. P. N. Brooks, *Thomas Cranmer's Doctrine of the Eucharist* (London, 1965).

30. J. Calvin, *Corpus Reformatorium*, XXXIII (Braunschweig, 1866) col. 460. ET in J. K. S. Reid, *Calvin: Theological Treatises*, LCC Vol. XXII (London, 1954), p. 166. Cf. P. Brooks, p. 68.

31. F. Clark, *Eucharistic Sacrifice and the Reformation*, 2nd edn (Oxford, 1967). The second edition contains an introduction pointing out 'the very wide measure of acceptance and scholarly agreement' with which the book's first publication had been greeted.

32. ibid., pp. 159–168.

33. E. T. by Francis Clark, ibid., p. 166, from Pole's *Epistulae*, 5 vols., ed. J. G. Schelhorn (Brescia, 1744–57), Pars V, p. 253.

34. F. A. Gasquet and E. Bishop, *Edward VI and the Book of Common Prayer*, pp. 400f. The authors wrongly observe that this argument, 'although somewhat unpleasant reading, has little to do with the main issue' (p. 162). On the contrary, it is important precisely because it is so crude.

35. Cranmer, *Works* (PS) ii, p. 453.

36. ibid., p. 62.

37. *The Acts and Monuments of John Foxe*, Vol. VI, pp. 511–520.

38. Cranmer, *Works* (PS) ii, p. 453.

39. Eugene K. McGee, 'Cranmer and Nominalism', *Harvard Theological Review* 57 (1964): pp. 189–216 attempted to argue that the difference

was Cranmer's supposedly Nominalist frame of reference. In reply W. J. Courtenay, 'Cranmer as a Nominalist', *HTR* 57 (Oct. 1964): pp. 367–380, shows that this is to misinterpret the actual doctrines of those philosophers generally considered to be nominalists.

40. See the fascinating discussion of 'the very creative act of breaking the rules that capture the illumination we wish to convey' in the exchanges between G. Egner (= P. J. Fitzpatrick) and H. McCabe in *New Blackfriars* 53 (1972): pp. 354–359, 399–409, 546–554, and idem, *New Blackfriars*, 54 (1973): pp. 171–80.

41. J. Pelikan, *The Christian Tradition* Vol. 4, *Reformation of Church and Dogma* (1300–1700) (Chicago, 1984), pp. 158–60.

42. *First and Second Prayer Books*, p. 393. Although the rubric was thought to be totally unnecessary by Cranmer, and was published without his permission or that of convocation, solely on royal authority, this sentence undoubtedly expresses his own doctrine.

43. The text is given in Strype's *Memorials of Archbishop Cranmer*, Vol. II (Oxford, 1848), pp. 597–611; this quotation, pp. 601f. But Strype, relying on Foxe, is not accurate in some parts; see the remarks of R. W. Dixon, *History of the Church of England*, Vol. III (London, 1902), pp. 244f.

44. *First and Second Prayer Books*, p. 127.

45. Cranmer, *Works* (PS) i, p. 398.

46. *First and Second Prayer Books*, p. 224.

47. Victor Turner, 'Passages, Margins and Poverty: Religious Symbols of Communitas', in *Dramas, Fields and Metaphors* (Ithaca, NY, 1974), pp. 231–71.

48. Quoted in Dixon, *History of the Church of England*, Vol. III, pp. 476–77.

49. See D. M. MacKinnon, 'The Notion of Presence' in *The Problem of Metaphysics*.

50. Cranmer, *Works* (PS) i, p. 306.

51. Cranmer, *Works* (PS) ii, p. 169.

52. 1552; *First and Second Prayer Books*, p. 383.

53. Lord William Paget, cited in A. G. Dickens, *The English Reformation* (London, 1964), p. 255.

54. M. Douglas, *Natural Symbols* (London, 1971), p. 21.

55. J. Strype, *Memorials of Cranmer*, Vol. III, p. 222.

56. ibid., p. 241.

57. G. Rupp on Thomas Cranmer in *Six Makers of English Religion* 1500–1700 (London, 1957), p. 49.

58. Strype, *Memorials of Cranmer*, Vol. III, p. 222.

59. *The Works of Thomas Cranmer*, ed. G. E. Duffield (Appleford, Berks, 1964), p. 326.

60. Latin text in Cranmer, *Works* (PS) ii, p. 565.

61. Strype, *Memorials*, Vol. III, p. 255. Strype conflated two sources, attributed to a Catholic writer known by the initials 'J.A.'; see R. W. Dixon, *History of the Church of England*, Vol. IV, pp. 532–33.

3

'LOVE BADE ME WELCOME'

One of the gifts of God to Anglicans, and through them to the whole Church, is the poetry and prose of George Herbert (1593–1633). There are many whose Christian faith and life have been nourished by Herbert's wit, insight and devotion, and who have warmly responded to Richard Baxter's view of him as 'a man who speaks to God like one that really believeth a God, and whose business in the world is most with God'.[1] Herbert has appealed to a very wide spectrum of readers, from non-Anglican Puritans, to devout Anglicans and Roman Catholics. Recently there has been something of a tussle to identify his sources of inspiration as predominantly either patristic and medieval or, on the other hand, reformed and Protestant. The debate has lasted for more than 40 years, since Rosemond Tuve's *A Reading of George Herbert* (Chicago, 1952), which strongly stressed the medieval theological and liturgical background, to Barbara Lewalski's *Protestant Poetics and the Seventeenth Century Religious Lyric* (Princeton, 1971) and Richard Strier's *Love Known* (Chicago, 1983), both of which turned to Reformation sources.

Perhaps, however, we should be readier to say simply that Herbert was an Anglican. In *A Priest to the Temple (APT)* he advanced the Anglican view that 'the country parson hath read the Fathers also, and the Schoolmen, and the later writers, or a good proportion of all' (*Ch. V 'The Parsons Accesory Knowledges'*).[2] There are no grounds for thinking that Luther and Calvin and other Protestant authors could not have been included among the 'later writers'; nor grounds for supposing that Herbert would not be discriminating in his use of Protestant theologians, to whom he would feel indebted without being subservient. Recent research has also given us good reason for thinking that those same theologians had reflected deeply upon both patristic and medieval writers, and that they also used them both critically and appreciatively. Richard Todd has recently argued that Herbert can be illuminated by consideration of patristic and medieval tradition, specifically in respect of an Augustinian understanding of signs, without underestimating the need for an historical understanding of seventeenth-century English Protestantism.[3] The early seventeenth century was a period when Anglicans began to achieve a somewhat more self-conscious sense of their own identity. Indeed some of Herbert's own somewhat chauvenistic lines in 'The British Church' express what subsequently came to be seen as the Anglican *via media*.

> A fine aspect in fit aray,
> Neither too mean, nor yet too gay,
>> Shows who is best.
> Outlandish looks may not compare
> For all they either painted are,
>> Or else undrest.[4]
> . . . But, dearest Mother, what those misse,
> The mean, thy praise and glorie is,
>> And long may be.

One of the ways in which we may appreciate how thoroughly Herbert is embedded within the still-developing Anglican tradition is to examine thoroughly one of his poems, 'Love III'. A testimony to the power of this brief piece both to reflect and to deepen the experience of faith lies in the work of Simone Weil. In a letter to a friend she wrote:

> I enclose the English poem, Love, which I recited to you. It has played a big role in my life, because I was repeating it to myself at the moment when Christ came to take possession of me for the first time. I thought I was only reciting a beautiful poem but, unknown to me, it was a prayer.[5]

The letter to which the above is the postscript contains an almost unbearable description of the writer's physical suffering and state of mind, and of her sudden sense of 'a presence more personal, more certain, and more real than that of a human being' (p. 140). Love had been the centre of her effort of will, and love was the content of the unlooked-for experience.

I quote the poem in full.

Love bade me welcome: yet my soul drew back,
    Guiltie of dust and sinne.
But quick-ey'd Love, observing me grow slack
    From my first entrance in,
Drew nearer to me, sweetly questioning,
    If I lack'd any thing.

A guest, I answer'd, worthy to be here:
    Love said, You shall be he.
I the unkinde, ungratefull? Ah my deare,
    I cannot look on thee.
Love took my hand, and smiling did reply,
    Who made the eyes but I?

Truth Lord, but I have marr'd them: let my shame
    Go where it doth deserve.
And know you not, sayes Love, who bore the blame?
    My deare, then I will serve.
You must sit down, sayes Love, and taste my meat:
    So I did sit and eat.

'Love III' closes the central section of *The Temple*, entitled The Church, and follows Death, Doomsday, Judgement and Heaven. It is at once apparent from this placing that there are a multiplicity of levels on which the poem can be read. In order to explore these as fully as possible, I propose in what follows to give the poem three 'readings': from the standpoint of biblical interpretation, in relation to Anglican liturgy, and as Christian doctrine.

I

George Herbert's explicit attitude to Scripture was that it provided the 'chief and top' of the Parson's knowledge, being 'the storehouse and magazine of life and comfort' (*APT* IIII). Accepting the requirement of the Ordinal that priests should read and weigh the Scriptures daily and thereby 'wax riper and stronger' in their ministries, Herbert held that the way to do it was to make 'a diligent collation of Scripture with Scripture'.

51

For all Truth being consonant to itself, and all being penned by one and the self-same Spirit, it cannot be, but that an industrious, and judicious comparing of place with place must be a singular help for the right understanding of the Scriptures (*APT* IIII).

This passage reflects in positive terms the requirement of Article XX (Of the Authority of the Church), forbidding the Church from so expounding 'one place of Scripture, that it be repugnant to another'.

'The Holy Scriptures II' speaks of the way in which all 'lights' in the 'constellation' of the Scriptures combine to tell a single, complete and intelligible narrative. It also recalls the biblical verse: 'The heavens declare the glory of God: and the firmament sheweth his handy-work' (Ps. 19:1, Coverdale). Herbert characteristically allows a biblical resonance ('Oh that I knew how all thy lights combine,/And the configurations of their glory!') which in one sense is fanciful, but in another has a core of appropriateness.

> This verse marks that, and both do make a motion
> Unto a third, that ten leaves off doth lie:
> Then as dispersed herbs do watch a potion,
> These three make up some Christian's destinie:

This is a typically multi-layered utterance, comparing biblical interpretation to astrological speculation or the concocting of medicines. When the word of God is said to be 'a book of stars' lighting the believer to eternal bliss, we are within the range of the central biblical metaphor of the light ('Thy word is a lantern unto my feet: and a light unto my paths', Ps. 119:10, Coverdale; 'I am the light of the world', John 8:12). Biblical events, metaphors, parables and analogies combine in Herbert's imagination to clarify and deepen his own experience and the figured world which he inhabits.

The core experience reflected in 'Love III' is that of hospitality, which is specifically an attribute of a Christian way of life (see Rom. 12:13; 1 Tim. 3:2; Titus 1:8; Heb. 13:1–2; 1 Pet. 4:9). More precisely the action of the poem is the way in which Love (the host) turns a stranger into a guest at table. Hospitality (*philoxenia*) is literally 'a love of strangers'. In the poem the host refuses to allow that the one who is welcomed should continue to construe himself as a stranger, but should rather accept the status of Love's guest. The biblical references here are numerous, especially in relation to Jesus' practice of dining with sinners (Luke 5:27–32; 19:1–10) and to the parable of the great supper (Luke 14:16–24; Matt. 22:1–14, the latter with its reference to the wedding garment).[6] But in the light of the eschatological setting of the poem in the section The Church, we must also reckon with the promise of the messianic banquet (Luke 13:29; 12:35–40; Matt. 26:29; Rev. 3:20; 19:7–9). Luke 12:37 specifically envisages the returning master glad to find his slaves alert at his late arrival, and ready to have them sit down to eat a meal which he himself will serve. This is a passage with a strong eschatological significance, which also would provoke a sense of strangeness and reversal in the master's actions. Herbert specifically connects that willingness to invite the slave to sit down and be a guest, with the moral quality of love. Helen Vendler draws attention to the portrayal of love in St Paul's ecstatic hymn in 1 Corinthians 13. 'By his [the host's] action, we deduce the nature of Love: Love is welcoming, Love is observant, Love is solicitous, Love is kind, Love is long-suffering, Love is not easily provoked, Love is not vainglorious, Love never fails.'[7]

If it be allowed that Herbert's guest may represent the Church at the marriage feast of the Lamb, then we are reminded of the traditional ecclesiological interpretation of the Song of Songs. Here the bride-groom brings his beloved into the banqueting house, 'and his banner over me was love' (Song of Sol. 2:4). Here also there is a certain emphasis on sitting; 'I sat down under his shadow with great delight, and his fruit was sweet to my taste' (2:3). The same source reflects a confession of unworthiness (1:5), traditionally attributed to the Church.

To be 'guilty of dust and sin' alludes to the twofold character of the natural human condition, which is mortal ('Dust thou art, and unto dust shalt thou return', Gen. 3:19, see also 2:7 and 3:14) and prone to evil thoughts and deeds. Addressing God, Abraham excuses himself as 'but dust and ashes' (Gen. 18:27). The final destiny of humanity being to disintegrate, the question arises in the mind of the Psalmist, 'Shall the dust give thanks unto thee: or shall it declare thy truth?' (Ps. 30:10, Coverdale). The thought that God does not deal with us in proportion to our sins is rooted in another psalm, 'He hath not dealt with us after our sins: nor rewarded us according to our wickedness' (Ps. 103:10, Coverdale), and is the starting-point of another poem, 'Sighs and

Groans'. Here the explanation that dust signifies frailty is made explicit ('But I am frailty, and already dust;/O do not grind me').

We have already noted the confession of unworthiness in the Song of Songs, but the self-reproaches of the biblical prophets are a much more widely diffused pattern of response to the divine invitation. Moses in Exodus 4 bewails his lack of authority and eloquence, and is asked, for his pains, who made the human mouth (Exod. 4:11; compare, 'Who made the eyes but I?'). Isaiah protests his unfitness as 'a man of unclean lips' (Isa. 6:5). Jeremiah insists that he cannot speak the word of the Lord, 'for I am a child' (Jer. 1:6). Not looking upon God is the theme of a number of biblical passages ('there shall no man see me and live', Exod. 33:20; Manoah after an angelic vision says, 'We shall surely die, because we have seen God', Judg. 14:22; Isaiah is in dread because 'mine eyes have seen the Lord of hosts', Isa. 6:5).

The holiness of God is the background to both of the guest's protestations, 'I cannot look on thee' and 'let my shame/Go where it doth deserve'. Shame, of course, is associated with Adam's fallen consciousness (Gen. 3). 'Whither shall I cause my shame to go?' was Tamar's protestation against Amnon's lecherous intentions (2 Sam. 13:13). It is no accident that all these examples derive from the Old Testament, since Herbert is moving the ground away from a religious system based on what is deserved, to one grounded on what grace and redemption have achieved; 'and know you not . . . who bore the blame?'. This is a direct reference to the New Testament interpretation of Isaiah 53 ('surely he hath borne our griefs' v. 4, 'for he shall bear their iniquities' v. 11), in such passages as 1 Peter 2:24, 'Who in his own self bare our sin in his own body on the tree', Hebrews 9:28, 'So Christ was once offered to bear the sins of many', and Matthew 8:17 – a direct quotation of Isaiah 53 – 'He himself took our infirmities, and bare our sicknesses'.

For all the particular allusions, 'Love III' goes far beyond a pastiche of scriptural references. It is a combination of a biblical scene, the messianic banquet, and a narrative of how self-exclusion has been overcome by grace. The drama of redemption acquires a specific location and the whole is shot through with conscious and unconscious biblical allusions and echoes, the result of Herbert's profound knowledge of, and affection for, the 'storehouse' of Scripture. Bloch appropriately comments on Herbert's 'imaginative freedom', in bringing together disparate and even contradictory passages in new configurations, elaborating upon their suggestions, and ranging them dramatically, so that what they say strikes us with the force of discovery.[8]

But it was, in his case, a Scripture already mediated to him in the Liturgy; and this fact gives us the opportunity for a second 'reading' in relation to his *Book of Common Prayer*.

II

The liturgical reading depends upon the interpretation given by the *Book of Common Prayer* (1559) to Jesus' parable of the marriage feast.[9] In the Lukan version, the invited guests 'all with one consent began to make excuse' (Luke 14:18). The Order for the Administration of the Lord's Supper or Holy Communion provides the curate with an exhortation, based on this parable, when he sees the people 'negligent to come to the holy Communion'. There follows a series of sentences which contain words woven by Herbert into his poem (in italic in what follows):

> We be come together at this time, dearly beloved brethren, to feed at the Lord's supper, unto the which in God's behalf I *bid* you all that are here present, and beseech you for the Lord Jesus Christ's sake, that ye will not refuse to come thereto, being so *lovingly* called and *bidden* of God himself. Ye know how generous and *unkind* a thing it is, when a man hath prepared a rich feast, decked his table with all kind of provision, so that there *lacketh* nothing but the *guests to sit down* . . . If any man say, I am a grievous *sinner*, and therefore am afraid to come, wherefore then do ye not repent and amend. When God calleth you, are ye not *ashamed* to say ye will not come?

The verbal echoes are striking: but what is also unmistakable is that the tone has altered. There is nothing in Herbert to correspond to the minatory words, 'Now if you will in no wise thus do, consider with yourselves how great injury ye do to God, and how sore punishment hangeth over your heads for the same.' These sentences from the Exhortation are a reasonable reflection of the Matthean version of the parable which includes a robust description of the punishment of the ungrateful invitees – 'They which were bidden were not worthy' (Matt. 22:8). But in Herbert's version it is the guest himself who pleads his own unworthiness ('I the unkinde, the ungratefull'); here the address is subtly phrased to apply to one who wants to be present at the feast, but feels unworthy.

The Prayer Book provides yet another Exhortation which identifies the danger to the believer of unworthy reception. In this text the priest says, in interpretation of 1 Corinthians 11:29 ('he that eateth and drinketh unworthily, eateth and drinketh damnation to himself'):

> For as the benefit is great, if with a truly penitent heart and lively faith we receive that holy sacrament (for then we spiritually eat the flesh of Christ, and drink his blood, then we dwell in Christ and Christ in us, we be one with Christ and Christ with us:) so is the danger great, if we receive the same unworthily.

This is the source of the anxiety of Herbert's guest. The poem addresses itself to the apparent requirement of a state of *prior* worthiness, as a condition of receiving the sacrament.

In *A Priest to the Temple*, indeed, Herbert identifies the celebrant's own *aporia* as to how to approach the Holy Communion ('Especially at Communion times he is in a great confusion, as being not only to receive God, but to break and administer him', Ch. XXII 'The Parson in Sacraments'). The priest's duty is to insist that the worshippers approach the sacrament with reverence. Herbert deals with the long-controversial matter of posture in the following way:

> The Feast indeed requires sitting, because it is a Feast; but man's unpreparedness asks kneeling. Hee that comes to the Sacrament, hath the confidence of a Guest, and hee that kneels, confesseth himself an unworthy one, and therefore differs from other Feasters: but hee that sits, or lies, puts up to an Apostle: Contentiousness in a feast of charity is more scandall than any posture.

In this passage there is a manifest tension between confidence and unworthiness. The Prayer Book instructed communicants to receive the Communion kneeling; but it also required that they not approach the Sacrament unworthily. The dialogue between host and guest in 'Love III' reflects this tension. Indeed in a somewhat programmatic way one may say that the oscillation between confidence and unworthiness is imposed upon the conscientious Anglican by the very requirements of *The Book of Common Prayer.*

Consider the following five stages through which a worshipper might well pass:

1. A warning to the 'negligent' and first invitation ('In God's behalf I bid you all . . .').
2. The exhortation to self-examination and private confession of sin, delivered a week before the celebration.
3. Invitation at the celebration to 'draw near with faith' and make public confession.
4. Welcome at the Lord's Table to all who do not trust in their own righteousness (Prayer of Humble Access).
5. Reception of the Sacrament, kneeling.

At each stage of this process there is a combination of invitation and warning, of confidence and of a sense of unworthiness. Two examples illustrating the close relationship between the stages of *The Book of Common Prayer* and the drama of 'Love III' may be taken at points 3 and 4. The invitation at Holy Communion is phrased in the following way: 'Ye that do truly and earnestly repent you of your sins . . . draw near with faith.' This may be compared in 'Love III' with the host's affirmation of the suitability of the guest to be a worthy guest, 'You shall be he.' But then, in the celebration, follows the confession of sin: 'We acknowledge and bewail our manifold sins and wickedness', which may be compared with the guest's protest, 'I the unkinde, ungratefull? Ah my deare,/I cannot look on thee'. But with the Absolution and Comfortable Words, Love takes the guest's hand, and affirms again that the redeeming God is the source of all true vision. The celebration then lifts the believer into the heavens to share the praise of the angels. But even here there is consciousness and unworthiness. The liturgy now invites the worshippers to admit that they do not presume to come to the Lord's Table trusting in their own righteousness. They are of themselves not worthy so much as to gather up the crumbs under his Table. Similarly, in Herbert's poem the guest is still inclined to ask that his sense of shame requires that he should not be present at the table – but perhaps under it, with the dogs identified by the Syrophoenician woman as eating the family's crumbs?

With this objection Herbert's drama has reached its turning point. There is nothing left but for the host to appeal directly to the death of Christ as the final grounds of acceptance: 'And know you not, sayes Love, who bore the blame?' And at this point the celebration of Holy Communion invokes the 'full, perfect and sufficient, Sacrifice, Oblation and Satisfaction for the sins of the whole world'. Now that the grounds and terms of the guest's status have been unambiguously articulated, the guest finally capitulates (though he has characteristically one more cavil to enter).

It is not my intention to suggest that Herbert has consciously moulded 'Love III' so that the reader should identify the dialogue as moving him or her through the stages of approach to the Holy Communion. There are no sufficiently persuasive verbal clues to substantiate any such claim. Nor would it be consistent with Herbert's methods, which are allusive and indirect rather than pedantic and pedagogical. In any case we have observed an important difference of tone between the unambiguously threatening language of *The Book of Common Prayer* and 'Love III'. Nonetheless I should want to claim that Herbert's experience of praying the Liturgy, and his example of encouraging his parishioners to be confident guests at the Holy Communion, informs the dialogue which the poem contains. This leads us directly to consider the doctrinal question concerning justification by faith, which specifically identifies the tension which the believer endures, as *simul iustus et peccator*, at one and the same time justified by grace, but a sinner.

III

In giving the poem, thirdly, what I call a doctrinal reading, it should not be understood that 'doctrine' can successfully be separated in our minds, let alone in Herbert's, from both biblical interpretation and liturgy. But it is one of the notable advantages of Richard Strier's *Love Known, Theology and Experience in George Herbert's Poetry* (1986), that we are invited to understand the human content of the poetry in relation to, not apart from, the theology which Herbert professes. Specifically in respect of 'Love III', we are now in a position to see that the poem addresses the problem, which *The Book of Common Prayer* exacerbates, that the doctrine of justification by faith can be undermined, not just by works and claims for merit, but also by a certain type of protestation of unworthiness. As Strier puts it, 'Herbert knew that the doctrine of grace alone was almost impossible to keep sharply and constantly in focus; he knew the belief that it merely advocated an internalized form of work would always haunt it'.[10] 'The Holdfast' openly expresses the amazing discovery that 'ev'n to trust in him, was also his:/We must confesse that nothing is our own.' Nor is a merely verbal protestation adequate to our situation; 'To have nought is ours, not to confess/That we have nought.' At this point the explanation is advanced that Christ's humanity is the guarantee that human faith, in all its poverty and insecurity, will be accepted as adequate; 'that all things were more ours by being his'. Objectively, therefore, the source of confidence is not the purity of our professions of unworthiness and faith, but Christ's own inclusive humanity. 'All things were more ours by being his./What Adam had, and forfeited for all,/Christ keepeth now, who cannot fail or fall.'

Similarly, 'The Thanksgiving' articulates the *aporia* of the forgiven sinner looking for an appropriate way of responding in gratitude to the crucifixion (we note that it follows the long poem of reproaches, 'The Sacrifice'). Boldly the poet proposes to revenge himself on God's love by responding to it with equal, even great generosity. He enumerates all the love-inspired actions he will undertake: alms, celibacy, asceticism, public philanthropy, the use to God's glory of all his musical or literary talents, and studious attention to Scripture. Excitedly he claims that he has turned back upon God God's own love, and won victory in the contest. But then, suddenly, he remembers the passion of Jesus.

> Then for thy passion – I will do for that –
> Alas, my God, I know not what.

There is no response adequate to the enormity of the grace of Christ in the cost of our redemption.

'Love III' presupposes this grasp of the uniqueness of what Christ has done for humankind. It sets up what begins as a 'courtesy contest', in which, by stages, self-denial becomes a form of assertiveness. At the first stage the guest utters a conventional demurral; he is covered in dust from the journey. At the second stage, however, he insists on becoming the focus of interest, with his insistence on being identified as guilty. At the third stage the courtesy has become a debate, and, as Strier appropriately observes, Herbert demonstrates 'a strong sense of the arrogance implicit in this humility'.[11] So the response of the host switches the focus away from the sinner to the one who bore the blame. The objectivity of Christ's atoning act is the final reason why the guest is welcome as a guest, and is accounted righteous.

It is at this point that the guest offers to serve at the table. This is the final cavil, and it embodies a contention of some subtlety. Now that the penny has dropped, and the guest has realised that neither merits nor protestations of unworthiness are the basis of his acceptability, but the deeds of Christ, he proposes an *imitatio Christi*. For it was Christ himself who said that he was among his disciples as one who serves (Luke 22:27; 'For whether is greater, he that sitteth at meat, or he that serveth? is not he that sitteth at meat? but I am amongst you as he that serveth.') It is Jesus who girds himself with a towel and washes his disciples' feet (John 13:1–17). It is the divine Son of God who takes upon him the form of a servant and humbles himself (Phil. 2:5–8). How can the guest be reproved for insisting on being a Christlike servant?

And yet this position of servanthood is also denied. The guest, like the slaves of Luke 12:37, must sit at table. At that table, to which he has been graciously invited, the host will at the same time be both the servant and the food. The meat is the flesh of the Son of God (John 6:55, 'for my flesh is meat indeed, and my blood is drink indeed'); and to sit and be served is a reminder that the priest at the Lord's Supper does not act in his or her own person, but in Christ's. The place of the guest is one of joyful helplessness, signified in the six blunt monosyllables, 'So I did sit and eat'. There is a sort of comic undertone of astonished enjoyment of status in the eyes of the other, an experience familiar to lovers. Eventually it dawns on the guest that he does not have to impress the host. The whole dialogue of 'Love III' occurs within the heart of the believer, who is trying to construe not just the position of the believer as a guest at God's board, but also of God in his love constructing the believer as one who is beloved by God. Herbert wants us to understand that even those who pursue the most scrupulous self-examination will never get to the bottom of the matter of sin and thereby impress God with the sincerity of their repentance. The situation is serious, but at the same time, comic. One has both to do one's best by way of repentance, and yet also to admit its insufficiency. The ground of hope is God alone; 'we love him, because he first loved us' (1 John 4:19).

IV

To this exposition may be added two contemporary comments. The first concerns the charge of negativity against the liturgical inheritance of the 1662 *Book of Common Prayer*'s Order of Holy Communion. At the time of its revision in many Provinces of the Anglican Communion it was frequently said that the worshipper was never allowed to escape from his or her own sense of sin. The exposition of Herbert's 'Love III' suggests that someone brought up on the 1559 *Book of Common Prayer* might well have seen the matter differently. It is true, of course, as our study has shown, that serious attention has to be paid by any faithful Anglican communicant to the reality of sin, to self-examination, to the necessity of confession and to restitution. But what is also apparent is that, in Herbert's way of interpreting the doctrine of justification by grace to be received by faith, sin certainly does not have the last word. The case is rather that precisely because of the place accorded to sin in that doctrine, joy and even humour can spring out of the process of self-examination.

Serious self-examination need not be seen as negativity or self-preoccupation. Indeed, as we have seen, Herbert himself seems to have transmuted the threats of the Exhortation against those who receive unworthily, into the gentler idiom of self-doubt. Modern liturgy needs to guard, however, against too great a swing of the pendulum. There is a vital point in our continuing to reflect, before participation in the Eucharist, on our personal and social culpability, our involvement in and condoning of individual and corporate wrong-doing.

We may go further. It would be spectacularly inappropriate to our age to become casual in our preparation to receive the Holy Communion. At the heart of the modern refusal to recognise the point of emphasising the fact of unworthiness and the real grounds of worthiness lies a disinclination to consider the holiness of God. We misunderstand the nature of God's love if we view it as no more than avuncular tolerance, in the presence of which we can be presumptuously casual. Such an attitude mirrors all too well a contemporary cultural style. Herbert, on the other hand, shows us a priest 'in great confusion' especially at Communion times, 'as being not only to receive God, but to break and administer him' (*APT* XXII 'The Parson in Sacraments'). That such breath-taking language might co-exist with intimacy and a sense of one's own comic absurdity has everything to do with our understanding of grace. 'Cheap grace' remains, as Bonhoeffer maintained, an abiding temptation to the professionally religious.

The second comment concerns the gender of the host. The guest is identified as 'he'; the host is only ever called 'Love'. Chana Bloch has suggested that the poem reminds one of 'a sexual encounter between an inhibited or impotent man and a gently loving, patient woman'.[12] Even if we set aside a patent piece of modernism, we may agree that the poem is shot through with feminine imagery – 'my deare', 'quick-ey'd Love', 'sweetly questioning', 'took my hand', 'smiling did reply'. But the matter and manner of Love's responses strike one as feminine in gender construction, rather than specifically female. Indeed, of course, if the guest be the Church, then, according to the traditional imagery of the Songs of Songs, she is the bride, and Christ is the bridegroom, or host. But if the content of the host's disposition, word and actions is feminine in gender, we have no reason to think that the term 'he', which identifies the guest, is not inclusive of both men and women. From the standpoint of what is at stake for Herbert in the life and ministry of the priest presiding at the Holy Communion, it is pure gain that Love's welcome is offered by Christ, as host, in a feminine voice.

NOTES

1. 'The Epistle to the Reader', *Poetical Fragments* (1681) with a note by V. de Sola Pinto (Westmead, 1971), sig. A. v.; cited in R. Strier, *Love Known: Theology and Experience in George Herbert's Poetry* (Chicago and London, 1983), p. 166.

2. G. Herbert, *The Works of George Herbert*, ed. F. E. Hutchinson (Oxford, 1945). This volume contains both the poetry of Herbert, *The Temple*, and *A Priest to the Temple*.

3. R. Todd, *The Opacity of Signs: Acts of Interpretation in George Herbert's The Temple* (Columbia, 1986), pp. 10–13.

4. On Herbert's Anglicanism, see Heather Asals, *Equivocal Predication: George Herbert's Way to God* (Toronto, 1981), p. 5.

5. S. Weil to Joe Bousquet, 12 May 1942, in *Simone Weil: Seventy Letters*, tr. and ed. R. Rees (Oxford, 1965), p. 142.

6. Chana Bloch, 'George Herbert and the Bible: a Reading of "Love III" ', *English Literary Renaissance* 8 (1978), pp. 329–340, has pointed out that previous editors and critics had failed to notice how much the poem owes to the Bible (pp. 330f). What follows is indebted to Bloch's article, and also to the later work *Spelling the Word* (Berkeley, 1985).

7. Helen Vendler, *The Poetry of George Herbert* (Cambridge, Mass., 1975), p. 275 I am indebted to the Revd Ben de la Mare for this reference, and for his very careful comments upon and assistance with this paper.

8. Chana Bloch, op. cit., p. 340.

9. For general background see J. E. Booty, 'George Herbert: *The Temple* and *The Book of Common Prayer*', *Mosaic* 12 (1979), pp. 75–90, and R. M. Van Wengen-Shute, *George Herbert and the Liturgy of the Church of England* (Oegstgeest, 1981).

10. R. Strier, op. cit., p. 70. See Parker Johnson, ' "Worthy to be here": Protestant Sacramental devotion and Herbert's "Love III" ', *George Herbert Journal* Vol. 13, Nos. 1 and 2, pp. 54f, on the long line of devotional writers from Calvin who attempt to assure believers that they were in fact worthy to attend the Lord's Supper.

11. *Love Known*, p. 80. See also Joseph H. Summers, *George Herbert, His Religion and Art* (Cambridge, Mass., 1954), p. 89.

12. Chana Bloch, 'George Herbert and the Bible: A Reading of "Love III" ', in *English Literary Renaissance* 8 (1978), pp. 338f.

4

THE FUNDAMENTALS OF CHRISTIANITY

The Modern Position

Within Anglicanism there is a long tradition of direct appeal to the 'fundamentals of Christianity', or to 'the fundamental articles of the faith' (the two are not necessarily the same). As we shall see, it is quite mistaken to believe that such an appeal distinguishes the Anglican from other communions. What does seem to be the case, however, is that there are good reasons why the contrast between fundamentals and non-fundamentals found a ready home among Anglicans, and has been in use in various contexts and in various ways to the present day.

Examples of modern use of the distinction are to be found in both the Malta Report and the Final Report of the Anglican-Roman Catholic International Commission,[1] of which Archbishop Henry McAdoo, a distinguished contemporary exponent of this tradition, was Anglican co-chairman.[2] The connection between fundamentals and the comprehensiveness of the Church is made clear in the Report of one section of the 1968 Lambeth Conference: 'Comprehensiveness demands agreement on fundamentals, while tolerating disagreement on matters in which Christians may differ without feeling the necessity of breaking communion.'[3]

A final indication of the importance of the notion of fundamentals and a possible way of construing it is to be found in the formulation and adoption by the 1888 Lambeth Conference of what has become known as the Chicago-Lambeth Quadrilateral. The four elements of this statement (Scripture, the creeds, two sacraments and the episcopate) have received repeated endorsement up to the present, though lately with qualifications and amplification.[4]

As we shall see, there are considerable complexities hidden in the proposal that all Christians do, can or should agree on fundamentals, a proposal which on the surface appears to be self-evident, or at least highly desirable.[5] There is no ready-made precision in the content of the fundamentals, and despite its deployment by some leading Roman Catholic theologians, among them Karl Rahner, it has been regularly dismissed as a Protestant theory, contrary to the unity of the Church as instituted by Christ and unrealisable in practice without an infallible authority to determine its content.[6] The tradition whose history we are to trace is neither redundant nor parochial; nor are all Anglicans agreed about it.

For example, in a sharp and clarifying appendix, 'On the Doctrine of Fundamentals', in his 1838 *Treatise on the Church of Christ*, the learned Tractarian, William Palmer (of Worcester College, Oxford), wrote:

> This term is capable of so many meanings as applied to Christian doctrine, and it actually is, has been, and must continue to be, used in so great a diversity of senses, that it is morally impossible to avoid perplexity while it is employed in controversy. As an ambiguous term, as conveying no one definite notion, it seems unqualified to be of any practical utility in questions of controversy.[7]

This is a challenge which must be taken seriously.

The Reformation Tradition

The reason for the Reformed Church of England's interest in 'the fundamentals' is plain enough: it derives from the charge against the Church of Rome that it has departed from the standards of the early Fathers, of the apostles and of Christ, and the corresponding claim that 'we have called home again to the original and first foundation that religion which hath been foully neglected and utterly corrupted' (Bishop Jewel's *Apology of the Church of England*, 1564).[8] The recall to fundamentals is a motif capable of being expressed in a variety of metaphors, of which 'foundation' is only one of the possibilities – but an important one, because it recalls a series of impressive biblical texts. ('If the foundations are destroyed what can the righteous do?', Ps. 11:3; 'Behold I am laying in Zion for a foundation, a stone, a tested stone',

Isa. 28:16, cited in 1 Pet. 2:6; the parable of the men who built houses with and without proper foundation, Matt. 7:24–27; Luke 6:47–49; 'No other foundation can any one lay than that which is laid, which is Jesus Christ', 1 Cor. 3:11; 'So then you are . . . built upon the foundation of the apostles and prophets, Jesus Christ himself being the chief cornerstone', Eph. 3:20.)

At the very start of the Reformation we are introduced to a dispute which has constantly returned to complicate the recall to fundamentals. Erasmus held that it should be possible for Christians to agree upon those few and simple truths which were intimately connected with practical Christian living. Much else, including the complexities of the reformers' view of the human condition and the terms of salvation, could be left to theological debate. Luther vehemently disagreed with such agnosticism. What he was teaching, he asserted, was simply the plain content of the Scriptures, proclaimed openly to the world and taught to the heart internally by the Holy Spirit.[9] Throughout his voluminous and unsystematic writings there are scattered numerous different ways of summarising the foundation, the chief article, the head, the heart and so forth of the Gospel. For Luther the whole Christian faith hangs together, like a chain, or a ring, or a bell. No one part could be lost, if the whole is to survive.

Erasmus' proposals were ignored by the Council of Trent, but were widely influential in England. So also was another idea, closely related to that of the fundamentals, but with a long and independent history, namely the fact that there were certain matters in relation to which Christians had freedom. These *adiaphora*, or things indifferent, became of great importance to the entire Reformation tradition.[10] Luther, for example, in reply to Henry VIII's *Assertion of the Seven Sacraments* (1521), had argued that whatever went beyond the Scriptures was a matter of indifference and should not be turned into a 'necessary doctrine'.[11] The term *adiaphoron* (plural, *adiaphora*) was frequently used by William Tyndale, and certain doctrines, notably those of purgatory or transubstantiation, became tests of what was necessary and what indifferent. John Frith (*c.* 1503–33) carefully explained, while awaiting death by burning, that he was convinced that the Christian was free to disagree with the view, held by his episcopal interrogators, that transubstantiation was 'an undoubted article of the faith, necessary to be believed under pain of damnation' ('Articles Wherefore John Frith

Died', 1533).[12] Three years later, after issuing his Ten Articles, Henry VIII was instructing his bishops 'in no wise to treat of matters indifferent, which be neither necessary to our salvation . . . nor yet to be in any wise contemned'.[13]

Within England, of course, power was sufficiently centralised for instructions of this kind to be enforced, and one should not underestimate the importance of political pressure for eliminating disagreement. Militating against wider Protestant concord over fundamentals was the fact that the politically separate parts of the movement of reformation accustomed themselves to different solutions of the question. The sixteenth, seventeenth and eighteenth centuries are replete with sincere and devoted persons seeking ecclesiastical agreement between the separate branches of Christendom on the basis of agreements on fundamentals. But the political forces keeping the Churches apart were stronger than good intentions. The separate political entities became accustomed to different usages, and resistance to change from outside hardened.

In the early years of the Reformation, however, matters were not so settled. From the Lutheran side, notably Philip Melanchthon (1497–1560) sought to define an area of common ground with Rome.[14] From the Roman Catholic side, solidly in the Erasmian tradition was the remarkable Georg Cassander (1513–66), a Flemish lay scholar who lived latterly in Cologne and devoted himself to the exploration of ground for restoring peace between Roman Catholics and Protestants. In the tireless (and fruitless) work of both there is a discernible emphasis on the cognitive content of Christianity, upon fundamental *articles* of belief as supplying the only secure basis for reconciliation. Thus the Augsburg Confession of 1530, largely the work of Melanchthon, is an article-by-article distillation of Reformation teaching in its most moderate and eirenic form. And Cassander's appeal was to the Creed and the faith of the Church of the first six centuries in agreement with the formula of St Vincent of Lérins (the so-called Vincentian canon; 'What has been believed everywhere, always and by all'), as supplying the qualifying basis for a Church to be reckoned a true Church.

Seventeenth-century Anglicanism

Stress has been laid on the non-Anglican treatment of fundamental articles in order to place the Anglican reception of this tradition in its proper content. Given Cranmer's knowledge of the Fathers and his comparative liturgical conservatism, Cassander's outline of the basis for reconciliation had obvious apologetic value. A work of the Swiss Reformer, Bullinger (1504–75), the *Decades*, was also highly esteemed in England for its demonstration that the Reformed religion was none other than that professed in the creeds and councils of the primitive Church.

But however much subsequent Anglicans owed to Roman Catholic, Lutheran and Calvinist predecessors, it is important that we observe the possibility of a *de facto* settlement of the question of fundamentals as well as a written theological apologetic. Use can determine what is held to be fundamental, as well as theory. The means by which refor-mation came about impinge closely on this question; these means include the authorisation and imposition of Books of Common Prayer, the successive versions of the Articles of Religion, the issuing of authorised homilies, and in due course the provision of a *Book of Canons* – all these were imposed with the authority of King-in-Parliament and the consent of the clergy in Convocation. Although the Thirty-nine Articles refer to Scripture as the criterion of things necessary to sal-vation, in none of these instruments of settlement is there a final and authoritative formulation of the fundamentals. That too is significant, as is the eminently reformable and progressive character of the work.

From the last years of the reign of Elizabeth I onwards there developed a considerable apologetic literature to explain and justify the nature of the English Reformation. We have already referred to Bishop Jewel's *Apology*. A little later Richard Hooker himself formulated what he termed 'the essence of Christianity' (in the earliest English use of that phrase known to me) as the God-given unity of the visible Church in the profession of one Lord, one faith, and one baptism.[15] The one faith is constituted by those few articles of Christian belief confessed by such early fathers as Tertullian and Irenaeus. Hooker, who was already embroiled in controversies with moderate Puritans still part of the comprehensive Church of England, is at once drawn into detailed argument about whether one complete form of church polity has been laid out in Scripture, thus forming part of what must be maintained as necessary to salvation. Against such a view, Hooker's position is clear. The articles of the Christian faith and the sacraments of the Church of Christ are absolutely necessary to salvation. The accessories are things which discretion will teach the Church how to decide, and decisions may vary from place to place and time to time without contradicting their God-given basis in natural reason.

In the seventeenth century, the appeal to the undivided Church of the first five centuries commended itself to a number of prominent persons, among them the Dutch jurist and theologian, Hugo Grotius, and the Genovese Calvinist, Isaac Casaubon (1559–1614), who immigrated to England in 1610 and contributed warmly to an apologetic for the Church of England. Georg Calixtus (1586–1656), who met Casaubon in London in 1612, was a German Lutheran likewise impressed with this argument, to which he linked the criterion provided by the Vincentian canon and a certain stress on practical Christian living deriving from Erasmus.

But the fundamental articles tradition lent itself also to the exposition of a strict Lutheran orthodoxy, which it received at the hands of Nicholaus Hunnius (1585–1643). In one of the most penetrating analyses of different kinds of fundamental, Hunnius distinguished between the *substantial* foundation, which is God and Christ, the *organic*, which is the holy Scriptures, and the *dogmatic*, the content of Christian doctrine. The last named is then subdivided between primary articles which all must confess, secondly articles which none must deny, and non-fundamentals which may be ignored or disputed. The point of this treatment is to show that though Lutherans and the Reformed might be agreed about the substantial and the organic fundamentals, there are fundamental differences in primary and secondary articles of doctrine. Here we come face to face with the fact that *per se* appeal to the notion of fundamentals is not, of itself, an ecumenically hopeful procedure. The problems are to be seen in the career of the remarkable Scottish ecumenist, John Durie (1596–1680), whose attempts to achieve European Protestant unity on the basis of agreement on fundamentals were frustrated by a combination of denominational intransigence and political rivalries.

In England the context in which the fundamentals or fundamental articles were principally deployed was that of controversy with Roman

Catholic theologians. Bishop Lancelot Andrewes (1555–1626) addressed himself to the attack of the Jesuit Ballarmine on the claim of King James I to be a Catholic. Adopting the theory already advanced by Calixtus, he held that the profession of the creeds and canons of the first four Councils was a sufficient title for the Church of England. His definition of the boundaries of Anglicanism occurs in a sentence later to become famous:

> One canon reduced to writing by God himself, two testaments, three creeds, four general councils, five centuries, and the series of Fathers in that period – the centuries that is, before Constantine, and two after, determine the boundary of our faith.[16]

Andrewes was in touch with both Casaubon, to whom he showed his reply to Bellarmine, and somewhat less cordially with Grotius.

Twenty years later William Laud (1573–1645) conducted a famous controversy with a Jesuit theologian, John Fisher (1569–1641), subsequently published as *A Relation of the Conference between William Laud and Mr Fisher the Jesuit* (1639). Against the proposition advanced by Fisher that all points defined by the Church are fundamental, Laud insists that the term 'fundamental' can only apply to the articles of the Creed. There may be many true deductions from the Creed, of which simple people are unaware, but which it may be necessary for others, more learned, to believe. But nothing is fundamental merely because the Church says it is so, but only because it is of itself. Picking up Andrewes' stress on Scripture and reflecting the earlier work of Protestant controversialists, Laud asserts that the belief that Scripture is the word of God and infallible is a preceding, prime principle of faith to be held along with the Creed. That the Church of England's positive articles are grounded in Scripture, he is content to be judged by the joint and constant belief of the Fathers of the first five centuries:

> To believe the Scripture and the Creeds, to believe these in the sense of the ancient primitive Church, to receive the four great Councils so much magnified by antiquity, to believe all points of doctrine, generally received as fundamental in the Church of Christ, is a faith in which to live and die cannot but give salvation.[17]

Others who wrote in the same sense included Archbishop James Ussher

(1581–1656), and later Bishop Jeremy Taylor (1613–67) and Henry Hammond (1605–60).

But did the testimony of the Fathers cohere quite precisely as these apologists claimed? Some held that it did not. A group of scholars in England, known as the Tew Circle, believed that resort to the Fathers only produced confusion, a view which received strong support from the work of the eminent French Protestant patristic scholar, John Daillé, *On the Use of the Fathers* (French, 1632). The argument of William Chillingworth (1604–44), who was Laud's godson, but who for a period had become a Roman Catholic influenced by the arguments of Fisher, shows a certain withdrawal from the patristic reference. In a controversial writing of 1638, *Religion of Protestants a Safe Way to Salvation*, he attempts to explain the relation between Scripture and the fundamentals. Once a person is persuaded that Scripture contains all things necessary to salvation (a quotation of Article VI), then it is enough if that person strenuously attempts to find and to believe the true sense of it. There is no final catalogue of all the truths which one must believe, because, on his argument, there is a vital moral component in all believing deriving from human autonomy. Chillingworth insisted, at the same time, upon the simplicity of the essentials of the faith.[18]

The clarification of an important point, at this time, was the work of another apologist, Edward Stillingfleet (1635–99), replying to the Jesuit account of the controversy between Laud and Fisher. In *A Rational Account of the Grounds of Protestant Religion* (1664) Stillingfleet distinguished between things which are necessary to the salvation of persons as such, in their individual capacities, and things which are necessary to be acknowledged by Christian societies, or as the bonds and conditions of ecclesiastical communion. The discussion of fundamentals had, he held, wavered uncertainly between the two, but they should not be confused. Concentrating upon the latter of the two uses, a later defender of Stillingfleet, William Sherlock (1641–1707), undertook to define 'fundamentals' in the following way:

> A *fundamental doctrine* is such a doctrine as is in strict sense of the *essence* of Christianity, without which the whole building and superstructure must fall; the belief of which is necessary to the

71

very being of Christianity, like the *first principles* of any *art* or *science*.[19]

Redefinitions: The Eighteenth and Nineteenth Centuries

If, as suggested earlier, we must be alert to usage as well as to theory, then it must be noted that the seventeenth-century Restoration, which saw the ejection of some 1,760 incumbents from their parishes, set clear bounds to the 'comprehensiveness' of the Church of England. The fact that the Anglican Ordinal insisted that its priests be episcopally ordained must be related to its view of the fundamentals. But how?

One learned, and ecumenically active, contributor to the discussion, Archbishop William Wake (1657–1737), was ambiguous on the point. He had read both Cassander and Grotius and was persuaded that the method of separating out the fundamental articles from the others was, for all its admitted difficulties and dangers, the only feasible way to the restoration of communion, alike with Roman Catholics and within Protestantism.[20] He corresponded extensively on this basis with friendly Roman Catholic theologians in the Sorbonne, but on the quixotic assumption that the Gallican Church would be ready to throw off papal supremacy. The Pope, Wake asserted, had wrongly claimed for himself alone the episcopate 'which Christ bequeathed in part to each several bishop to be held in common.'[21] But Wake had already committed himself enthusiastically to the view, against the Roman Catholic Bossuet's charge of incoherence in Protestantism, that Protestants are already united in whatever is fundamental in the faith (Sermon of 1689).[22] Wake stood solidly in the tradition of Hooker, Whitgift and Andrewes in holding that the kind of government of the Church was not a matter affecting the being of the Church, and that although episcopacy is a divine right, it does not follow that a non-episcopal Church is no Church. He commended the institution of episcopacy to his Reformed and Lutheran friends; he reordained those with Presbyterian orders; but at the same time he wrote that Article XXXVI of the Thirty-nine Articles 'only asserts the validity of our Book of Ordination, but does not affirm the necessity of the three orders which we retain in our Church' (Letter of 1720).[23] Despite extensive correspondence with Swiss theologians notable for their support of the method of defining few fundamentals as a condition of union, the plans came to nothing. Wake found, as others have done since, that far from agreeing on the few Articles in common, many not of his persuasion insisted on laying the greatest emphasis on the points of difference.

A further contribution of major importance to the subject was made by a Cambridge theologian, Daniel Waterland (1683–1740), whose calm and analytic mind illuminated a number of disputes in the eighteenth century and whose works were reprinted constantly into the nineteenth century. In *A Discourse of Fundamentals* (1735), he tackles the question of what should be held to belong essentially to the 'fabric' of Christianity. His solution to the complexities is the work of a systematician. On the premise that Christianity is a covenant, it follows, he argues, that what is essential to Christianity is everything that inheres in the covenant, the two parties, the agreement, the person of the mediator, and the conditions, means and sanctions attaching to the covenant.[24] For the idea of the centrality of covenant, and for numerous features of the argument, Waterland refers to a German Lutheran and disciple of Grotius, Samuel Pufendorf (1632–94).

Following Chillingworth, Waterland asserts that no catalogue of fundamental truths is possible. It is adequate to give examples of fundamentals, which must include matters of worship and conduct as well as belief, and a rule for establishing them. If difficulties arise then it is wiser to choose the side of peace and latitude. In the case of doubt the burden of proof lies on those who would assert something to be fundamental.

Waterland acknowledges that other rules have been proposed for deciding upon what is fundamental, and undertakes to support his argument with a brief but radical refutation of alternatives. Notable among those he dismisses are: the definitions of the Church, even of the primitive Churches; the whole of Scripture or even all matters expressly taught in Scripture; the Apostles' Creed (here Waterland acknowledges his disagreement with, amongst others, Calixtus, Chillingworth, and Stillingfleet); the mere confession of Jesus as Messiah (with reference to John Locke);[25] and the universal agreement of Christians. His central theological proposal of the notion of covenant as the most comprehensive way in which to determine the terms of Church communion leaves open, he believes, the question of the terms of salvation for each individual.

In the second half of the eighteenth century a new set of ideas emerged in European Protestantism to account for the changes in successive historical forms of Christianity. For this way of thinking it became axiomatic that no one historical embodiment of the Christian faith was, or could be, normative for all time, especially no series of propositions. The reasons for this new development were complex, partly the result of investigations into biblical and patristic history which showed internal variety and disagreement, and partly the impact of a new non-cognitive theory of religion, which the Romantic Movement planted indelibly within European Christianity. The result was a need to identify, if possible, an abiding essence behind the changing forms. When Schleiermacher in his epoch-making definition of the 'essence of Christianity' (*Speeches on Religion*, 1799) spoke of Christianity as having an intuited 'principle of coherence', at the same time he denied that it could be constituted by a 'particular quantity of religious matter', a coded way of referring to the fundamental articles tradition.[26]

These European developments coincided with a period in the life of the Anglican Church when the Church of England was at its most self-preoccupied and isolated. The foundation of an independent episcopate overseas occurred through the agency of the Church in Scotland. And welcome though this *de facto* modification of what had hitherto been widely assumed to be fundamental, namely a particular relationship with the sovereign power, might be, it had the effect of intensifying Anglican efforts to explain its own distinctiveness. By the beginning of the nineteenth century, for those groups out of which the Tractarian Movement developed, it was axiomatic that an Anglican defence of its stance as a Church must be different from a commonly Protestant one. The altered state of affairs is nicely illustrated in the title of a work by the Irish bishop of Limerick, John Jebb (1775–1833), *Peculiar Character of the Church of England: as distinguished both from other branches of the Reformation, and from the modern Church of Rome*. It was this work which was given as an example of Anglican apologetic by a young friend of John Henry Newman, Benjamin Harrison, to a French abbé whom he had met at a dinner party in Paris in 1834. Jager engaged first with Harrison and then with Newman himself in public controversy over the claim of the Church of England.[27]

The dispute eventually came to centre upon the issue of the fundamental articles. When Newman became involved at the end of the year he had to read himself into the Anglican history we have reviewed, especially the relevant works of Laud, Stillingfleet, Chillingworth and others. In his first intervention, Newman explicitly invokes the idea of fundamentals and continued to justify it throughout the controversy. In his own mind he was merely reproducing the views of Bishop Stilling-fleet. But it is now evident, and was evident also to Harrison, that his line of defence amounted to his own theory of fundamentals, a theory which developed into a theory of development, and which eventually helped in his transfer to the Roman Catholic Church.

Jager, who had read some of the *Tracts for the Times*, was evidently astonished to discover that an Anglican was prepared to defend the distinction between fundamentals and non-fundamentals, for him a quintessentially Protestant apologetic. Newman, though his theory of religion was of a mystery lying hid in language, was still keen to insist on the existence of a central immutable core of truth, infallibly taught by the Church. But characteristically he introduced into the discussion a very considerable measure of flexibility and uncertainty about the difference between the core, which he called the apostolic tradition, and exploratory elaborations of it, which he called the prophetic tradition. The theory was indeed his own, and when he wrote it up in full as *Lectures on the Prophetical Office of the Church Viewed Relatively to Romanism and Popular Protestantism* he took pains to emphasise that what he was defending was not Protestantism.[28]

His Tractarian colleagues were more definite. W. H. Froude characteristically told a friend that he nauseated the word fundamental.[29] More seriously, as we have already seen, William Palmer offered to demonstrate the internal inconsistency of the use of the word in the works of Chillingworth, Laud, and Waterland. From the last named person's review of the varieties of opinion Palmer concluded the impossibility of arriving at any adequately agreed rule, and criticised the arbitrariness of thinking that human beings could stand in judgement on divine revelation, a criticism which Karl Barth was to echo a hundred years later.[30] Quoting Keble, Palmer concluded that the only safe way of proceeding was to insist on guarding the whole faith of Christ.

The undoubted advantage of Newman's theory of development was its capacity to absorb the impact of historical relativism. Consistency over time, he argued, required change. Newman's Anglican critics for the most part reverted to earlier static theories. The Church can only be what it has always been, and profess what it always has professed. The works of many of the theologians we have reviewed were reprinted, among them those of Andrewes, Laud, Taylor, Henry Hammond, Herbert Thorndike (1598–1672) and Bishop John Cosin (1594–1672), and were accorded a kind of normative status within Anglicanism. Their defence of fundamental articles preserved a style of theological argument which had ceased to be current in the European context. Although, as we have seen, in its origins it was a tradition shared with a large number of Protestant theologians both Lutheran and Reformed, and a smaller group of Erasmian Roman Catholics, by the nineteenth century it had the appearance of being distinctively Anglican. Both the term 'Anglicanism' and some of the standard definition of its distinctiveness owe much to these developments.

With the challenge of biblical criticism to the doctrine of biblical infallibility, the scriptural basis of the fundamentals became problematic. It was an important development, therefore, when Charles Gore and the *Lux Mundi* school both accepted criticism, and yet continued to defend the truth of all the articles of the creed. Modern interpretation of the fundamentals tradition is at some pains to argue that the use of reason (as justified by, among others, Hooker and Chillingworth) is part of the method of holding to fundamentals, and that the *Lux Mundi* theologians are the natural heirs of this Anglican tradition.[31] The twentieth century, however, has seen a number of acute controversies relating to doctrines affirmed by the creeds, especially the virgin birth and the (bodily) resurrection of Christ, which raise in an acute form the adequacy of this defence.

Modern Problems and Solutions

At the beginning of this essay it was remarked that the fundamentals of Christianity are not necessarily to be identified with the fundamental *articles* of Christianity. In the history we have traced, distillation into articles of belief has played a very important part, and is evidently the consequence of an approach to religion which emphasises its cognitive aspects.[32] A major objection to the fundamental articles tradition is that it is based upon an unbalanced account of what the Christian religion actually is, ignoring or relegating its experiential, ritual or cultural aspects. But there are further difficulties with the appeal to fundamentals *per se* which must also be faced.

First, as Palmer observed, there is no common agreement about what the fundamentals are. Nor is there any agreed rule for determining what they are. Waterland's proposal is ingenious, but in the face of equally plausible competitors it is, *prima facie*, arbitrary.

The charge of arbitrariness raises the question of authority, insistently posed of the fundamental article tradition by apologists for the Roman Catholic Church. Anglican responses which invoke the tradition of the undivided Church, the creeds, or the Vincentian canon bear the aspect of private judgement masquerading as tradition. On close inspection they can be found to furnish either too much or too little.[33] They all suffer alike from what has been called the 'Myth of Christian Beginnings', which were anything but homogeneous.[34]

The recitation of the history of the fundamentals also rarely enough emphasises the repeated failure of this tradition to solve ecumenical problems. Nor, if Anglicans are honest, does it solve the problems of inner-Anglican ecumenism, the reconciliation of differences over the application of biblical criticism or hermeneutics to matters like the gospel miracles or the patriarchalism of the Scriptures.

Nonetheless, contemporary ecumenism has shown a desire to reinvoke the notion of fundamentals and some of its inherent problems may yield to renewed thought. Anglicans have good reason to reflect on the Chicago–Lambeth Quadrilateral. Here, after all, is not just a list of miracles of belief, but a series of usages, the use of Scripture in public in the vernacular, the use of creeds in worship, the celebration of the sacraments, and the practice of episcopal government. It is important to stress that all these presuppose the Church's life of active discipleship, worship and witness, centred upon Christ. It assumes also the normal Christian activity of faith seeking understanding, attended, as it always has been, by theological argument and dispute. Agreement upon usage can, as Anglican experience testifies, be hospitable to conflict about belief. Indeed the use of the Bible as the 'prime principle of faith', to cite Laud, *provokes* disagreement, including disagreement about boundaries between acceptable and unacceptable expressions of belief. The history of enquiry in the fundamentals of Christianity contains ambiguities, confusions and errors. But it is not for that reason to be set aside.

NOTES

1. Malta Report in A. C. Clark and C. Davey (eds.), *Anglican/Roman Catholic Dialogue* (London and New York, 1974), pp. 107–15; ARCIC, *The Final Report* (London, 1982). Esp. 'Ministry and Ordination', para. 17 (p. 38). The Malta Report is reprinted in *The Final Report*.
2. See esp. *The Spirit of Anglicanism: A Survey of Anglican Theological Method in the Seventeenth Century* (London, 1965); and *The Unity of Anglicanism: Catholic and Reformed* (Wilton, Conn., 1983).
3. *The Lambeth Conference 1968* (London, 1968), p. 140. It should be made clear that Reports to the Conference carry only the authority of those by whom it was approved, in this case some one-third of the assembled bishops.
4. *Bonds of Affection*, Proceedings of Anglican Consultative Council-6 (London, 1984), pp. 70–75.
5. Heinrich Fries and Karl Rahner, *Unity of the Churches* (Philadelphia, 1985), pp. 7, 13–23.
6. A. Tanqueray, 'Articles fondamentaux (système des)' in *Dictionnaire de Théologie Catholique* I. iii (Paris, 1923), pp. 2025–35, and the encyclical of Pius XI, *Mortalium animos* (1927), DS 3683, cited by Congar, *Diversity and Communion*, p. 118.
7. *Treatise on the Church of Christ* I (London, 1838), p. 122.
8. *Apology of the Church of England* (1561), ed. J. E. Booty (Charlottesville, 1974), p. 121.
9. From the Preface to the *Bondage of the Will* (Weimar Ausgabe 18, p. 603; American edn, 33, p. 5). In J. Dillenberger (ed.), *Martin Luther: Selections from his Writings* (New York, 1961), p. 170.
10. For an outline of the history of the term see B. J. Verkamp, *The Indifferent Mean: Adiaphorism in the English Reformation to 1554* (Ohio and Wayne State University Presses, Athens, Ohio, Detroit, Mich., 1977), p. 22.
11. ibid., p. 96.
12. ibid., p. 103.
13. ibid., p. 51.
14. On Melanchthon's use of fundamentals see F. Hildebrandt, *Melanchthon: Alien or Ally* (Cambridge, 1946).
15. Richard Hooker, *Of the Laws of Ecclesiastical Polity*, III, i. 4.
16. L. Andrewes, *Opuscula quedam Posthuma*, Library of Anglo-Catholic Theology (Oxford, 1852), p. 91.
17. *A Relation of the Conference between William Laud and Mr Fisher the Jesuit*, Library of Anglo-Catholic Theology (London, 1849), p. 361.
18. See R. L. Orr, *Reason and Authority, The Thought of William Chillingworth* (Oxford, 1967), p. 96.

19. *Vindication of the Defence of Stillingfleet* (London, 1682), p. 256.
20. Norman Sykes, *William Wake, Archbishop of Canterbury, 1657–1737* (Cambridge), vol. i, p. 252.
21. ibid., vol. i, p. 271.
22. ibid., vol. ii, p. 2.
23. ibid., vol. ii, p. 19.
24. *The Works of the Rev. Daniel Waterland* (Oxford, 1823), p. 95.
25. Locke's reductionist proposals were contained in his *Second Vindication of the Reasonableness of Christianity* (London, 1697).
26. F. D. E. Schleiermacher, *On Religion, Speeches to Its Cultured Despisers* (New York, 1958), p. 218. On the history of essence definition see S. W. Sykes, *The Identity of Christianity* (London and Philadelphia, 1984), chs. 4–8.
27. L. Allen, *John Henry Newman and the Abbé Jager* (London and New York, 1975).
28. J. H. Newman, *Lectures on the Prophetical Office* (London, 1837); he reissued this work as a Roman Catholic with a new preface and notes, *The Via Media of the Church of England* (London, 1877) vol. i. See S. W. Sykes, *Identity of Christianity*, ch. 5.
29. Cited by J. H. Newman in 'Palmer on Faith and Unity' (a review of Palmer's work on the Church, see n. 7), in *Essays Critical and Historical* (London, 1871), p. 174.
30. Barth's discussion of the fundamental articles tradition is to be found in the *Church Dogmatics* I. ii (Edinburgh, 1956), pp. 863–6.
31. See esp. the argument of P. E. More in 'The Spirit of Anglicanism' in P. E. More and F. L. Cross, *Anglicanism* (London and New York, 1935), p. xxxi; also followed by McAdoo (see n. 2).
32. Note esp. G. A. Lindbeck, *The Nature of Doctrine* (London and Philadelphia, 1984).
33. See H. B. Swete, *The Holy Catholic Church* (London, 1915), p. 241.
34. R. L. Wilkens, *The Myth of Christian Beginnings* (London, 1979).

BIBLIOGRAPHY

Congar, Y., *Tradition and Traditions* (London, 1966). Esp. Excursus B, 'Scripture and the "Truths Necessary for Salvation" ', pp. 508–19.
Congar, Y., *Diversity and Communion* (London, 1984). Esp. ch. 11, 'Agreement on "Fundamental Articles" or on the Positions of the Early Church', pp. 107–25.
Joest, W., 'Fundamentartikel' in *Theologische Realenzyklopädie* XI (Berlin and New York, 1983), pp. 727–32.
Leclerc, J. SJ, *Toleration and Reformation*, 2 vols. (New York and London, 1960).
Neill, S. C. and Rouse, R. eds., *A History of the Ecumenical Movement* (London, 1967). Esp. essays by M. Schmidt, 'Ecumenical Activity on the Continent of Europe in the Seventeenth and Eighteenth Centuries', and N. Sykes,

'Ecumenical Movements in Great Britain in the Seventeenth and Eighteenth Centuries'.

Rowell, Geoffrey, 'The Confessions of Faith of the Early Church as Seen in the Classical Anglican Tradition' (Reply, G. W. Bromiley, pp. 329–33), *Anglican and Episcopal History* 60 No. 3 (September 1991), pp. 305–32.

Valeske, U., *Hierarchia Veritatum* (Munich, 1968). Esp. ch. 3, 'Das Problem der Fundamentalartikel in der Theologiegeschichte der nichtrömischen Kirchen'; and bibliography.

5

RICHARD HOOKER AND THE ORDINATION OF WOMEN TO THE PRIESTHOOD

A more dutifull and religious way for us were to admire the wisedome of God, which shineth in the bewtifull varietie of all things, but most in the manifold and yet harmonious dissimilitude of those wayes, whereby his Church upon earth is guided from age to age, throughout all generations of men.[1]

I

When Anglicans confront the fact that the Roman Catholic Church deems the ordination of women to the priesthood not to be in accordance with God's plan for his Church,[2] they are obliged to reflect on their own understanding of the Church. There are many Anglicans, perhaps a majority, for whom the firm opposition of the Pope and the Sacred Congregation for the Doctrine of the Faith is a most serious obstacle. Among these will undoubtedly be some who hold more or less secretly that the Churches of the Anglican Communion have no basis of authority independent of the Papacy, and for whom, therefore, a papal veto is simply final. Their identity as Anglicans will, of course, be severely tried by a decision to ordain women to the priesthood. But since they make no intellectual case for their present allegiance, they can hardly complain of any inconsistency in such an Anglican development. A much larger and more serious number of Anglicans, however, hold strongly the argument from tradition, in which Roman Catholics and Eastern Orthodox agree, and will feel on ecumenical grounds the inadvisability of any movement which increases the gulf between Anglicans and the non-Protestant world.

I have on a number of occasions attempted to point out how misleading is the mental map which simply spreads the denominations out in a straight line, and places Anglicanism midway between Rome and wherever it is thought the headquarters of undifferentiated Protestantism may lie.[3] There have been at least three versions of *via media* Anglicanism. In the sixteenth century, Anglicans, together with Lutherans, saw themselves as midway between Rome and Anabaptism. By the mid-seventeenth century the Church of England was developing an apologetic self-understanding over against independency and presbyterianism, as representative of left-wing Protestantism, which in the Tractarian recension became *the via media* between Rome and 'popular Protestantism', as defined by John Henry Newman. The history of these variations demonstrates the instability and inadequacy of the model, which is, in any case, on any rational reflection unacceptably crude. It has, moreover, inhibited Anglicans from the necessary attempt to articulate their own understanding of the Church. Knowing that some Anglicans are 'virtually' Protestants and others 'virtually' Romans, the straight line model has suggested that Anglicanism can be 'comprehensive' by the simple expedient of adopting the ecclesiologies of others. But this is an illusion, the poverty of which is rapidly disclosed by ecumenical contact. For, one discovers, the Orthodox, Roman Catholics and Lutherans all claim 'comprehensiveness' – and accuse Anglicans of incoherence. Anglicans have to learn that a comprehensive Church needs to articulate a doctrine of the Church precisely in order to justify its very comprehensiveness.[4]

One needs, therefore, an Anglican doctrine of the Church in order to understand what it is that Anglicans are doing in ordaining, or proposing to ordain, women to the Church's priesthood. An 'Anglican doctrine of the Church' is not the same thing as a doctrine of the Anglican Church. The latter would be, however useful in practice, inadequate for the task of interpreting what it is that is done when people are ordained to the 'ministry of Christ's Holy, Catholic and Apostolic Church'.

What is required is a Christian doctrine of the Church, making claims to evangelical and catholic truth, which Anglicans, who are as a matter of fact a distinct denomination in Christendom, can accept as true. Whether such a doctrine strikes other people as 'distinctively Anglican' is for them to judge. What is needed is an understanding of the Church corresponding to the norms of catholic doctrine as Anglicans believe them to be, and which makes sense of their witness, experience and hope.

II

One part of such a reflection should entail the examination of the acknowledged classics of Anglican theology of the past. The acute failure of theological nerve precipitated by the violent internal polemics of the nineteenth century assuredly did not afflict Anglicans of earlier centuries. Among the theological justifications of the stance of the Church of England offered then, Richard Hooker's apologia for the Elizabethan settlement, *Of the Laws of Ecclesiastical Polity*, is pre-eminent. Moreover Hooker is precisely that kind of theologian against whose understanding of the Church Anglicans should test these modern proposals, since his encounter with what has recently been named 'moderate puritanism'[5] made him sensitive to those particular issues relating to tradition which cause modern Anglicans such anxiety when confronted by the innovatory ordination of women to the priesthood.

The thesis of this paper is that it is entirely consistent with the theological method of the most famous Anglican writer perhaps of the whole of Anglican history, Richard Hooker, that women should be ordained to the priesthood. It is an argument whose intention is to take seriously the objection that such ordinations constitute a break of the invariable tradition of the Church from the days of the apostles. I have two further objectives in mind. The first is to exhibit the thought of a major Christian theologian wrestling with the problem of church order in such a way as to show how it can and should be related to particular times and places. And the second is to demonstrate that it is possible to hold both that a particular church order is divinely ordained and also that it is not immutable. The severing of this particular connection is of especial importance, for those who like myself cannot draw from the conclusion that the Church must today ordain women to the priesthood the inference that it was in error not to do so in earlier centuries. The genesis of this paper lay in a question and a hunch. Based on the realisation that Richard Hooker and William Shakespeare were contemporaries, the question arose whether the theologian showed any signs of interest in the debate about women which so fascinated Tudor and Elizabethan society.[6] On the speedy discovery that virtually all of Hooker's references to women were of a sturdily conservative kind, as we shall see, the hypothesis presented itself that, despite this standard sixteenth-century patriarchalism, the position espoused by Hooker on the broader issue of order in the Church might lend itself to serious treatment of the grounds for the ordination of women. What follows is the result of the pursuit of this hunch. Begun perhaps in a somewhat light-hearted desire to enlist the support of one of the supposed 'fathers' of Anglo-Catholicism, it has resulted in an increased respect for the profundity and subtlety of Hooker's theological stance, and especially for his readiness to take seriously the social reality of the Christian Church in time and history; so that I have found my growing conviction of the importance of the study of social history for the Christian Church at every stage of its life to be met and deepened by Hooker's insistence on the dual character of the Church, 'being both a societie and a societie supernaturall'.[7]

III

There are three pages in the *Laws* in which Hooker makes passing but explicit references to the status of women. The first is in the Preface, where Hooker acknowledges the fact that women were prominent as recruits to the Puritan cause, but takes this to be an indication of the inferiority of the rational grounds for puritanism, on the assumption that the judgements of women are 'commonlie weakest by the reason of their sex'.[8] Hooker admits the 'eagernesse of their affection' and their 'naturall inclination into pittie', but observes with some disdain the opportunities women enjoy 'to procure encouragements for their brethren' and the delight they take 'in giving verie large and particular intelligence, how all neere about them stand affected as concerning the same cause'.[9] They are, in a word, gossips.

In the second passage, the point at issue is the emergency baptism of infants by women, especially by midwives. The immediate background to this was the objection of the Admonitioners that the Prayer Book had not specifically forbidden such baptisms, as had Calvin and Bullinger, on the grounds that it was a superstitious use of the sacrament.[10] Hooker's view followed Luther, Tyndale and the general Catholic tradition in accepting the legality and validity of baptism by women, as part of his defence of the view that baptism is 'generally [i.e. universally] necessary to salvation'. Lay baptism in cases of urgent necessity is consistent with this stance, and Hooker strenuously resists the apparent corollary that women can be 'ministers in the Church of God' which, he tartly remarks, would be a 'grosse absurditie' in the light of the Apostle Paul's injunctions not to let women teach (quoting 1 Tim. 2:12 and 1 Cor. 14:34). Here Hooker refers to the (fourth-century) document entitled the *Apostolic Constitutions*, which he held, together with the majority of his contemporaries, to have been written by Clement of Rome in the first century. In this document we find a specific injunction that a woman may not baptise, which Hooker is at some pains to gloss as a prohibition designed to deter the rash and presumptuous from turning what is lawful in necessity into something more common.[11]

The last example of a reference to women occurs in the section on matrimony in Book V, where Hooker is attempting to meet Puritan objections to the ceremonies retained in the Anglican rite. Here Hooker invokes a highly traditional argument concerning the divinely appointed end or goal of matrimony, namely the replenishing of the earth with blessed inhabitants and ultimately of heaven with saints. If the having and bringing up of children is the goal, the means requires the 'subalternation' of women to men. This is naturally grounded upon the inequality of the sexes, 'because thinges equall in everie respect are never willinglie directed one by another'. Woman is thus not merely brought into being after man, but is 'inferior in excellencie' to him. Thus the delivering up of the woman by her father is one of the customs which have a true and sufficient reason, rooted as it is in the ancient authority of husband, father or tutor over all women. The ceremony accordingly reminds women 'of a dutie whereunto the verie imbecillitie of theire nature and sex doth bind them, namelie to be allwaies directed guided and ordered by others, although our positive lawes doe not tie them now as pupils'.[12]

IV

These uncompromising expressions of female subordination to male power are, nonetheless, utterly incidental to the course of Hooker's argument. He is apparently not in the least interested in the theoretical questions about the status of women which had already surfaced in European discussion.[13] Hooker is a traditionalist for whom no serious question arises which might lead him to place women in any other position than that accorded her in the standard theory. The subordination of women was integral to that theory, as it was for most leading Roman Catholic and Protestant writers of the age.

It is essential to the argument of this paper to note the interlocking character of the disciplines whose arguments contributed to the theory of female inferiority. This theory was composed of a variety of elements from law, philosophy, ethics and medicine as well as from theology, as Ian Maclean's most impressive treatment of the theme has demonstrated.[14] One example will suffice. Hooker's reference, noted above, to women's 'imbecillitie' is not a gratuitous insult, but a standard piece of legal theory deriving from the *Digest*, where woman's disbarment from succession, office and privilege, the legal consequence of her *deterior conditio*, is justified by her alleged *levitas, fragilitas, imbecillitas* and *infirmitas*.[15] The French jurist, André Tiraqueau, compiled in his seminal treatise on marriage law a list of occurrences of these words in Roman Law. But the work itself is full of references to theology, medicine, ethics and ancient literature, as well as to law, all in support of female inferiority.[16] The marriage of Aristotle's anatomical and ethical theories to the patristic understanding of the creation and fall had contrived to produce a synthesis according to which woman was an incomplete version of the male (a *mas occasionatus*).[17] Her weaker powers of reason are the grounds for her being deceived, this explanation cohering with the *deterior conditio* of woman in law.[18] Maclean describes the relationship between the disciplines as 'molecular' as well as 'hierarchical'.[19] Thus although Aristotelian medical theory provides a basis for morality, and medicine and ethics underlie law, the synthesis of Aristotelian and Christian theses is full of ambiguities, apparent and real contradictions and open possibilities which make it responsive to slow change. Hooker's participation in the synthesis was total, informing every aspect of his minimal references to women. But he wrote at a time when for the first time the scholastic synthesis came under attack as a whole. And his significance is that he provides the Church with a way of understanding what it might mean to come to new terms with the new view of woman which was shortly to develop in modern Europe.

The case that can be argued in this connection rests on Hooker's awareness that certain aspects of church law can properly vary with time and place. But it is important not to overstate the point. His thought is permeated with Aristotelian assumptions and there is nothing to suggest a willingness in him to entertain in relation to the place of women even contemporary ideas which conflicted with the scholastic synthesis. As we have seen in Hooker's treatment of marriage the necessity of a relationship of superiority/inferiority, which is ultimately derived from Aristotle's dualities, is simply assumed as axiomatic. Although we now have been forced to separate Aristotle's ethics from his physics in order to give any kind of future for Aristotelian thought at all,[20] Hooker could not have envisioned how this could be done. The most that can be said is that just as our treatment of Aristotle is likely to be eclectic, so was Hooker's though in different proportion; it is perhaps relevant to add that we are no more obliged to accept or reject Hooker's scholaticism *in toto*, than Hooker was to adopt Aristotle's entire political philosophy.

V

The issue, then, that we have to investigate is Hooker's approach to church polity. As is well known, he adopted from Jewel, Whitgift and other Anglican writers the distinction between things necessary to salvation and matters indifferent.[21] It was already conventional Lutheran apologetic that rites and ceremonies belonged to matters indifferent. Hooker agreed, and it is the purpose of Book III of the *Laws* to carry his point against the Puritans, who, he holds, insist that discipline and church government belong to things necessary to salvation.

Hooker's position as it unfolds is differentiated and subtle. Although at first sight it looks as though he is going to argue quite simply that what he prefers to call 'church-politie'[22] is a matter of indifference to be decided by each national or regional body for itself, by means of a fundamental analysis of different types of law he shows to what extent the Church must rely on Scripture and to what extent and how she must develop her own positive regulations. In chapters 1–4 of Book III all that is in mind is the sharp distinction, which he needs for polemic purposes, between what he calls 'the verie essence of Christianitie' (the earliest use in English known to me of this phrase), by which he means one Lord, one faith, and one baptism,[23] and ceremonies, such as marrying with a ring, the use of the sign of the cross at Baptism, kneeling at the Eucharist and so forth.[24] From ceremonies are excepted 'Sacramentes, or anie other the like substantiall duties in the exercise of religion'.[25]

In chapter 5 Hooker turns his attention to the Puritan use of the phrase 'commanded by the word of God', and asks the pertinent question, What is the proper use of Scripture?

> When that which the word of God doth but deliver historically, wee conster without any warrant as if it were legally meant, and so urge it further then wee can proove that it was intended, doe we not adde to the lawes of God, and make them in number seeme moe then they are?[26]

The argument is plainly *ad hominem*, in that it represents the Puritans as multiplying 'lawes' without due grounds, the very charge they brought against the conformists. But we should note that the exegetical sensitivity which refuses to quote 'by-speeches in some historicall narration or other' as though they amounted to the 'most exact forme of lawe' is the precursor of a type of historical relativism.

'Commaunded by the word of God', then, is an inadequately refined tool for the proper use of Scripture, and Hooker uses this fact as a pretext for a general argument in favour of the use of reason in Scriptural interpretation. It is, he says, the Church which first instructs us to treat the Scripture as authoritative, which enquiry and experience then confirm. Reason in this context can both refute error and build up faith, aided and directed by the Holy Spirit. Reason, therefore, can also be used in the same context for the formulation of the laws of church polity. This is precisely the point which Hooker desires to make. No church polity is good unless God be the author of it. But God may be the author of it in two ways, either by supernatural revelation, or by the Holy Spirit's guided use of the natural light of reason ('those thinges which men finde out by helpe of that light, which God hath given them unto that ende').[27] Thus though Scripture itself contains many laws, there are a number of matters for which the scripture hath not provided by any law, but left them unto the carefull discretion of the Church; . . . and what is so in these cases, partely scripture and partly reason must teach to discerne.[28]

At this point Hooker brings to bear on his argument the analysis of the different types of law which he has already provided in Book I. The three types of law which concern this argument are the law of reason (which Hooker also calls the law of nature), the divine law revealed in the Scriptures, and human law. The last of these, which includes all church constitutions, is subject to the criterion of the former two.[29] The complicating factor is the evident fact that Scripture contains a variety of material, both precedents and examples, natural laws and 'positive laws'. The last are called positive, rather than human law, to signify the fact that their role is not merely to instruct, but to enjoin and constrain.[30] There are two kinds of 'positive' laws, those which are 'mixed' and which amount to the ratification of natural law, and those which are 'merely' positive, that is, are within the province of human societies to determine as seems convenient.[31] But, and here is the rub, it is not self-evident from Scripture itself which kind of material is which.

> When scripture doth yeelde us precedents, how far forth they are to bee followed; when it giveth naturall lawes, what particular order is thereunto most agreeable; when positive, which waye to make laws unrepugnant unto them; yea though all these shoulde want, yet what kind of ordinances woulde be moste for that good of the Church which is aimed at, al this must be by reason founde out.[32]

Church polity is the area of 'positive law', but it is not, for that reason, arbitrary or, in the modern sense, a matter of indifference. But positive law is mutable, and Hooker is at pains to do justice to the complexity of this issue. The mere fact that a law is given in Scripture is not itself a decisive consideration. Sometimes positive law is given with an indication as to how long it is to remain in force. But if not, we can only judge the question of whether change is permissible or not by considering 'the ende for which it was made, and by the aptnese of thinges therein prescribed unto the same end'.[33] The three types of Jewish laws show these principles at work. The *moral* law is unchanged because the matter of it continues as before, the *ceremonial* law is at an end because, although the matter continues, the end or purpose has ceased; the *judicial* law is mutable, because though the end continues, yet the matter is in some respects altered.[34]

By these means Hooker reaches the paradoxical-sounding conclusion that

God never ordeyned any thing that could be bettered. Yet many things he hath that have bene chaunged, and that for the better. That which succeedeth as better now when change is requisite, had bene worse when that which now is chaunged was instituted. Otherwise God had not then left this to choose that, neither would now reject that to choose this, were it not for some new growne occasion making that which hath bene better worse. In this case therefore men doe not presume to chaunge God's ordinance, but they yeelde thereunto requiring it selfe to be chaunged.[35]

The importance of this principle of change for our argument is obvious. According to it, it may be agreed that the restriction of the priesthood to males at one time was the ordinance of God. But at some 'new growne occasion' that same positive law may become the worse course for the Church to follow. The fact that the first law was indeed the law of God, and given by his authority, by no means demonstrates its unchangeableness.[36] The question would be whether or not the positive law given in the Scriptures had such a connection to natural law that its maintenance did not acquire the extra force of universality. But whether that is so or not, would, on Hooker's own argument, be a matter for reason itself to determine.

How would Hooker himself have interpreted the question of the ordination of women to the priesthood? The answer is hardly in doubt, and precisely illustrates his method of argument. The idea that women would be 'teachers in the house of God', he holds, as we have seen, to be 'a gross absurdity' in the light of the apostolic injunctions. This would be, in other words, an instance of Scripture giving a clear positive law. Moreover, for Hooker, such a law would undoubtedly have been a case of 'mixed' positive law, since natural reason also taught women's inferiority. Such at least is clear from his traditional handling of the place of women in marriage, which closely follows the terms of the scholastic synthesis. But if Hooker's own position on the question, had it occurred to him to raise it, cannot be in doubt, neither can the fact that it was being undermined, even as he wrote, by the fact of the rule of Queen Elizabeth, whose supremacy in the Church as monarch was likewise a matter of positive law. Hooker must surely have known of the fierce debate about the propriety of the government of women such as not merely Elizabeth I, but also Catherine de Médicis and Mary, Queen of Scots.[37] He can scarcely have been ignorant of the argument produced in 1588 by an Oxford scholar, John Case, in favour of feminine rule where the ability is present, and denying that the distinctively feminine humours adversely affect the mind.[38] He lived at a time when the Aristotelian doctrine of inherent female inferiority, rooted in logic and physiology, was already proving itself to be impermanent.

VI

But what of the question of ordination? Was that, too, for Hooker a matter of positive law, or was it a sacrament covered by the faith content of the Gospel? Although Hooker does not give ordination the explicit title of a sacrament, he sings a paean of praise to the authority and power of the ministry, which God alone can bestow.[39] By the time he came to write Book V, Hooker had come to accept the doctrine which was relatively new to Anglican apologetic that the origins of episcopacy lay in the distinction which Christ had made between the Twelve and the Seventy.[40] This had been argued by Hadrian de Saravia in his *De Diversis Ministrorum Evangelii Gradibus* of 1590, and it proved increasingly attractive to many Anglicans (including Hooker) in place of the Jeromian theory held by most Elizabethan divines that episcopacy was first introduced after the death of the Apostles.[41] But he makes abundantly clear that his argument does not depend on the former view, since we may claim the ministry to be of divine origin even if it be of human institution, provided that it has divine approbation.[42]

It is, therefore, quite consistent with Hooker's basic theory for him to say that there are conditions under which it would be legitimate to vary the form of church polity. The Tractarians found it a difficult passage to swallow, and Anglo-Catholics have choked on it ever since, but it is plain enough. Compared with matters necessary to salvation, the Scriptures are not so insistent or clear on matters relating to ecclesiastical polity that 'much which it hath taught [might] become unrequisite, sometimes because we need not use it, sometimes also because we cannot'.[43] Then follows the admission that the failure of the reformed Churches of France and Scotland to retain episcopacy, though a defect, could not be considered a cause of serious reproach or blame. This is a clear example of Hooker's readiness to judge of times and seasons.

A similar interpretation can be given to Hooker's discussion of the Jeromian theory. Even if it is by custom that bishops hold authority in the Church, none the less what has long continued in the Church without alteration is an integral part of its being considered a divine institution. The conclusion is that the power of bishops may be taken away if their behaviour becomes 'proud, tyrannical and unreformable'.[44] For Hooker, ever sensitive to the exigencies of history,

> the whole body of the Church hath power to alter, with general consent and upon necessary occasions, even the positive laws of the apostles, if there be no command to the contrary, and it manifestly appears to her, that change of times have clearly taken away the very reasons of God's first institution.[45]

Likewise in particular emergencies the Church may ordain someone where there is no bishop who could do so.

> We are not simply without exception to urge a lineal descent of power from the Apostles by continued succession of bishops in every effectual ordination.[46]

In these exceptional cases, and Hooker, we should note, draws their conditions very tightly, the crucial factor is the consent of the Church. Hooker did not believe in episcopal government of the Church, nor even in clerical government. The power of the government, he lays down in Book I, apart from the consent of the governed is no better than tyranny, and a principle he applies to both Church and State.[47] It is for this reason that he gives Parliament as well as Convocation a role in the making of ecclesiastical law. Hooker by no means anticipated the secularisation of the Church; as Cargill Thompson pertinently observes, 'had he done so, he would hardly have approved of the continued survival of Parliament's right to make laws for the Church'.[48] But it cannot seriously be doubted that he would have regarded the participation of the laity in synodical government as a normal and desirable state of affairs, conducive to that testing of consent without which no form of government is secure.

Nothing in Hooker's treatment of ordination would lead us to the conclusion that it could be an area of church polity exempt from the general considerations relating to positive law which he advanced. He anticipates the fact that different contexts will give rise to different decisions, and this he labels an 'harmonious dissimilitude'.[49] What is permanent in the ministry is the task of teaching the Gospel of Christ.

As an example of what may properly be considered a temporary measure he instances Paul's instructions to Timothy concerning the choice of widows (1 Tim. 5:9). God's clergy are a permanent state to carry out the laws governing the administration of the word and sacraments. To this necessity he adds the hierarchical distinction of degrees among the clergy so as to secure order, and the necessity of ordination. The rest are matters on which the Church has the right to make positive law in accordance with scriptural principles and right reason.

The point of this enquiry is that it shows Hooker to be the architect of an understanding of church polity which can seriously consider the necessity of change, even in an institution as traditional as an all-male priesthood. It does not, of course, turn Hooker into an advocate of women's ordination. But on his own principles Hooker would undoubtedly have been ready to consider an argument which destroyed the status of the doctrine of women's subordination as a deliverance of natural reason. The point can be made more precisely. The issue is not patriarchy (the rule of the father in the household), but male dominance. Aristotelian physiology and psychology are entirely general in their application to womankind, and are the basis upon which the impropriety of female dominance can be urged. Once this generalised basis was abandoned (and it must be said to have lingered in psychology long into the twentieth century), the support from 'natural reason', essential to Hooker's prescription for a mixed positive law, evaporates. When generalised female subordination ceases to make sense medically or empirically, the route must be open for a reappraisal of the scriptural positive law concerning the impropriety of female teachers.

This is not merely a matter of the ordination of women. A consistent modern application of the scholastic synthesis would be such as to preclude the participation of women in *any* form of public office or leadership role. Those who urge the Church's tradition as an argument against women's ordination are inconsistent with that tradition in failing to deplore female monarchs, prime ministers, members of parliament or members of church synods, heads of church colleges, and chairpersons of bodies of great power in State and Church. To have capitulated in this arena in order to preserve a *cordon sanitaire* around the Church's ministry is absolutely to have abandoned Hooker's position.

What we discover, then, in Hooker is an undeniably Anglican doctrine of the Church which enables us to reflect seriously upon the implications for church polity of the new understanding of the female-male relationship. It is a position which has no obligation to be unremittingly hostile to the church tradition in order to satisfy the instincts of radical feminism, nor, on the other hand, is it obliged to assume the immutability of laws even of divine origin. It is a position, moreover, which has a high doctrine of the apostolic ministry, and no *a priori* objection to the existence of a hierarchy. It would not feel obliged to impose the same structures upon all cultures at the same time, and could enjoy what Hooker describes in a felicitous phrase as the 'manifold and yet harmonious dissimilitude of those wayes whereby his Church upon earth is guided from age to age'.[50]

With these considerations in mind one may return to the question of the official response of the Roman Catholic Church. The documents, both the Declaration and the Commentary, seem plainly of a provisional character, striving both to start and end on a positive note, though conscious of the apparent negativity of their central teaching. The Declaration, *Inter insigniores*, recalls the opposition of the Second Vatican Council to discrimination based upon sex. The Commentary notes that it would have been desirable to have inserted into the Declaration a more general presentation on the question of the advancement of women; but, it adds, 'the time is not ripe for such a comprehensive exposition, because of the research and work in progress on all sides'.[51] But both publications are characterised by an extreme reluctance to present an historical picture of the traditional scholastic synthesis, claiming that the 'undeniable influence of prejudices unfavourable to women' or the presence of arguments 'that modern thought would have difficulty in admitting or would even rightly reject' can be easily separated from the Church's constant tradition.[52] One can have no such confidence.[53] So long as the status accorded to women remains in doubt, the isolation of the Church's priesthood from a general theory of the natural relations of the sexes strikes the reader as defensive, and in a strict sense uncatholic.

The argument of this paper brings one to the point where, without denying what the Church has maintained in the past or imposing an unhistorical interpretation upon it, an Anglican can freely face the challenge of recapturing the vision of a 'discipleship of equals', which is also part of the scriptural portrait of the nature of the Church. It may be that this vision could not have survived the Church's inculturation in the Graeco-Roman world, in which it was only wealthy widows who could exercise any kind of leadership through patronage. The self-interested character of the male medical science which asserted the natural imbecility of women can readily be recognised, and even excused. Equality, even in the Church, had little currency value until women acquired equal access to education and wives freedom from the burden of involuntary pregnancy. A new-grown occasion is upon us, and Richard Hooker provides us with the fundamental equipment with which to face it.

NOTES

1. *Laws* III, xi, 8. Quotations from Hooker are from the Folger Library Edition of his works (Cambridge, Mass., 1977–).
2. *Woman and the Priesthood*, Declaration on the Question of the Admission of Women to the Ministerial Priesthood, Sacred Congregation for the Doctrine of the Faith (Vatican City, 1977), p. 11.
3. The obvious candidates, Geneva or Wittenberg, identify the brand of Protestantism too closely. Perhaps we should suggest Marburg, on account of the cacophony of squabbling Protestant voices to be heard at the Colloquy (1529), and therefore conforming to this kind of Anglican prejudice.
4. See S. W. Sykes, 'Have Anglicans no special doctrines of their own?', *The Franciscan*, Vol. XXX, No. 1 (1988), 32–7.
5. By Peter Lake in his *Moderate Puritans and the Elizabethan Church* (Cambridge, 1982).
6. On which see Louis B. Wright, *Middle Class Culture in Elizabethan England* (Chapel Hill, N. Carolina, 1935), ch. xiii, 'The Popular Controversy over

Woman'; Ruth Kelso, *Doctrine for the Lady of the Renaissance* (Urbana, Illinois, 1956), esp. ch. 2, 'Women in the Scheme of Things'; Ian Maclean, *The Renaissance Notion of Women* (Cambridge, 1980); Simon Shepherd, *Amazons and Warrior Women* (Brighton, 1981); Linda Woodbridge, *Women and the English Renaissance, Literature and the Nature of Womankind 1540–1610* (Brighton, 1984); and Lisa Jardine, *Still Harping on Daughters: Women and Drama in the Age of Shakespeare* (Brighton, 1983).

7. *Laws* I, xv, 2.
8. Preface iii, 13. This coheres with Thomas Aquinas' opinion that the natural piety of women is not a particular mental attribute, but a lack (a *defectus contemplationis*) resulting in a tendency toward credulity (*Summa Theologica* 2a 2ae 83, 3). That there were both gains and losses to women in the Protestant Reformation is nicely argued by N. Z. Davis, in her essay 'City Women and Religious Change', *Society and Culture in Early Modern France* (Stanford, California, 1975), pp. 65–95.
9. *Laws*, Preface iii, 13. The more independent role of women in the Puritan movement has frequently attracted comment. See 'Women and Puritanism', ch. 5 of Shepherd, op. cit. (n. 6).
10. See Calvin's *Institutes*, 4, 15, 20 and Bullinger's *Decades* (Parker Society 4) pp. 370–72; as noted by John E. Booty in Vol. 4 of Folger Library edition of the *Laws* (Cambridge, Mass., 1982), pp. 209–10.
11. *Laws* V, lxii, 1–3, and 22. In the last paragraph of this chapter Hooker refers to 'divers reformed Churches' which do allow women to baptise in cases of necessity. These, doubtless, would be Lutheran churches, perhaps those of Hesse and Brandenberg-Nuremberg. So Booty, op. cit., p. 210.
12. *Laws* V, lxxiii, 1–5. It should be added that Calvin had also asserted the need for the wife to be subject to the husband, in order to guarantee the subordination of both to the authority of God (*Commentary on the Epistles of Paul the Apostle to the Corinthians* (Edinburgh, 1900), pp. 232f.
13. Henry Cornelius Agrippa's *De nobilitate et praecellentia foeminei sexus . . . declamatio* (1529: E. T. *A treatise of the nobility and excellency of womankind*, London, 1542) is an example. But its radicalism is usually interpreted as an exercise in rhetoric, perhaps because the idea of women's equality could be treated in no other way. See Maclean, *Renaissance Notion of Women*, pp. 80 and 91.
14. See note 6 above.
15. The main passage relevant to women's legal status reads as follows: 'Women are excluded from all civil and public offices; and thus they may not be *judices*, nor magistrates, nor advocates; nor may they intervene on another's behalf in law, nor act as agents' (*De regulis juris antiqui*, 50, 16, 2). In a volume published in Lyons in 1593, five eminent scholars comment on the position of women in Roman, Holy Roman and Canon Law, and references to the *imbecillitas* of women are frequent. Cf. I. Maclean, *Women Triumphant, Feminism in French Literature, 1610–1652* (Oxford, 1977), pp. 13ff.
16. *De Legibus connubialibus* (1513) I, 1, 70–6 in *Opera omnia* II, 15–17, discussed by Maclean, op. cit. (n. 6), pp. 3 and 83.

17. Maclean, *The Renaissance Notion of Women*, pp. 8f., referring to Thomas Aquinas, *Summa Theologica* 1a, 92, 1.
18. Maclean, op. cit., p. 15, referring to Peter Lombard, *Sententiae* II, 20 and Thomas Aquinas, *Summa Theologica* 2a 2ae, 163, 4, and 165, 2.
19. Maclean, op. cit., p. 83.
20. Here one thinks primarily in modern times of Alasdair MacIntyre's powerful argument in *After Virtue* (London, 1981).
21. For what follows I am especially indebted to the lucid analysis of Hooker's political philosophy in W. D. J. Cargill Thompson's essay 'The Philosopher of the "Politic Society": Richard Hooker as a Political Thinker', in his (posthumous) *Studies in the Reformation*, ed. C. W. Dugmore (London, 1980), pp. 131–91.
22. For the interesting and significant reason that it lays too much weight on 'the exercise of superiority peculiar unto rulers and guides of others', *Laws* III, i, 14.
23. *Laws* III, i, 4. On the history of this term see H. Wagenhammer, *Das Wesen des Christentums* (Mainz, 1973) and S. W. Sykes, *The Identity of Christianity* (London, 1984), esp. pp. 211–38 and 250–61.
24. Other examples are given in *Laws* III, v. 1.
25. *Laws* III, iii, 4.
26. *Laws* III, v. 1.
27. *Laws* III, ii, 1.
28. *Laws* III, ix, 1.
29. 'All our controversie in this cause concerning the orders of the Church is, what particulars the Church may appoint. That which doth finde them out is the force of man's reason. That which doth guide and direct his reason is first the generall law of nature, which law of nature and the morall law of Scripture are in the substance of law all one', *Laws* III, ix, 2.
30. *Laws* I, x, 8.
31. *Laws* I, x, 10.
32. *Laws* III, ix, 1.
33. *Laws* III, x, 1.
34. *Laws* III, x, 4.
35. *Laws* III, x, 5.
36. 'I therefore conclude that neither God's being author of laws for government of his Church, nor his committing them unto Scripture, is any reason sufficient wherefore all churches should for ever be bounde to keep them without chaunge', *Laws* III, x, 7.
37. See Maclean, *Women Triumphant*, p. 58.
38. 'Nature often makes women shrewd, hard work makes her learned, upbringing makes her pious, and experience makes her wise. What, therefore, prevents women from playing a full part in public affairs? If one is born free, why should she obey? If one is heiress to a kingdom, why should she not reign? Divine law, the history of nations, ancient institutions, and examples drawn from Holy Writ all support such arguments', *Sphaera civitatis* (Oxford, 1588, I, 3, p. 33; cited in Maclean, *The Renaissance Notion of Women*, p. 61 (Latin, p. 95).

39. *Laws* V, lxxvii.
40. *Laws* V, lxxviii, 5. See W. D. J. Cargill Thompson's discussion in 'Anthony Marten and the Elizabethan Debate on Episcopacy' in G. V. Bennett and J. D. Walsh (eds.), *Essays in Modern English Church History in Memory of Norman Sykes* (London, 1966), pp. 44–75.
41. Hooker acknowledges his conversion to the new theory in *Laws* VII, xi, 8.
42. *Laws* VII, xi, 10.
43. *Laws* III, xi, 16.
44. *Laws* VII, v, 8.
45. *Laws* VII, v, 8.
46. *Laws* VII, xiv, 11.
47. *Laws* I, x, 8.
48. 'The Philosopher of the "Politic Society" ', p. 190.
49. *Laws* III, xi, 8.
50. *Laws* III, xi, 8.
51. *The Ordination of Women, Circumstances and Origin of the Declaration Women and the Priesthood* (Catholic Truth Society, Do. 494; London, nd), p. 4.
52. *Women and the Priesthood*, pp. 5–6.
53. Indeed in one place the Commentary leaves wholly ambiguous whether or not the proposition of St Thomas Aquinas that *mulier est in statu subjectionis* is 'scarcely defensible' or the direct (and presumably defensible) exegesis of the first chapters of Genesis and 1 Timothy 2:12–14.

PART II

THE ANGLICAN DOCTRINE OF THE CHURCH

6

ANGLICANISM AND THE ANGLICAN DOCTRINE OF THE CHURCH

Do Anglicans have no special doctrines of their own? If so, then plainly the title of this contribution which refers to 'the Anglican Doctrine of the Church' is confused. But the argument of this essay is intended as a direct challenge to the denial that Anglicans have doctrines of their own. The claim will be made not merely that it would be interesting or convenient were Anglicans to attempt to write up their doctrine of the Church, but that their previous justifications for not doing so are false. It might be instructive for a church historian to trace the origins of this denial, which would not, I hazard a guess, have occurred to many pre-nineteenth-century Anglican theologians, least of all to Richard Field (1561–1616), friend of Richard Hooker and author of a multi-volume work, *Of the Church* (1606–10). Modern Anglicans, I shall argue, have the materials to write such a doctrine and need to be shown why they must have the courage and humility to do so.

What has this to do with the Chicago-Lambeth Quadrilateral?* Much in every way. For the Quadrilateral, in either of its forms, is confidently said to be inadequate, not merely as a definition of Anglicanism, which was never its purpose, but even as a basis for ecumenical discussion, which was the ostensible reason for its promulgation by Lambeth 1888. Anglicanism, we are told, has now gone beyond the bare Quadrilateral in its ecumenical discussions, because these have demonstrated the degree to which the mere listing of four bases masked a host of problems.[1] The supposed inadequacy of the Quadrilateral was also the theme of some urgent debate forty years ago by theologians of the American Church Union, who saw in the

*This essay first appeared in the symposium *Quadrilateral at One Hundred* (1988).

101

changing terminology with which the Quadrilateral was described and recommended an open threat to 'Catholic principles'. They argued that the prime defect of every plan for union (necessarily at this stage with Protestant Churches) was the failure to present the partners with a clear statement of the doctrine, discipline, and worship of the Anglican Communion. It is one thing, they said, to present the Quadrilateral as 'basic elements of an organic whole' comprising the faith and order of the Church (which is how, they claim, Chicago 1886 understood the matter); it is quite another to present it as 'a basis upon which approach may be . . . made' (the terms of Lambeth 1888).[2]

It is not my intention further to discuss the justification for these complaints. But it will become clear that there is a close connection between the contents of the Quadrilateral (in either version), the denial that Anglicans have special doctrines of their own, and the need to supplement the Quadrilateral with something – with, I shall argue, the attempt to articulate the Anglican doctrine of the Church. The first section of this essay will deal with traditional denial. Here I shall argue, as formally and rigorously as possible, that the claim is demonstrably false. In the second part I shall turn to the central issue in the erroneous tradition, which concerns the nature of doctrine. At this stage it will be necessary to reformulate the theological connection between the Scriptures and the creeds, the first two elements of the Quadrilateral. Finally we shall consider the application of the previous arguments to the project of the Anglican doctrine of the Church, and provide one brief illustration of what might be involved in its development.

Have Anglicans No Special Doctrines of Their Own?

It is a major and central feature of modern Anglican apologetic to deny that Anglicans have special and peculiar doctrines of their own.[3] A typical example of this view occurs in Bishop Wand's standard work, *Anglicanism in History and Today* (1961). Here, in the context of a distinction between Anglican theology, whose existence he affirms, and Anglican doctrines, Wand asserts that it is part of the glory of Anglicanism that 'we claim to believe what is in the Creeds and in the Bible, that is to say, what is common to all Christendom.'[4] Somewhat earlier Bishop Stephen Neill had been more sweeping still, denying not merely that there were special Anglican doctrines, but even that there existed a 'particular Anglican theology'. The Church of England, he affirmed, 'teaches all the doctrines of the Catholic Faith, as these are to be found in Holy Scripture, as they are summarized in the Apostles', the Nicene, and the Athanasian Creeds, and as they are set forth in the decisions of the first four General Councils of the undivided Church.'[5]

It is the sole purpose of this part of the essay to show that the NSD ('no special doctrines') claim is fallacious. What follows from such a demonstration can only be properly considered when Anglicans have thoroughly mastered the reason why it has to be given up. It emerges as a thoroughly confused and confusing piece of Anglican apologia whose paradoxical purpose was to distinguish Anglicanism from all other denominations and one of whose astonishing consequences has been to create a view of the catholicity of the Church private to Anglicans. It is of no small consequence to disabuse our minds of this venerable absurdity.

We must enquire, in the first place, what a 'special doctrine' would be. As already indicated, Wand holds that it is Anglicanism's 'glory' that we have 'no special and peculiar doctrines of our own.' Neill indirectly glosses the notion of 'special doctrines' when he instances as 'additions to the Catholic Faith' the dogmas of the Infallibility of the Pope and of the Corporal Assumption of the Blessed Virgin Mary. The idea that some denominations have made *additions* to a body of doctrine *common* to all Christendom is a form of apologetic highly characteristic of Anglicanism. It suggests the following mathematical interpretation of the NSD claim: namely that whereas Eastern Orthodoxy professes doctrines A, B, C, D and E, F, G, H, and Roman Catholicism professes doctrines A, B, C, D, E, F, G, H, and I, J, K, L, Anglicans profess merely A, B, C and D. Protestant denominations are, on this analogy, sometimes represented as affirming more than the basic quantity of doctrines, for example Lutherans as insisting on a special doctrine of the Eucharist, or Calvinists on double predestination, while at least some Congregationalists may entirely fail to teach the orthodox doctrine of the Trinity. On this gloss of the NSD claim, Anglicanism turns out, somewhat paradoxically, to be 'mere Christianity', unhyphenated Catholicism without omission of anything essential or addition of anything inessential.

At this point, of course, objection might be raised to quantifying doctrines in this way. Is it really the case, it might be asked, that

Christian doctrines can simply be listed in a crassly numerical manner? The objection has powerful theological weight to it, but there are very good reasons in the history of Anglicanism why the claim should be interpreted as implying the possibility of enumerating the basic Christian doctrines. It was the whole point of the 'fundamental articles' tradition, in which Anglican apologists invested heavily in the sixteenth, seventeenth and eighteenth centuries, that the 'necessary doctrines' could be distinguished and enumerated with enough clarity to distinguish them from 'additions' and 'matters indifferent'. The NSD claim and the Anglican attempt to identify fundamentals belong to the same world of discourse.

The position which we are to examine in this paper, therefore, is the one taken by both Wand and Neill which glosses the NSD claim in traditional Anglican fashion by assuming that doctrines may be expressed one by one in propositions. The demonstration, which I shall provide, that this claim is false is one of the reasons for *not* holding such a view of Christian doctrine. The revision of this viewpoint will concern us below; but in the meantime we must demonstrate the untenability of the NSD claim in the form in which I have given it.

The argument I shall advance proceeds on the basis of the same assumptions as held by Wand and Neill. The reason why the claim fails is that it is unable to provide an account of the extent of true doctrine. It is notorious from the history of the Church that there have been disagreements about doctrine. On the mathematical metaphor some denominations hold a larger, and some a small body of propositions. All denominations are, therefore, obliged to justify their own claims by showing: (a) that their view of the extent of Christian doctrine is a sufficient expression of the catholic faith, and (b) that their denomination has the authority to declare that body of doctrine to be the full expression of the catholic faith.

There is enough evidence that the first of these claims is commonly made by Anglicans. In both of the original texts of the Chicago-Lambeth Quadrilateral the word 'sufficient' is to be found (Chicago, article 2, 'The Nicene Creed as the sufficient statement of the Christian Faith'; Lambeth, article 2, 'The Apostles' Creed as the Baptismal Symbol; and the Nicene Creed, as the sufficient statement of the Christian faith'). It is worth briefly pausing to consider this term in this context. Two antecedents suggest themselves. The first is the well-known declaration of sufficiency (*satis est*) in the Lutheran Augsburg Confession.

> For the true unity of the church it is enough to agree concerning the teaching of the Gospel and the administration of the sacraments (translation of Latin text of Article VII).[6]

If the Quadrilateral's use of the word 'sufficient' is a reflection of Augsburg it is an unconscious and indirect one, though experience of Anglican-Lutheran dialogue confirms that the differences between the Quadrilateral and the Augsburg Confession are a central area of difficulty.

A second antecedent is the prolonged Anglican use of the terms 'essential' and 'necessary' in relation to the doctrines of the creed. 'The visible Church of Jesus Christ', affirmed Richard Hooker, 'is therefore one, in outward profession of those things, which supernaturally appertain to the very essence of Christianity, and are necessarily required in every particular Christian man.'[7] The 'fundamental articles' tradition, of which this is an early instance, first asserted the necessity to salvation of believing the apostolic faith, qualifying it subsequently to affirm the necessity for the Church to be the Church of its acknowledgement of the same apostolic faith. But there is, of course, a difference between 'necessary' and 'sufficient', and the phrase 'the sufficient statement of the Christian faith' prompts the same sort of commentary that the term 'sufficient' has aroused in its Lutheran context in the Augsburg Confession.

Be that as it may, the Anglicans who used this language in the 1870s and 1880s could certainly not have claimed that their definition of what constituted a 'sufficient statement of the Christian faith' would have been generally agreed to by Christians. To appreciate the intentionally controversial nature of this statement we have only to contrast it with the words of the 1870 Dogmatic Constitution, *Pastor Aeternus*, which declared the Pope's infallibility:

> We, therefore, with the approval of the sacred Council, judge it necessary, for the protection, the safety and the increase of the Catholic flock, to propose to all the faithful what is to be believed and held, with regard to the establishment, the perpetuity and the nature of this sacred apostolic primacy, in which is found the

strength and solidity of the entire Church. Likewise we judge it necessary to proscribe with sentence of condemnation the contrary erroneous opinions so detrimental to the Lord's flock.

Here is exemplified both a different statement about what might be said to be the content of the faith, and also the claim of a different body to speak with exclusive authority for the entire Church.

Anglicans, of course, have been both reticent and elusive on the subject of their authority to define what is a sufficient statement of the Christian faith. But it is apparent that it could not be adequate merely to *assert* a certain number of doctrines as though their sufficiency was a self-evident fact. Anglicans have certainly attended with considerable vigour to the historic justification of this claim, with copious reference to the consensus of the so-called undivided Church. But again it has proved not to be self-evident that a certain fixed number of centuries contain that consensus, and even Anglican definitions of the fundamentals have varied widely.[8] The issue of the authority of the Church of England, and of the Churches in communion with her, to declare in the absence of contemporary Christian unanimity that such-and-such constitutes a sufficient statement of Christian faith is unavoidable. For this right to exist in the way Anglicans believe or assume that it does, it must exist in the Church as such. That is to say, on the very assumptions of Wand and Neill, there must be a theology of the Church according to which the Churches of the Anglican Communion have the right to make controversial declarations about the extent of the content of the Christian faith. Even though doctrines A to D are affirmed, and even though these doctrines may be held in common with all other Churches, the affirming of these doctrines to be sufficient entails a further doctrine, M, which can only take the form of an Anglican doctrine of the Church. But *this* doctrine could not, by definition, be common to other bodies, except those which defined the Church's doctrines in precisely the same way. Anglicans, therefore, must have at least one special doctrine of their own.

The fact that the NSD claim is internally inconsistent is unsurprisingly supported by the discovery that in the past Anglicans have conspicuously felt able to offer a more articulated doctrine of the Church. This is most strikingly the case in respect of commentary upon the Thirty-nine Articles. No one reading the relevant passages in William

Beveridge's *Discourse on the Thirty-Nine Articles*, posthumously published in 1710, could doubt for a moment that he believed himself to be expounding the Anglican doctrine of the Church.[9] Furthermore he makes it abundantly clear that the Articles are the basis for such a doctrine precisely because they were the result of a decision of a Church council, and authoritative for Anglicans in the same way that the decrees of the Council of Trent were for Roman Catholics. Moreover he uses the opportunity provided by commentary on this article for listing the ways in which the doctrine of the Church of Rome is in disagreement with that of the Church of England.

Other commentators, for example the late-nineteenth-century Anglo-Catholic, Dr Gibson, have noted what they deem to be significant differences between the Anglican article XIX and the phrasing of the Augsburg article 7 (to which we have already referred).[10] It is ironic that the contrast is said to lie in the fact that the Anglican article is more precise and guarded and has nothing to correspond to the Lutheran *satis est*. Gibson's commentary also includes discussion of the fact that the article contains no reference to the 'invisible Church', an omission whose doctrinal implications he weaves into a clear statement of the doctrine of the Church.

One of the contributory factors in the formulation of the NSD claim is the decline in the status of the Thirty-nine Articles. Already in 1888 the Lambeth Conference had declared that the newer missionary Churches should not necessarily feel obliged to accept them in their entirety. Wand adduces in support of his NSD contention that the Articles and Catechism occupy a 'lower level of authority than the creed.'[11] That is indisputably the case. *De facto* the Articles have lost authority by being either ignored or relativised to a particular period of history. The sort of claim which Beveridge made for the Articles would be most unlikely to command the assent of any but a very few Anglicans today. But that fact is itself interesting. For what it means is that one (and not the only) traditional basis for the development of the Anglican doctrine of the Church has lost status as an indication of the standpoint to which Anglicans are corporately committed. It could not imply that Anglicanism *per se* is not committed to a special doctrine of the Church. And it would be as logical to infer that the consequence of the Articles' lost status is that Anglicans must now work harder at developing their own doctrine on the basis of the sources and norms to which they are still corporately committed.

We must, therefore, press the question whether the fact that some prominent Anglicans recently have declined to articulate the Anglican doctrine of the Church is a contingent matter, or (as they assert) inheres in the nature of contemporary Anglicanism. It must be assumed that promulgating doctrines of their own is something which Anglicans could do. If that were not even possible, let us say on the grounds that only that would count as a doctrine which was taught by the *whole* Church, then the NSD claim would simply be tautologous. Anglicans would then have no special doctrines simply because 'doctrine' would not be the kind of thing which only Anglicans could advance. But if it is possible that there could be such a thing as an Anglican doctrine of the Church then it is also possible that, though there was not one at the moment, there could be one in the future; and if, as I have argued, there is such a doctrine, then what we would expect to find is a state of affairs in which an Anglican doctrine of the Church, special to Anglicans, was *implicit* in the professions of faith.

That this is indeed the case arises from credal profession of belief in the Church. For any Church to profess a belief in the One, Holy, Catholic and Apostolic Church must be taken to be self-referential; that Church includes this Church. Thus it is implied by Anglicans saying the creeds that the Church in which they believe is one in which the Churches of the Anglican Communion participate. This is clearly stated in the case of English Anglicans by Canon A1 of the Church of England (corresponding to canon 3 of the 1603 Canons):

> The Church of England, established according to the laws of this realm under the Queen's Majesty, belongs to the true and apostolic Church of Christ; and as our duty to the said Church of England requires, we do constitute and ordain that no member thereof shall be at liberty to maintain or hold the contrary.

But this proposition *must* imply an Anglican doctrine of the Church. Furthermore it is because Anglicans affirm and believe such a doctrine that they are in a position to go on to assert, as they do, controversially, that a certain limited number of doctrines constitute a sufficient statement of the apostolic faith. This proposition, moreover, contains within itself the necessary claim to possess the authority to delimit the extent of the content of the faith, which, as I have argued, is the basic requirement of doctrine M, the Anglican doctrine of the Church.

The conclusion of this argument is now clear. What Anglicans have to assert is that the Church to which they belong has the authority to determine that a specific number of doctrines constitutes a sufficient statement of the Christian faith. Since that position is not acceptable, for example, to the Roman Catholic Church or to the Eastern Ortho-dox Churches, it cannot be the case that this implied Anglican doctrine of the Church is common to all Christians. Therefore, again it cannot be the case that there are no Anglican doctrines. The NSD claim is false.

It will be said that this argument rests upon a disputable premise, that Christian doctrines are capable of being enumerated. There is indeed wide-ranging contemporary debate on the nature of doctrine, about which the authorities cited for the currency of the NSD claim are innocent. It is time, of course, for Anglican apologetic to rejoin modern theological discussion and cease the pretence of being above the denominations. This absurdity reaches into the heart of the solemn assurances which Anglicans sometimes give of what the 'catholic Church' may or may not do, on a definition of catholicity private to a particular party within Anglicanism. It is time that we grew up enough theologically to realise that there is dispute between the denominations about what the catholicity of the Church signifies, and that if we, as Anglicans, have a view worth considering on this matter, we must take the risk of advancing an Anglican doctrine of the Church, as a special doctrine of our own in dialogue with, and not above, those of our contemporaries.

The Scriptures and Creeds in Anglicanism

What is needed by way of assistance out of this impasse is a revised understanding of the nature of doctrine. It is the intention of the second part of this essay to reformulate the connection between Scripture and the creeds, and to do so in a way which is more convincingly and consistently Anglican than the venerable, but mistaken, tradition which we have analysed.

As we have already seen, the NSD claim is related to the way in which Anglicans have traditionally formulated the fundamental articles of Christianity. It has seemed for a very long time to be an attractive way of resolving inter-Christian dispute that one should propose or presuppose the existence of unchallengeable fundamentals. Three centuries of disagreement about the precise extent and content of such verities taught at least some Anglicans one lesson, that no declaration of the fundamentals could possibly be unchallengeable. What account, then, ought to be given of the status of the articles of the creeds? And how are they related to the way in which a much larger number of doctrines has been formulated in the history of the Church, which are to be found in, or might be deduced from, the Holy Scriptures?

In attempting to answer these questions we face the relationship between the first and the second pillars of the Quadrilateral. We quote them in both of their forms:

1. The Holy Scriptures of the Old and New Testament as the revealed Word of God (Chicago, 1886); (compare)
    A. The Holy Scriptures of the Old and New Testaments, as 'containing all things necessary to salvation,' and as being the rule and ultimate standard of faith (Lambeth, 1888).
2. The Nicene Creed as the sufficient statement of the Christian Faith (Chicago, 1886); (compare)
    B. The Apostles' Creed, as the Baptismal Symbol; and the Nicene Creed, as the sufficient statement of the Christian faith (Lambeth, 1888).

One advantage of the changes introduced by Lambeth 1888 is that they bring the text of both of the sections closer to Anglican *practice*, to the practice of using the Scriptures as Anglican article VI (quoted in A above, from Lambeth 1888) prescribes and to the practice of using the Apostles' Creed at Baptism. Merely to hold the Holy Scriptures to be the revealed word of God might imply nothing distinctive as to their use. They might quite consistently be regarded as the property of the Church, to be studied and interpreted only by an authorised élite. Article VI, however, contains a precise and significant reference to the Anglican practice of publicly reading the Scriptures to the whole people in their own language. It runs as follows:

Holy Scripture containeth all things necessary for salvation; so that whatsoever is not *read* therein, nor may be proved thereby, is not to be required *of any man*, that it should be believed as an article of the Faith, or be thought requisite or necessary to salvation (*my emphases*).

This is the principle which underlies the rubric relating to the public reading of Scripture.

Then shall be read distinctly with an audible voice the first Lesson, taken out of the Old Testament . . . ; He that readeth so standing and turning himself, as he may best be heard of all such as are present (Morning Prayer, 1662 *BCP*).

It is because the whole congregation hears the reading of Scripture that they are actually in possession of everything 'necessary for salvation.'

This practice necessarily makes the whole Church into students of the Scriptures. Doubtless it is true that some, even many, are not very diligent. Nonetheless the requirement of attention to what is read is plain enough; it must be heard, marked, learned and inwardly digested (Collect for the Second Sunday in Advent, 1662 *BCP*). Illiteracy is, in principle, not an insuperable obstacle to the kind of attention demanded of the laity, though the surmounting of this hindrance is a natural activity for the Christian mission. Nor is the sort of proficiency required in Scriptural knowledge beyond the reach of people of average or even limited intelligence. For the God who is clearly portrayed in Scripture is not the kind of tyrant who might require human beings to judge certainly between interpretations of difficult places in Scripture on pain of damnation. William Chillingworth (1602–44), the Anglican theologian who thought out this matter with considerable clarity and force, laid particular stress on the notion of sufficiency:

It is sufficient (he said) for any man's salvation to believe that the Scripture is true, and contains all things necessary to salvation; and to do his best endeavour to find and believe the true sense of it.[12]

There is a morally humane character to the diligence required of hearers of the word.

In the language of more recent theology, it would surely be right to interpret the assertion of Lambeth 1888 that the Scriptures are the 'rule and ultimate standard of the faith' in terms of their narrative or story quality.[13] That is to say, what gives the Scriptures ultimacy is the fact that they present an overarching narrative which cannot be replaced by any abstract philosophical or theological propositions. The Scriptures constitute a single narrative world, the world of God's creative and redemptive love, told in manifest and complex ways through particular stories. It is because it is in story form that it is communicable and accessible even to children and others of limited intellectual attainment. It is because it is in story form that it is also so taxing and so fascinating to those trained and alert to the problems of anthropomorphism.

The fact that the Scriptures present us with a *single* narrative world gives us the clue to the relation between the Scriptures and the Christian creeds. For the two creeds referred to in the second part of the Quadrilateral are both in narrative form. Their central section is composed of a summary of the deeds of Christ, which is itself contextualised by statements about first and last things, creation and eschaton. They constitute, therefore, not a self-contained statement of the Christian faith, but a *sufficient* statement, bearing in mind their reference to the narrative world of the Scriptures.

Here again the explicit recollection in Lambeth 1888 of Anglican practice in speaking of the Apostles' Creed as the 'Baptismal Symbol' is a useful addition. For here is the point of entry upon the Christian life of every believer, so that the repetition of the Creed in the public workshop of the Church should constitute an implicit reminder of baptism. The reading of the Scriptures (at Morning and Evening Prayer), followed by the saying or singing of passages of Scripture expressive of the believer's response, is crowned by the public recitation of the faith of the Church. The canticles are a hermeneutic for the passages of Scripture which have been read, a hermeneutic largely of communal praise. The creeds which follow provide the total context for the passage, a context which may not have been explicitly alluded to in the reading. They are, therefore, an important reminder that the Church has generally held that there exists a hierarchy of truths, and that not everything read in Scripture is of equal importance. The use of *both* Scriptures *and* creeds is alike a moral activity, requiring the kind of effort, judgement and commitment that such a God might properly demand of his creation.

The Anglican Doctrine of the Church

The application of these remarks to the Anglican doctrine of the Church must now be considered. We have established that the reference of the creeds to belief in One, Holy, Catholic, and Apostolic Church is not a self-contained proposition, but a way of referring to the Church of the Scriptures, the people of God of both Old and New Testaments. It is, above all else, a statement about the narrative world in which not merely they, but also we, live. To profess belief in this Church is, as we have argued, necessarily to affirm that we ourselves, the people making this profession, belong to the same pilgrim people.

We must attend, however, in greater detail to the summary statement made above that it is a consequence of such a self-involving profession that there must be an Anglican doctrine of the Church. As we have seen, Anglicans have felt some diffidence (to put it no more strongly) about such a proposal. I now wish to show that there is some real content to this diffidence, despite the fact that it has been presented in the wholly unconvincing and disastrous guise of the NSD doctrine.

We may have to admit to a difference between the sense in which one can speak of Anglican doctrine and that in which one can speak of Lutheran or Roman Catholic doctrine, *provided* that what is meant by doctrine is conceived in principle to be the elucidation of a document or documents specific and fundamental to a denomination. *If* the characteristic of Lutheran or Roman Catholic doctrine is the interpretation of the *Confessio Augustana* or the Decrees of the Council of Trent, of Vatican I and II, and of the *ex cathedra* utterances of the popes, then it is plain that contemporary Anglicans have nothing to correspond to such an activity. At least we can say that we have nothing *precisely* to correspond to that kind of interpretation; but it would be more hazardous to say that we had nothing analogous.

An example will make the point clearer. In a volume of denominational 'statements' on *The Nature of the Church*, published in 1952, Professor Leonard Hodgson, Regius Professor of Divinity at Oxford, contributed a piece which he meticulously entitled 'The Doctrine of the Church as held and taught in the Church of England'.[14] The reason for the caution, he asserted in his first sentence, was 'so as not to suggest that there is any specifically Anglican doctrine'. In further elucidation he added that the English Reformation (by presumed, but, alas, not uncontroversial distinction from German, Swiss, French, Danish, Swedish or Norwegian reformations) aimed at 'reforming abuses in the continuing life of the existing Church,' and did not proceed 'by logically developing a theological or ecclesiastical system from some basic doctrine or premise'.

Despite this claim, the entire content of the rest of Hodgson's statement consists of the citation of relevant extracts from the Thirty-nine Articles, the 1662 *Book of Common Prayer* and the Canons Ecclesiastical, followed by carefully phrased interpretations of them. The penultimate paragraph contains a ringing declaration beginning with the words, 'In the mind of the Church of England the universal Church is . . .', and the final paragraph expresses what 'the Church of England believes itself to be'. Moreover, the interpretations of the citations from the formularies are replete with statements designed to show, in particular, how the Church of England's positions differ from those of both Protestants and Roman Catholics.[15]

What, then, are we to make of Hodgson's original denial that there is any specifically Anglican doctrine? Here we have formularies, cited as official and given careful interpretation; we have clear emphasis upon the differences which distinguish Anglicans from others; we have a statement of what is said to be 'the mind of the Church of England'. Why, then, does not all this amount, in Hodgson's view, to Anglican doctrine? There are, it seems, two reasons for his diffidence. The first, which he gives explicitly, consists of a denial that the official formularies of the Church of England constitute 'confessions'. They are not "foundations documents" setting out a specifically Anglican *corpus* of doctrine to be the starting-point of all later Anglican teaching.'[16] The second reason for diffidence is his insistence on trying to do justice to two differing canons of Scripture interpretation, according greater or lesser weight to the early Fathers and to the reformers. Both of these interpretative strategies, he insists, can be held with loyalty by members of the Church of England; and it is futile to attempt to construct 'Anglican doctrine' 'by paring away what is distinctive of each and concentrating on what is common to both.'[17]

Hodgson's grounds for caution in formulating Anglican doctrine are entirely reasonable. But neither of them amount to a case for radically distinguishing Anglicans from other denominations. As we have seen, theologians of earlier times have had no scruples in treating the Articles in the way Hodgson claims that Anglicans cannot. We are then dealing with a modern development. But the fact is that the same modern developments have occurred in other denominations, so that in practice the Thirty-nine Articles are treated by Anglicans analogously to the way in which the *Confessio Augustana* is dealt with by Lutherans. That is to say, they are used as a weighty source (not, of course, the sole source) for interpreting the Scriptures and the creeds. They are both placed in historical context and viewed relative to controversies of the time. They are by no means regarded as infallible.

Nonetheless a difference lingers, and it has been well formulated thus:

> It is not simply that they (that is, the Articles) are supposed to be read in conjunction with the Book of Common Prayer. There is a more important difference, which is that the Anglican doctrinal tradition, born of an attempt (neither wholly successful nor wholly unsuccessful) to achieve comprehensiveness within the limits of a Christianity both catholic and reformed, is not susceptible to the kind of textual definition which the Confessions (on the Protestant side) and the conciliar decrees (on the Catholic) afford. One might almost say that Anglicans have taken the authority of the Scriptures and the Catholic creeds too seriously to be comfortable with another single doctrinal norm.[18]

With this remark about 'textual definition' we return to the hypothetical remark with which we first analysed the difference. But even if Lutherans or Roman Catholics are *more* textually oriented than Anglicans, it is still true that Anglicans consider *their own* Prayer Books (not the Lutheran or Roman Catholic ones) and write interpretive books about *their* articles (not about the *Book of Concord*). The differences in effect are, at the most, a matter of degree, and their consequence is not that Anglican doctrine is an unthinkable phenomenon.

A similar remark may be made of Hodgson's other anxiety, the pressure to bury the historic dialectic of Anglican interpretations behind a synthetic statement of 'Anglican doctrine'. Here, too, it would be impossible to distinguish contemporary Anglicans from contemporary Roman Catholics or Lutherans on the grounds that only the former knew of differing interpretations of their authoritative documents. In this matter modern developments in all denominations have greatly increased the fact of internal diversity. Most denominations have bodies which make decisions on disputed matters and though they accord them various degrees of authoritativeness, none of them prove to be *de facto* unchallengeable.

The further complication of the autonomy of Anglican Provinces adds a certain complexity to the task of formulating Anglican doctrine. In some Provinces no mention is made of the Thirty-nine Articles. All Provinces have their own Prayer Books, some, such as the USA, having adopted a new *Book of Common Prayer*. A serious attempt to do justice to an Anglican doctrine of the Church would have to refer to a plurality of such books and documents. It is, indeed, thinkable that the actions of Provinces which take no care to establish a perceptible coherence between the prayer books of the different Churches could effectively frustrate the enterprise. But the completion of the task is not impossible in principle, however complex in practice. Nor would it distinguish Anglicanism from Lutheranism, which also has known the development of contrasting traditions of interpretation, differing ecclesial practices and liturgies. No modern Lutheran writing on the Lutheran doctrine of the Church would today expect to go unchallenged by her or his contemporaries.

What is finally needed in the presentation of this case for the existence of Anglican doctrine, specifically of an Anglican doctrine of the Church, is an illustration. A patient reader may even have agreed with the arguments deployed hitherto, without being persuaded that a credible account could be given of such doctrine. Lacking the time or competence to offer a complete outline of the Anglican doctrine of the Church, one ought none the less be willing to provide at least an example of one element in it.

The example needs to be taken from something that is relatively uncontroversially and uniformly characteristic of Anglicans in all parts of the world, and no better case exists than Books of Common Prayer. In terms of a doctrine of the Church, what are they? They are first and foremost a way of *ordering the worship* of the people of God. In other words, they resolve the problem of potential disorder in worship, a phenomenon already known in the churches of St Paul. Disorder includes not merely unruly conduct, but also discrepant conviction. Common worship is thus relevant to doctrinal dispute, a phenomenon chronic in the history of Christianity. Such dispute, of course, may be resolved by analytic enquiry undertaken by Christian theologians and promulgated by authoritative decision. No such decisions, however, are in principle void of ambiguity and all may give rise to further dispute. This is where the importance of common worship according to an authorised text is so significant. For prayer is not in the analytic mode. It contains doctrine, but it does not insist on resolving ambiguity. Its characteristic language is the primary symbols of the Scriptures. It leaves the worshipper free to make his or her own associations. It is a pedagogical instrument, but is not didactically driven. Unity in prayer and praise is qualitatively different from the discursive unity of a doctrinal formulation.[19]

One should expect, therefore, the Prayer Books of the Anglican Communion to express with a certain clarity, but not with overdefinition, the principal features of an understanding of the unity of the Church. This unity is implicit, of course, as much in the rubrics as in the text. The rubrics prescribe certain actions, forbid others and permit yet others. All these conditions of worship have reasons to do with order in the congregation, an order conceived not as decorum for its own sake, but as inhering in the search for conformity to the mind of Christ, and to *koinonia* with God and with one another. Needless to say, it is always possible that the imposition of certain kinds of order may have more to do with cultural taste than with the Holy Spirit.

The linguistic and behavioural order of the congregation needs to express and embody the *priority of Scriptural symbols*. By symbols is meant here elements of a system of communication which more or less effectively realise what they symbolise. Anglicans take care to read the Scriptures of the Old and New Testaments publicly (and, one hopes, effectively) in the hearing of the whole congregation. They then reinforce by the device of repetition (in which the congregation joins) the major symbols involved in the act of praising God (the hymns and canticles of the Church). After this they evoke the entire overarching framework of the system of communication in the words of the creed.

All these activities involve the priority of Scriptural symbols over later Christian thought, though there is no objection in principle to the presence of the latter in a subordinate position. The fact that the symbols are part of a system of communication, that they must proclaim and embody 'the Gospel', implies that they are in need of revision, since cultures have their own symbol systems, some of which make it

117

impossible for the Gospel to be heard. Constant and fussy revision, however, undermines the significance of repetition, which is a key factor in the way in which human beings are embedded within the Christian world of meaning. Élite groups within the Church are occasionally insensitive to the fact that their manipulation of variety or alteration of common texts is an affirmation of their dominance over 'lower' participants in the Church. The repetition of the symbols constitutes a major way in which the whole Church exerts subversive power within a culture, and the preservation of a common text is the delivery into the hands of the whole people of God of an equal share in the resources which all will need for their 'vocation and ministry'.[20]

Ordered worship is thus also *a nurturing environment* which seeks to gather people from a single locality, male and female, old and young, high and low, rich and poor, and fashion them into a community which learns from one another. Where particular educational events necessarily are related to the needs and abilities of sub-groups within a congregation, worship invites the community into a catholic whole, in 'one communion and fellowship' (collect for All Saints' Day, 1662 *BCP*). It is a unity of prayer based upon common attention to the Word in Scripture. The point is made in the collect for St Simon and St Jude's day.

> O Almighty God, who hast built thy Church upon the foundation of the Apostles and Prophets, Jesus Christ himself being the head cornerstone: Grant us so to be joined together in unity of spirit by their doctrine, that we may be made an holy temple acceptable unto thee.

This collect, which is probably of Cranmer's own composition, is based on Scripture, notably Ephesians 2:20–22 and 4:3, with a side reference to the pastoral epistles which make so much of the word 'doctrine'. It has survived from the 1549 Prayer Book (where the Lutheran word 'congregation' figured for 'Church'), and in the American *BCP* was 'promoted' from the obscurity of a Saints' Day to be one of the collects for a Sunday after Trinity.

The reference in the collect to the symbol of the 'Temple' undergirds the last feature of the Anglican doctrine of the Church which we shall mention. It arises from the Prayer Books in the fact that they insist upon a *unity of worship and practice within the theological category of sacrifice.*

The degree to which Anglicans are at home with sacrificial imagery can be seen in the immensely influential work of George Herbert, *The Temple* (1652), whose centre and focus is precisely the unity of the 'temple of the heart' with the 'temple of the congregation', and the practical life of self-sacrifice issuing from both. The determination of Anglicans to sustain sacrificial imagery in the theological life of the Church can be demonstrated both from the debate in the seventeenth and eighteenth centuries about the eucharistic sacrifice, and from the attention given in the nineteenth and twentieth centuries to atonement theology. The continuing importance to Anglicans of kenotic Christology also needs to be interpreted as a fundamental investment in the understanding of sacrifice.[21]

The doctrinal features to which I have briefly alluded are *elements* in the Anglican doctrine of the Church. They plainly require substantial development, and such further consideration of them would have to face difficulties, controversies and objections. For example, it could be said that Anglicans have, as a matter of fact, *over*-emphasised order in worship; that they have never provided an adequate theology of the laity; or that their concern for sacrifice has been cultic in the pejorative sense, and has blunted their appreciation of issues of social justice. The degree to which any of these charges may be true of the past ought not to discourage Anglicans from their task. It is a mistake to think that a prime function of any denominationally specific doctrine of the Church is to gloss the historic failures of that Church. The purpose of writing an Anglican doctrine of the Church would be, rather, to raise to consciousness those aspects of the Church's life which are worthy, justifiable, Christian, and true. It would articulate an open criterion by which failure in the past and present could be judged. It would give Anglicans the opportunity of arguing with one another, with reference to the acknowledged 'ultimate standard' of their corporate life, in a way which could only be constructive and healthy. It would provide non-Anglicans with a clear, even if controversial, rationale for comparing and unifying traditions with differing histories.

We have to face the uncomfortable fact that traditional Anglican diffidence in presenting its doctrine of the Church, in so far as it is not merely the consequence of the factors already discussed above, strikes Christians of other allegiances not as the fruit of modesty, but of pride and fear: pride, in desiring to occupy a place which no other communion in Christendom occupies, and fear of the consequences, internal and external, of having to formulate a responsible account on behalf of a body which has got out of the habit of taking its theology seriously. The Inter-Anglican Theological and Doctrinal Commission correctly perceived the ever-present danger for a Church which has consciously attempted to embrace pluralism. 'For too long Anglicans have appeared willing to evade responsible theological reflection and dialogue by acquiescing automatically and immediately in the coexistence of incompatible views, opinions, and policies.'[22] My argument is that it is both possible and desirable for Anglican theologians to attempt to formulate the Anglican understanding of the Church. The Chicago-Lambeth Quadrilateral is no substitute for such an undertaking, and its very ambiguities should illustrate to us the urgency of the task.

NOTES

1. The 1984 proceedings of the sixth meeting of the Anglican Consultative Council, published as *Bonds of Affection* (London, 1984), pp. 75–76, contain brief remarks on these lines.
2. Louis A. Haselmayer, *Lambeth and Unity*, A Study of the Lambeth Quadrilateral, Its Principles and their Application to the Problem of Unity (New York and London, 1948), pp. xiiff, and pp. 9, 14, 21, 28 and 158–159.
3. What follows in this section is an expanded version of an article which appeared in *The Fransiscan* xxx:1 (1988), pp. 32–37, entitled 'Have Anglicans no special doctrines of their own?' I would like to acknowledge the assistance of Christopher Hancock, Margaret Guite, Nicholas Sagovsky and Michael Sansom in generously providing me with acute observations on the first draft of that paper.
4. J. W. C. Wand, *Anglicanism in History and Today* (London, 1961), p. 227.
5. S. Neill, *Anglicanism* (Harmondsworth, 1958), p. 417.
6. T. G. Tappert (ed.), *The Book of Concord* (Philadelphia, 1959), p. 32. The German text is somewhat fuller.
7. *Laws of Ecclesiastical Polity*, Book III, i, 4.
8. Wiliam Palmer of Worcester College, Oxford, exposed the varieties of definitions of the fundamentals in an Appendix of his learned *Treatise on the Church of Christ*, Vol. I, (London, 1838), pp. 122–131. For treatment of the history of Anglican usage of 'fundamentals' and 'fundamental articles', see my article in S. W. Sykes and J. Booty (eds.), *The Study of Anglicanism* (London, Philadelphia, 1988).
9. Note the title given to the Discourse, *Ecclesia Anglicana Ecclesia Catholica*; or *The Doctrine of the Church of England consonant to Scripture, Reason and the*

Fathers. The first complete edition of this work was published in Oxford by the University Press in 1840; see Vol. II, pp. 97–139.

10. E. C. S. Gibson, *The Thirty-Nine Articles of the Church of England* 2nd edn (London, Methuen, 1898), p. 493.
11. Wand, op. cit., p. 227.
12. *The Religion of Protestants* complete edition (London, 1846). This passage is cited by R. R. Orr in his *Reason and Authority, The Thought of William Chillingworth* (London, 1967), p. 83, without a page reference, and I have been unable to trace it. A somewhat similar passage occurs in Answer III, section 81 (edition cited, pp. 223f).
13. See G. A. Lindbeck, *The Nature of Doctrine* (London and Philadelphia, 1984).
14. In R. Newton Flew (ed.), *The Nature of the Church* (London, 1952), pp. 121–146. The same volume contains a piece on behalf of the American Episcopal Church by L. C. Lewis, pp. 309–318.
15. Hodgson is particularly at pains to demonstrate the differences from Protestantism, and the essay, which is the outcome of some considerable consultation, is punctuated by footnotes containing respectful correction of his viewpoint by certain Evangelical Anglicans.
16. Hodgson, op. cit., p. 121.
17. ibid., p. 138.
18. Oliver O'Donovan, *On the Thirty-Nine Articles, A Conversation with Tudor Christianity* (Paternoster, 1986), p. 12.
19. I have attempted to argue this case in *The Identity of Christianity* (London and Philadelphia, 1984), ch. 11, 'Worship, Commitment and Identity'.
20. On this whole theme see the important work of D. Martin, *The Breaking of the Image, A Sociology of Christian Theory and Practice* (Oxford, 1980), esp. ch. 6, 'Profane Habit and Sacred Usage'.
21. See S. W. Sykes, 'The Strange Persistence of Kenotic Christology' in A. Kee and E. T. Long (eds.), *Being and Truth: Essays in Honour of John Macquarrie* (London, 1986), pp. 349–375.
22. *For the Sake of the Kingdom* (Anglican Consultative Council, London, 1986), para. 97, p. 60.

7

FOUNDATIONS OF AN ANGLICAN ECCLESIOLOGY

Sitting in the meeting of Affirming Catholicism called at the York Synod in July 1993, listening to the Dean of Exeter, I was suddenly struck by the extraordinary and perhaps unperceived importance of what we were doing. The first thing I want to say is that, despite the sometimes absurd pretentiousness of established English Anglicanism, it is not negligible in world Christianity for there to be a Church in England, claiming to be the Catholic Church of the English nation, going about its ordinary business of preaching and teaching the Catholic faith and celebrating the Catholic sacraments. It is only ignorant parochialism which pretends that there is something disgracefully disqualifying about the fact of our current disagreements and arguments – as compared with the supposed unanimity which obtains in all the serious Churches. On the contrary. I have come to the conclusion that, despite our smallness, something quite important in world Christian terms depends upon our living a quiet and confident Catholicism, which does not posture, strive or cry, which is serious about its prayer and self-discipline, which is energetic in its social witness, which understands secularity and accepts the obligation of honest evangelism, and which draws upon the intellectual and spiritual riches of the whole Catholic tradition.

I think it is undeniable that part of the importance of this movement derives from the anxious conservatism of the current leadership in Rome. There are many Roman Catholics, I know, who look to Anglicans to embody this confident Catholicism, not least in relation to women's ministry, but also in its continuing receptivity to, and testing of, good argument in biblical and theological scholarship. I hope this will be *one* of the strands of Affirming Catholicism, without of course allowing the movement to become a talking shop or mobile study group, but as a proper expression of that proper celebration and offering of the intellect which has always been a feature of Catholic faith. It is in that spirit that I want to offer a paper on Anglican ecclesiology, which has *one* presupposition and *three* points to make:

The presupposition is that there must be an *Anglican ecclesiology*, that is, the Anglicans cannot take their doctrine of the Church second-hand and unadapted from other sources.

The three points are:

(i)   That the Church is a visible sign of God's activity in human history.

(ii) That we have at all costs to keep contact with a sophisticated account of the understanding of the Church in the New Testament.

(iii) That the theology of baptism is foundational.

Since the General Synod's vote in November 1992 in favour of ending the rule restricting the priesthood to males, a great deal has been said about the Church of England in relation to Christ's One, Holy, Catholic, and Apostolic Church which is anything but ephemeral, and there are some important perspectives from systematic theology to be brought to bear in a more than opportunistic or political way.

The Anglican Doctrine of the Church

First, I should want to re-emphasise the importance of realising that Anglicans have an obligation to develop a doctrine of the Church. There is no such thing as a generalised 'Catholic' theology of the matter. This is the conclusion one must draw from an even cursory appreciation of modern Orthodox ecclesiological writing, for example John Zizioulas's *Being as Communion* (1985), and the response of Professor Oliver Clement to 'Some Aspects of the Church as Communion', a letter to the Bishops of the Catholic Church from the Congregation for the Doctrine of the Faith (1992). At crucial points, notably on the subject of the relationship between the local and the universal Church, Orthodox and Roman Catholic theologies simply part company, and these are points on which Anglicans are bound to have rather different sympathies and interests. As a consequence they cannot take over either Orthodox or Roman Catholic ecclesiology without significant modifications.

A single example will make this point, relating to the papacy. In the recent Letter to the Bishops of the Catholic Church from the Congregation for the Doctrine of Faith ('Some Aspects of the Church as Communion', 1992) it is apparent that the papacy is being presented in the document on the Church as Communion as the logically prior interior principle of unity in the Church: 'The ministry of the successor of Peter as something interior to each particular Church is a necessary expression of that fundamental mutual interiority between universal and particular Church' (para. 13). The argument had earlier been spelled out in an article by Cardinal Ratzinger entitled, 'The papal primacy and the unity of the people of God' (in *Church, Ecumenism and Politics* (1987)). Here it is asserted that it belongs inherently to the faith that the confession of Christ by the Church is as a community in which particular named persons bear personal responsibility. So Christian unity is represented in personalised form by Peter.

> In his new name that transcends the historical individual Peter becomes the institution which passes through history (since this ability of this institution to continue and the fact that it has continued is contained in this re-naming), but in such a way that this institution can only exist as a person and in personal responsibility tied to a particular name. (p. 36)

In this way theological anthropology is made to undergird the theology of primacy, so that the very act of confessing the faith entails what one might call a papal presupposition. 'Thus even when the claims of his office are disputed the pope remains a point of personal reference in the world's sight for the word of faith' (p. 44). The point being made is an important one. To put it in the form of a negation, it proposes that papal primacy should not be regarded as an extrinsic addition to conciliar fellowship. It wants to connect desire for the unity of the Church, which is implicit in the personal profession of faith, with the focal character of the papacy – an understandable apologetic aim, even if there are major gaps, and dangers, in the precise formulation of the argument. At the very least, however, Anglicans who apparently figure in the Congregation's document among 'those ecclesial communities which have not retained the apostolic succession and a valid

Eucharist' (para. 17) would be obliged to recast their understanding of the Church in a fundamentally different way.

The same is true in relation to the ecclesiologies of the modern Protestant Churches. Again the reason can be given very briefly. The episcopate in Anglicanism, though individual Anglican theologians have given differing accounts of it, has none the less functioned practically in such a way as to inhibit the growth of mutually tolerant recognitions of ministries. As a consequence, it is simply impossible to pass off a Reformed or Methodist doctrine of the Church as an Anglican one.

From both these examples I conclude that Anglican theologians have an inescapable responsibility to think through and to teach a doctrine of the Church. The present situation reveals this fact with painful clarity. There are still those who call for an account of authority in the Church, as though that could be provided apart from a doctrine of the Church, or who treat priesthood and episcopate as though these ministries were not rooted in the nature of the Church itself. None of this is remotely adequate to the case, and we have been badly served by those Anglican theologians who in the past have assured their all-too-willing public that 'Anglicans have no doctrines of their own'. These have included some of our most venerated names. And while it may have been true that there is no specifically Anglican Christology or doctrine of the Trinity, or even (though it could be disputed) doctrine of justification, it cannot be the case that there is no Anglican ecclesiology.

Some of us may be inclined to ask, how then have we been living all these years, convinced that we had no need of any such doctrinal support? The answer is instructive. It is perfectly possible for a Church to live out of the resources of what might be called an 'ecclesial instinct'. Explicit doctrine comes into its own in two situations, those of primary evangelism and of serious conflict. We need a doctrine of the Church at the present for both of these purposes. Men and women who come into new contact with the faith require a presentation of the nature of the Church appropriate to their situation. This must include an interpretation of conflict in the Church, and a way of living with the fact that Christians differ from each other. It will be part of my argument that the Anglican instinct on this matter is much clearer and more persuasive than we sometimes give ourselves credit for.

There is a further answer to the question of our apparently miraculous doctrineless survival, which is that we have, in fact, been far from inactive. There has been throughout the twentieth century a series of Anglican writers attending to ecclesiology, which has included Charles Gore, H. B. Swete, Norman Quick, Lionel Thornton, E. L. Mascall, F. W. Dillistone, Norman Pittinger, Stephen Neill and Michael Ramsey. More recently Paul Avis has provided very helpful studies of the ecclesiologies of the English reformers and of later Anglicanism, as well as making contributions in his own right, and Tim Bradshaw has put us in his debt with a wide-ranging and irenic study of varieties of Anglican ecclesiologies in *The Olive Branch* (1992). If only the profundity of much of this effort were more evident in the public discourse of the Church, we would be less despondent. As it is, the slogan and the sound-bite have achieved an altogether too great ascendency in our habits of speech and thought, and it is past time for us to dig deeper.

The Church as Visible Sign

A great deal of Western European theology since the Reformation, and especially since the European Enlightenment, has been developed on the assumption of a fundamental dichotomy between 'Catholic' and 'Protestant' principles. Friedrich Schleiermacher, the so-called 'father of modern theology', neatly encapsulated the alternative movement of faith either through the Church to Christ (the Catholic principle), or through Christ to the Church (the Protestant principle). The natural geographical context for such formulations is, of course, Germany, Holland, and Switzerland, where Catholic and Protestant communities live side by side. Contemporary ecumenism still produces a similar discussion about the existence of 'fundamental disagreements'.

Both the Orthodox and Anglicans are generally treated as marginal to this discussion. Anglicans, in particular, may feel themselves uncomfortable with the terms of the alternative. What, for example, do they make of the question of whether the Church is fundamentally and essentially visible in character? This is the question refined by centuries of Roman Catholic apologetic with a view to embarrassing Protestants. The Catholic tradition is to give an unequivocally affirmative answer, and to point to the Roman Catholic Church as its exemplification. Protestants, on the other hand, are supposed to believe that the true Church is invisible, because its extent is known only to God who alone can interpret a believer's faith. 'Church' occurs as and when God's promises and the summons to faith are offered in word and sacrament. In terms of their structures there can be many Churches, which can enjoy harmonious but autonomous membership in the One Church. Little justice though such an account does to more recent exposition of the ecclesiology of Luther or Calvin, such is popularly supposed to be the opinion of Protestantism. As a consequence it is polemically dismissed as 'individualistic'.

So much of the doctrine of the Church in the Western tradition has been argued out through the distorting lens of late medieval canon law, both in affirmation and negation, that it is a necessity to refer, time and again, to the Eastern tradition for the sake of balance and new insight. Under the subheading 'the "iconic" character of the ecclesial institutions', John Zizioulas argues for the importance of eschatology to all interpretation of the institutional character of the Church, including tradition, apostolic succession, scriptural foundation or actual historical needs. The Holy Spirit points beyond history, and as a result institutions become sacramental, losing their self-sufficiency, and existing *epicletically* (that is, they depend for their efficacy on prayer, the prayer of the 'community').

> It is not in history that the ecclesial institutions find their certainty (their validity) but in constant dependence on the Holy Spirit. This is what makes them 'sacramental', which in the language of Orthodox theology may be called 'iconic'. (p. 138)

To return to the blunt question of whether the Church is essentially visible or invisible, it turns out to be no mere evasion to say that it is both; and to insist (in Orthodox language) on the iconic character of its historical institutions and forms. We can go further. The dichotomy between visible and invisible is precisely one of those dualities or oppositions which are full of ambiguity, and which appear to require their own opposites. The Church's visibility is the necessary appearance in history of its beyond-historical character, to which it points. While it is not complete or perfect in its historicality, neither is its historical being inessential or lacking in instrumental power. The visible signs are never self-sufficient, but always and only effective in the context of prayer and by the action of the invisible Spirit, who both governs and gives life to the Church and is therefore its Lord.

We may well prefer the category 'sign' to that of sacrament or icon because it is a biblical way of speaking of Jesus' own ministry, especially in the fourth gospel. As C. H. Dodd has pointed out, for the writer of the fourth gospel there is no reason why a narrative should not be at the same time factually true and symbolic of a deeper truth.

> Whilst in the first intention the feeling of the multitude signifies the timeless truth that Christ, the eternal Logos, gives life to men, and the healing of the blind that He is the Bearer of light, yet in the development of the argument we discover that Christ's work of giving life and light is accomplished, in reality and actuality, by the historical act of his death and resurrection. In that sense, every *semeion* (sign) in the narrative points forward to the great climax. (*The Interpretation of the Fourth Gospel* (1953), p. 142)

This conclusion is fully consistent with recent work on the sectarian background to the fourth gospel's sacramentalism. Being baptised represents the threshold between the world and the community for John, as the believer publicly confesses allegiance to Christ as Son of God come down from heaven. The Eucharist reinforces the boundary this creates between believer and non-believer, and at the same time builds up solidarity between those who faithfully abide in Jesus. The 'sacraments' of baptism and Eucharist count as signs precisely because they point to the Passion of Christ and to the Resurrection. Together with Jesus' miraculous deeds (which continue in the experience of St Paul, see 2 Cor. 12:12, 1 Cor. 2:4, Rom. 15:19) these signs are part of the reality of divine sovereignty in history (see Luke 11:20). They are thus likewise eschatological and inseparably linked to the presence and activity of the Spirit. The Church fundamentally belongs to the sign-character of God's activity in human history.

Interpreting Biblical Ecclesiology

To understand the Church as visible sign helps us to interpret the multiple images of ecclesia in the New Testament. The astonishing profusion of metaphors and images from previous theology and ordinary experience which go to make up New Testament ecclesiology has frequently been studied, notably by Paul Minear. His classic *Images of the Church in the New Testament* (1960) identifies no fewer than 96 images or analogies. Fortunately there is something close to a consensus that four images are dominant, namely:

(i)   'the people of God';
(ii) 'the body of Christ';
(iii) 'the communion of faith, hope, and love'; and
(iv) 'the creation of the Spirit'.

Each of these has an irreducible contribution to make to the historic development of the classic ecclesiologies of the major traditions. The 'people of God' is an image which establishes Christianity's continuity with Israel, and embodies the essential narrative reference characterising the raw material of all Christian theology. Ecclesiology has always to be related to the specific experience of a concrete people in history, acting within the context of the covenant of God, whether in obedience or disobedience. The 'body of Christ' derives its power as an image from the crucifixion, death and resurrection, and is the natural vehicle for much of the sacramental mysticism of the Church's teaching. It is, therefore, intimately connected to the third of the images, that of a unity which is a social and ethical sharing in a common life. The three gifts of faith, hope, and love require and support each other, but it is love which binds everything and everyone together and completes the whole. Finally, the Church is the consequence of the activity of God's Holy Spirit, and there are a whole series of remarkable images of building a house or temple out of an assembly of persons.

In Ephesians 2 all the images are gathered together in a remarkable synthesis.

> The new *people of God* is not to exist at enmity with the old; both peoples are to be incorporated into *a single body* founded on the flesh and blood of Christ. This body is a true *communion*, in which there are no longer aliens and strangers but fellow citizens, members of God's household. And the bond or matrix of this building, household, temple, is the redemptive presence, the indwelling, the upbuilding, creative work of God as *Spirit*. (Hodgson, p. 34)

Inevitably the very richness and profusion of the metaphors and images have given rise to controversy, as one way of envisioning that the Church has achieved interpretative primacy over the others. But the acutest modern difficulty lies elsewhere, namely with how the remarkably exalted quality of the whole of biblical ecclesiology is to be interpreted in relation to the mundane reality of the actual Churches. The referent of these statements, after all, is not unknown to us from the letters of St Paul. Here it emerges unmistakably that the life of the Churches was not in every respect an edifying spectacle. Their members were capable of the grossest immorality and had a penchant for bitter factiousness. Even the most established leaders could be capable of being challenged and resisted. And we have no idea who presided at their Eucharists, which were, in any case, capable in Paul's withering phrase, of tending to do more harm than good (1 Cor. 11:17–22). There is a major problem here which has been ignored for too long.

Two interpretative manoeuvres prove inadequate. The first is to ignore the historical context of biblical ecclesiology as irrelevant, and to concentrate solely on the doctrine. That course is forbidden to us, because it denies the essential historicality of ecclesiology as such, namely the fundamentally narrative character of God's dealings with humankind. The great affirmations concerning the body of Christ are connected to the accounts of the actual behaviour of the Church within the category of sign. It is the same Church capable of disorder which also points to the unity of Christ's body. To extract the edifying doctrine from the mundane (but not merely mundane) reality is to create an abstract and idealised impression of the Church. In this way it becomes all too easy to legitimate the modern structures of the Church and covertly to ignore the fact that they, too, similarly participate in the ambiguities of history.

The second manoeuvre is to insulate the New Testament period from subsequent history, and fail to see the faith communities as undergoing developments of which the documents only contain adumbrations. It has been realised for a considerable time that the New Testament provides evidence for the way in which the Churches grow as institutions and resolve their problems (the 'routinisation of charisma' discussion). Of course, it is correct to say that one may not simply make of a sociological process a normative statement. The fact that the pastoral epistles have already turned charismatic leaders into ordained officials, if that is what they have done, does not imply of itself that the development was inevitable, still less a process guided by the Holy Spirit. But it is impossible to ignore the fact that during the New Testament period developments in the life of the Church were under way which had come to no final conclusion by the end of the first century, and which went on working themselves through as the Church grew in size, influence and complexity. All this means that solutions which might have been available to one Church community in the 60s and 70s of the first century were not available to the Church of the second and third centuries, still less to the modern Western European Churches. Inevitably we are committed to an effort of theological imagination to project the trajectory of the biblical Churches into the modern world.

Orthodox, Roman Catholics and Anglicans have understood this very well, but have offered characteristically different solutions. The Orthodox require a holistic doctrine of tradition, of which the ancient sees are the embodiment. Roman Catholics allow tradition to develop to the point where it has evolved a final question-deciding authority. The classic Anglican solution involved what has been called quinquesecularism, the doctrine that the unanimous consent of the first five centuries contain all that the Churches need to know about the faith, with neither deviation nor accretion. If none of these is any longer credible in its strictest form, I should want to affirm the Catholic instinct without hesitation on the ground of the historicality of the Church. That is to say, to be God's Church on earth is to be his sign in the midst of ambiguous and changing circumstances. Yet Anglicans are right to insist that we should under no circumstances lose contact with the biblical witness to the Church in its full historic reality. Processes in the Church cannot be turned into the equivalent of revelation. Although the Church requires a decision-making process, all the relevant criteria in matters relating to salvation are open to all believers because they are biblical. The biblical portrait of the Church, warts and all, remains foundational in the capacity to inform the minds of those who continue to discern the Church's way in new circumstances.

Baptismal Ecclesiology

To complete this paper, which is a most incomplete orientation on the doctrine of the Church, I wish to deal with one central topic on which Anglicans have, I believe, an instinct but not yet, or not adequately, a theology. It concerns the fate of the theology of baptism in the context of widespread agreement between the Orthodox and Roman Catholics on what is called 'eucharistic ecclesiology'. Associated with the work of Father Nicholas Afanasiev, and strongly developed in altered form by John Zizioulas, eucharistic ecclesiology is specifically mentioned in the Congregation for the Doctrine of the Faith's recent document. Here the Letter is at some pains to distance itself from one of the implications of a form of eucharistic ecclesiology, namely that it validates the assembly of the local Church 'in such a way as to render any other principle of unity or universality inessential' (para. 11). On the contrary, the document argues

> the oneness and indivisibility of the Eucharistic body of the Lord implies the oneness of his mystical body, which is the one and indivisible Church. From the Eucharistic centre arises the necessary openness of every celebrating community, of every particular Church. By allowing itself to be drawn into the open arms of the Lord, it achieves insertion into his one and undivided body. For this reason too the existence of the Petrine ministry, which is a foundation of the unity of the episcopate and of the universal Church, bears a profound correspondence to the Eucharistic character of the Church.

But even subject to this caveat, the root and centre of ecclesial communion is said to exist in the holy Eucharist (para. 5), because the eucharistic sacrifice 'receives the entire gift of salvation' (para. 11).

But what then of baptism? Since the Decree on Ecumenism of Vatican II, a Roman Catholic theology has been committed to a strong affirmation that 'baptism . . . constitutes the sacramental bond of unity existing among all who through it are reborn' (*Unitatis Redintegratio*, para. 22). But the question immediately arises whether one could be 'truly incorporated into the crucified and glorified Christ and . . . reborn to a sharing of the divine life' without also being a member of Christ's One, Holy, Catholic, and Apostolic Church? It is difficult to imagine how incorporation of the kind asserted could be distinguished from such 'membership', biblically conceived as being a limb or organ of Christ. In this case, a concept of 'Church' must exist to which baptised members of non-Roman Churches properly belong.

In this connection one may argue that Roman Catholic theology does not permit one to say, as has recently been suggested, that the decision to ordain women to the priesthood implies that the Church of England no longer belongs to the One, Holy, Catholic, and Apostolic Church. What Roman Catholic theology in fact asserts is that through faith and baptism every member of the faithful is 'inserted into the One, Holy, Catholic, and Apostolic Church' ('The Church as Communion', para. 10), and that this is an 'introduction' into 'ecclesial communion', involving 'a certain communion albeit imperfect' with Roman Catholic Christians. Again, one must say that the only form of 'communion', theologically conceived as the consequence of baptism, is communion *within* the body of Christ.

Of course, the same passage on the ecumenical importance of baptism immediately qualifies this affirmation with a strong reservation.

> Baptism, of itself, is only a beginning, a point of departure, for it is wholly directed towards the acquiring of fullness of life in Christ. Baptism is thus ordained towards a complete profession of faith, a complete incorporation into the system of salvation such as Christ himself willed it to be, and finally towards a complete integration into Eucharistic communion. (*Unitatis Redintegratio*, para. 22)

This raises several points of importance. First, one must agree that baptism is the point of entry into a life which involves growing into the full stature of Christ. That life may be stultified through various obstacles and impediments, among which may be a failure to make use of the available means of grace, especially the eucharistic sacrament. Baptism properly understood thus signifies a process of growth. I find this point nowhere better put than in the Public Baptism of Infants of *The Book of Common Prayer*, where the priest, after the baptism, exhorts the godfathers and godmothers in the following terms:

> Remembering always that Baptism doth represent unto us our profession; which is to follow the example of our Saviour Christ,

and to be made like unto him; that as he died, and rose again for us, so should we, who are baptised, die from sin, and rise again unto righteousness; continually mortifying all our evil and corrupt affections, and daily proceeding in all virtue and godliness of living.

In a certain sense it improperly diminishes baptism to speak of it as 'only a beginning'. Baptism represents the totality of the Christian life, and we live our way into it assisted by all the available means of grace. Again, in a certain sense it is misleading to speak of a further 'complete incorporation into a system of salvation' beyond baptism. One should rather reserve the word 'incorporation' for the baptismal event itself. Theologically, it would not be tolerable to hold that baptism is a partial incorporation into Christ, as if those who were 'only' baptised were incomplete in their membership of Christ. But, of course, complete incorporation into Christ in baptism is compatible with a growing realisation of the ramifications of that incorporation, and enjoyment of its consequences. Baptism, therefore, essentially belongs to the realm of sign, signifying a not fully realised communion with the risen Christ, a communion of which we have a foretaste, but not the whole, within human history and experience.

At the same time the Roman Catholic theological tradition is entirely justified on biblical grounds in asserting the unity of the sacraments of baptism and Eucharist. There are no first-century analogies for our modern situation in which Churches recognise one another's baptisms, but not their Eucharists. The growing normativity of infant baptism and the problem of the Donatist schism led to a separation of baptism from eucharistic communion which has plagued Western church life and theology from the days of Augustine. The choice is apparently to emphasise either eucharistic fellowship and correspondingly to diminish baptismal communion; or vice versa. The Roman Catholic tradition has consistently followed the former course, and speaks of 'wounds' of varying degrees of seriousness in those Churches which fail to acknowledge that communion with the Pope is one of the constituents internal to the life of communion in Christ's body, the Church. It is important to realise that Anglicans have never held this view, and that their instinctive ecclesiology gives a rather different account of the relation of baptism and Eucharist within the body of Christ. Anglicans hold, with the whole scriptural and early patristic witness, that initiation (a term here consciously preferred to baptism, and in explicit acknowledgement of the problematic relationship of baptism and confirmation) is initiation into the eucharistic community. On this basis, for example, canonical permission to partake of the Holy Communion is given to 'baptised persons who are communicant members of other Churches which subscribe to the doctrine of the Holy Trinity, and who are in good standing in their own Church' (Canon B15A(1)(b)).

The discrimination implied in the phrase 'which subscribe to the doctrine of the Holy Trinity' is directly related to baptism in the name of the Holy Trinity, and confirms the fact that judgement is required about the authenticity of the faith-community from which the potential communicant derives.

Consistent with this is the long, consistent and distinguished tradition in the Church of England which insists that other Churches, including trinitarian non-episcopal Churches, really participate in the One, Holy, Catholic, and Apostolic Church of Christ. That affirmation, made in the light of a common baptism, is compatible with a judgement that different Churches may be in various states of error, of varying degrees of seriousness, in relation to particular doctrines. The 'branch theory', first put forward in the nineteenth century, is a radical and highly disputable curtailment of that understanding, with a view to limiting 'the Catholic Church' to three 'branches', Eastern, Roman, and Anglican. It has been soundly criticised by numerous Anglicans, among them H. B. Swete and A. M. Ramsey, and has no title to be regarded as more than one privately advanced theological proposal within an Anglican spectrum. A more consistent judgement, and at the same time a more authoritative one, is contained in the Meissen Declaration in which the Church of England solemnly acknowledges the Churches of the Federation of the Evangelical Churches in the German Democratic Republic and of the Evangelical Church in Germany to be Churches 'belonging to the One, Holy, Catholic, and Apostolic Church of Jesus Christ, and truly participating in the apostolic mission of the whole people of God'.

In reflecting on these and similar judgements it appears that Anglican ecclesiology has been more deeply influenced by one of its Thirty-nine Articles than it is, perhaps, consciously aware. Article 19 on the Church is a curiously one-sided statement about the visible Church, from which, as Professor Oliver O'Donovan has pertinently observed, the invisible Church has disappeared. It then passes to what at first sight appears a discouragingly negative verdict on the Churches of Jerusalem, Alexandria, Antioch, and Rome. These, we are assured, have erred, not merely in living and ceremonies, but also in matters of faith. This proposition has the liberating consequence of denying the existence of error-free zones, and through it Anglicans have acquired a certain instinct for critical self-appraisal. As O'Donovan appositely comments:

> Every 'particular' Church that has ever existed or does exist has erred. It is for this reason that we must remain humble about our institutions and resist the temptation to identify this or that one with the Catholic Church. (*On the 39 Articles*, p. 95)

The reformability of each particular Church must patently include its ability to correct its own mistakes at reformation.

The tragic failure of the Churches to realise the intrinsic connection between baptism and Eucharist also involves Anglicans who are inextricably implicated in the consequences. But in this case there exists no motive to deny the full affirmation of the efficacy of Christian baptism on profession of trinitarian faith as bestowing membership in the body of Christ. This, as we have seen in the case of the Gospel of St John, establishes the boundary between Church and world, the passage from darkness to life and bondage to freedom. In terms of its significatory character the sacrament is both instrument and sign, both effecting radical change and pointing to more than is yet visibly realised. Nothing in the Churches' failure to keep eucharistic communion in harmony with the baptismal beginning should encourage Anglicans to diminish the life-altering character of the sacrament of baptism.

At the same time, the Anglican has no obligation to minimise the intrinsic connection which exists between the unity of Christ's body, the eucharistic sacrament, and the agent or enabler of eucharistic celebration, the bishop. Eucharistic ecclesiology, shorn of certain exaggerated nuances, still has a powerful message. Precisely because it is a repeated sacrament, the Eucharist actualises again and again the completed reality of the reconciliation of God and humankind in the cross. The eucharistic sacrifice is, as such, theologically inseparable from the baptismal sacrifice. It belongs intrinsically to the institutional reality of the Church to order baptism and Eucharist in such a way that this connection is constantly made clear. From this arises the task of the episcopate, to ordain by prayer and the laying on of hands those whose principal task it is to baptise and celebrate the Eucharist publicly with, for, and in the face of the whole Church.

It follows that those who perceive this connection are necessarily committed to the restoration of the visible unity of the Church. To defend this connection I take to be the ground of, and principal reason for, Anglican intransigence on the subject of the episcopate. At the same time such arguments do not entail the theories of defects or wounds in non-episcopal Churches, compensated for by mysterious toppings-up of uncovenanted mercies to account for the obvious signs of grace and holiness which they display. In terms of sacramental theology, the reality of baptism sufficiently accounts for the gracious presence and unstinting activity of the Holy Spirit in each of the Churches; and the mundane and ordinary failures of the historic institutions include their failure to agree about ordained ministry and the Eucharist, and so to preserve the unity established in the baptismal sacrifice. Despite this the eucharistic sacrament continues to be a sign and foretaste of the realisation of greater unity in the eschatological banquet; and in the episcopal Churches the structural unity of the episcopate, even in the unreconciled form of parallel jurisdiction, contains the promise of a future unity, including the potential of a universal primacy.

It is not for the sake of yet more argument about the sex of the priesthood that I have produced this paper. But there will be those who will want to know what conclusions might be drawn from such an ecclesiology in the context of our present situation. We have now to assume that Anglicans are, as a matter of fact, defining or redefining themselves ecclesiologically in every part of the world. It is, despite what its detractors say, not a negligible occurrence, and the rest of the world Church treats it as considerable. For me, something happened when the suffragan bishop of Namibia, speaking with the authenticity of the suffering Church of Southern Africa, told me that he wanted his Province to be the kind of place where those who were opposed to this development could feel they belonged and were honoured alongside those in favour. The Anglican Communion has plainly embarked on a vocation to which it is impossible to predict the end, and it has done so believing that it has acted in obedience to its Lord. Though opponents deny it, the actions are claimed to be totally consistent with continuing to transmit the essential priesthood and episcopate of the Catholic Church. In these orders priest and bishops, if women, will continue to intend to do what Christ has delivered to his Church to perform in the sacraments of baptism and Eucharist. The consequence that some Anglicans will not be able conscientiously to recognise these sacramental actions is seen as less damaging than disobedience to a vision of an inclusive ministry.

From the ecclesiology I have sketched I wish to draw one seriously critical and one positive comment. The critical remark concerns the damage done to the visible unity of the Church. The Roman Catholic Church's official pronouncements have been consistent in their warnings, and they have every right to their expressions of profound regret at a new and grave obstacle to reconciliation. Of course, it might be said that very little encouragement has recently been given by the Vatican to Anglican-Roman Catholic relations; or that there is absolutely no sign of change in relation to the papal pronouncement against Anglican orders as such. But the context of ecclesiastical diplomacy is not a self-sufficient world, and no Anglican has any right to do other than view with genuine dismay the widening gulf which separates us after explicit and repeated warnings. The ecclesiology I have sketched requires Anglicans to take the unity of the Church with the greatest seriousness and to see the ordained ministry as its enabler. It is inconceivable that this unity should be harmed without grave cause, or in a mood of absent-minded or light-hearted modishness. It will not do, therefore, to defend the development as anything other than an act of eschatological obedience to the future of the Catholic Church, a temporary act from one part of the Church in the cause of a greater and deeper eventual unity of the whole.

The second, positive comment I make in negative form. It could always be, on sound Anglican principles, that the Anglican Churches are in error. There is here something of a doctrinal crux for those who oppose this development. Either, it appears, they must reach the conclusion that so seriously is the Anglican Communion in error that it is evidence for the truth of another Church claiming immunity from errors of such gravity; or they must find a way of believing the teaching of a Church for whom the possibility of at least temporary error is part of its doctrinal stance. I have already defended the truth of the Article on error in the Church on the grounds that it permits Anglicans to be consistently self-critical, even of the Church's reformations. The essential point is the vulnerability of the truth, and it is this which makes self-congratulatory posturing wholly inappropriate. If we are open to his truth, God will not deny us his grace, especially not at his Eucharist. On that condition alone, I am prepared for my Church to be in error until such time as God vouchsafes it a new vision.

8

AUTHORITY IN THE ANGLICAN COMMUNION

There are two ways in which a topic of this kind could be tackled:

(i) By 'authority in the Anglican Communion' could be meant the actual or desired processes of decision-making within the Anglican Communion. A paper on such a subject could be expected to display familiarity with the constitutions and canons of the Provinces of the Anglican Communion, the status of the Lambeth Conferences, and the terms of reference of the Anglican Consultative Council and of the Primates' Committee. Such an approach is well beyond my competence, though I personally believe that a modern study of this kind (last carried out by a former Archbishop of Melbourne, Henry Lowther Clarke, in 1924) is urgently needed; indeed it must be a matter of great anxiety that quite radical developments proceed apace in individual parts of the Communion without any apparent community of reflection and criticism to undergird them. A second approach is, however, also possible.

(ii) By ' "authority" in the Anglican Communion' (note the re-punctuation) could also be meant the theological topic of 'authority', as it is articulated and reflected upon in the common stock of experiences shared by the Anglican family. It is this latter topic which I propose to tackle, conscious though I am of limitations of knowledge and, in particular, of perspective. It is in this sense that the problem of authority has become a central theological issue, especially in ecumenical dialogue and within these dialogues especially with Roman Catholics. Thus 'authority in the Church' was a vital part of that intense theological ferment within the

140

Roman Catholic Church, which led up to the Second Vatican Council.

It is precisely in this connection, however, that the question may not unreasonably arise whether 'authority' has become a typical preoccupation of *Western* theology. After all, it was the *Western* Church which developed through the long and involved history of medieval Europe a pattern and style of church government complementing (and in part reproducing) the pattern of civil authority. The Churches of the Reformation, in their turn, responded to and subsequently moulded their *Western* environment. Finally, it is political and intellectual developments in the *West* (both Europe and America) which challenged received structures of authority in both Roman Catholic and Protestant communities, and which led to the liberalised interpretations of authority characteristic of most, if not all, of the modern denominations. Is not the whole topic, from start to finish, Western in conception?

It is not, by any means, easy for a Westerner to become fully aware of the limitations imposed on his perspective by his own history and upbringing. Two points of immediate relevance, however, can be made. First, that 'authority' is a biblical term, and the problem of authority in the Church is bequeathed by the biblical documents to the *whole* Church – as we shall see. Secondly, that although there are different 'habits of authority' in different cultures, there are certain conditions in which Christian living flourishes, and others again which undermine it. These conditions are universal, because the Gospel itself is universal. Wherever the Gospel is preached, therefore, a potential tension is set up between it and whatever happen locally to be the assumptions about the proper exercise of authority within a human community. Local churches are always in dialogue with local culture; and this is as true of Western Churches as of those of Africa, Asia, or the West Indies. It is by comparing how the intrinsic and universal authority of the Gospel appears when proclaimed by the Church in the context of *different* cultures that progress is made in transcending the limitations of a single perspective.

Quite apart, therefore, from the obvious intellectual limitations of the author, what follows can only be offered as a *contribution* to the correct formulation of the question at issue. And it necessarily follows that if the Anglican Communion is serious about the potential of its contribution to the whole Christian world, then it must enable its scholars to exchange insights into the common problems of authority in understanding and being faithful to the Gospel of its Lord.

Subject throughout to the above limitation, my essay is to be set out in two major sections:

Authority as a theological problem. Here I wish to state clearly the way in which the biblical documents (which are our common heritage) bequeath to all subsequent Christian history the problem of authority in the Church. At the same time, in laying out the problem, I want to illustrate how the Anglican Communion (by its receptivity to the tradition of the early Church, and by the medium of its standard Books of Common Prayer) has provided an interpretation of the biblical data. *The Anglican experience of authority.* The whole modern Anglican Communion shares certain experiences, in particular certain documents (prayer books, ordinals and articles) and certain events (the circumstances of the creation of the Anglican family, and the major determinants of modern church history, most of which are reflected in one way or another in the Lambeth Conference documents). These experiences need to be set out and analysed if the present state of 'authority' in the Anglican Communion is to be given any historical depth.

These two, major sections prompt a number of critical and constructive conclusions, which round off the discussion.

Authority as a Theological Problem

(a) The divine source of authority

Authority, as inherited by the Anglican Communion from the undivided Church of the early centuries of the Christian era, is single in that it is derived from a single Divine source, and reflects within itself the richness and historicity of the divine Revelation, the authority of the eternal Father, the incarnate Son, and the life-giving Spirit.

(From the report on the Anglican Communion, Lambeth Conference 1948, p. 84.)

In affirming the single divine source of authority, the document's authors merely reflect the consistent biblical testimony to the oneness

142

and unity of God, and to derivation of all rule and authority from him alone. In referring, however, to the 'richness and historicity of the divine revelation', the authors are opening up something of the complexity of the biblical witness. One of the gains of contemporary biblical scholarship is the realisation that within the biblical documents there is a history to be traced of the constant reinterpretation of earlier traditions.

A pertinent example of this process of reinterpretation may be seen in the use of the term 'Lord of hosts'. The sanctuary at Shiloh, where the ark of the covenant was stationed, was the site of an annual sacrifice to 'Yahweh of hosts' (1 Sam. 1:3, 11). The ark itself had a vital function in the context of holy war, and the military meaning of the term is clearly seen in the reference to David's fighting in the name of the Yahweh of hosts, who is the 'God of the armies of Israel' (1 Sam. 17:45; cf. Ps. 24:7–10; 60:10). The meaning of the epithet is powerfully reinterpreted by the prophets, however, in whose writings the majority of the occurrences of the term is to be found. God, while continuing to accomplish his mighty deeds, also judges his own people. And a further theme is developed, namely that of Yahweh presiding over the host of heaven, his council (see 1 Kings 22:19; Job 1–2; Ps. 82). Indeed the prophets could claim that they, unlike the false prophets, had been drawn into this council, and thus could speak the authoritative, 'Thus says the Lord' (Jer. 23:18, 22; cf. Isa. 6:8; 40:6; Amos 3:7). The LXX, in translating 'Yahweh of hosts', frequently uses *kurios pantokrator* (Lord almighty), and it is this term which passes into the creed in Greek, and eventually into the Latin, *deus omnipotens*. The very process of translation is a process of reinterpretation, and it has been pointed out with justice that the English 'Almighty' and 'omnipotent' by no means are exact equivalents of the Greek, let alone the Hebrew terms.

What then are we to understand by the epithet, 'Lord of hosts'? First and basically, that God alone is Lord in heaven and on earth. This sovereignty has reference to creation, to the historical order, and to the last days, all of which provide examples of God's mighty works. Anglicans, whose spiritual life is or may be moulded by the recital of the Psalter, are daily confronted with words which 'ascribe power unto the Lord' (Ps. 68:34: all references are to the Liturgical Psalter), or which 'ascribe to the Lord the honour due to his name' (Ps. 29:2). Each of the canticles of the *BCP* Matins and Evensong contains the theme of thankfulness to God for his mighty acts, not least the New Testament canticles (from Luke), which explicitly see in the coming of Christ another, albeit final, act of salvation.

As far, then, as at least a very substantial and influential strand of biblical tradition is concerned, 'The Lord of hosts is with us, the God of Jacob is our stronghold' (Ps. 46:11).

(b) The way of the servant
The Psalms themselves, however, present us with a well-known problem. Many, who would unhesitatingly say

God is to us a God who saves:
by God the Lord we do escape death (Ps. 68:20),

falter at the verse which follows,

But God shall smite the heads of his enemies:
the hairy scalp of those that walk in their sins (68:21).

There is a Christological construction to be put upon the Psalter, which sees the power of God as expressed in the crucified Christ. Part of what is meant is already contained in the emphasis laid upon the 'constant goodness' of God.

God has spoken once, twice I have heard him say:
that power belongs to God,
that to the Lord belongs a constant goodness:
for you reward a man according to his works
(Ps. 62:11, 12).

Even here the principle of reward according to works is explicitly denied by St Paul, in his theological meditation upon the grace of God.

It is plain that there is a problem here. How is the power of God to be understood in the light of the ministry of Jesus, and in the light of the cross? At the least we must say that a process of transformation is taking place, yet again, in the understanding of divine power. This transformation is evident in three respects: (i) The actual practice of authority (lordship) in contemporary society is explicitly challenged as a model for the exercise of rule in the community; 'not so with you', the leader is to be one who serves (Luke 22:24–27). (ii) More fundamentally, the very power of God is the power of weakness, of humility, and of the cross (1 Cor. 1:18–31, cf. Phil. 2:5–10). (iii) Finally, those who themselves are helped, or even armed by the power of God, must expect to suffer, because suffering is the hallmark of the disciple of Christ (2 Thess. 1:5, Rom. 8:17, 2 Cor. 1:5, Phil. 3:10, 1 Pet. *passim*).

How does this affect our understanding of the power of God? It means, surely, that in the light of Jesus Christ, one trait by which we may recognise the contemporary 'mighty works' of God is where the Christian Church, or any member of it, in serving God, suffers. In 1 Peter, the author warns his Christian friends not to be surprised by the 'fiery ordeal' through which they were passing 'as though it were something extraordinary'.

> It gives you a share in Christ's sufferings, and that is cause for you; and when his glory is revealed, your joy will be triumphant (or overflow). (1 Pet. 4:13)

Paul is likewise persuaded both that suffering is normal here and now, and that the severest suffering bears no comparison with the as yet unrevealed glory (Rom. 8:18–39). In other words, belief in the ultimate triumph of God may be joyfully entertained in the very midst of suffering, *because righteous suffering itself is the route which God takes in his dealings with humanity.* There is no loss of belief in the power of God; but that power is now interpreted in the light of the cross. The only way to the triumph of the resurrection is by the cross. The very entry into Christian life, through the waters of baptism (symbolising at once creation and destruction), is by identification with the death of Christ and by participation in his resurrection.

(c) The power of the Gospel
The Gospel, in the memorable translation of the KJV, is 'the power [*dynamis*] of God unto salvation, to every one that believeth' (Rom. 1:16). Several comments must be made on this point. First, Paul evidently means that, for everyone who has faith, in the full sense of that word, the Gospel is triumphantly effective in the end. The Christian will certainly participate in the ultimate triumph of God, and this

certitude is able decisively to transform the experiences (of suffering) which any Christian now undergoes. Secondly, participation in the ultimately triumphant power of God is available to *everyone* who believes. Every believer is thus personally empowered by God. This is not to be construed individualistically. The writer of the deeply Pauline letter to the Ephesians sees that it is the Church which has been elected, in the plan and foreknowledge of God, to be the area of God's ultimately triumphant activity in Christ, its supreme head. And he prays that God will grant 'strength and power' (*dynamis*) to all his people so that they may attain fullness of being. It is by the immeasurably great 'power [*dynamis*] which is at work among us' that God himself is glorified in the Church and in Christ for us 'from generation to generation evermore' (Eph. 3:2f). The power centre is, thus, the whole Church, and every believer within it.

A third point needs to be made about 'the power of the Gospel'; and this arises directly from the theme of the previous section and specifically from 1 Corinthians. Against the demand of the Jews for more mighty acts of God ('signs') and of the Greeks for impressive argument ('wisdom'), Paul is determined to proclaim only Christ crucified. The impact of the Gospel contains a sufficient demonstration of spirit and power (*dynamis*), quite apart from any such embellishments. Amazingly, God has chosen the low and contemptible to overthrow the existing order (1 Cor. 1:18–2:5). The Magnificat, following the theme of several of the Psalms, makes the same point.

> He has cast down the mighty from their thrones:
>   and has lifted up the lowly.
> He has filled the hungry with good things:
>   and the rich he has sent empty away. (vv 6, 7)

Mary, in the liturgical use of this hymn of praise, and in the devotion of the Church becomes, by her gift of humanity to the divine Son of God, and in her reception of the grace of God, the mother of all the faithful, especially of the lowly. The God in whom she rejoices is no respecter of persons; he has no favourites (Acts 10:34; Rom. 2:11), and neither should we (Jas. 2:1–9). Precisely in the context of the heated discussion of his own status as apostle, Paul affirms that, in the light of Christ's loving self-offering unto death for all humanity, worldly standards have ceased to count in our estimate of any man . . . When anyone is united to Christ, there is a new world; the old order has gone, and a new order has already begun (2 Cor. 5:16f).

In short, the Gospel is the priceless possession and calling of every Christian. It is in virtue of the Gospel alone that any person has status in the eyes of God; it is by means of the Gospel alone that every member of the Church shares in the ultimate victory of God, and thus participates in his power. The basic act of the Anglican Reformation was the attempt to give access to the apostolic Gospel in the language of the people by means of a vernacular liturgy and Scriptures. Persuaded that 'both in the Old and New Testament everlasting life is offered to Mankind by Christ, who is the only Mediator between God and Man' (Article VII), no barrier of language could be allowed to prevent the Scriptures being heard, read, marked, learnt and inwardly digested (Collect for Advent 2). Developing his argument from St Chrysostom and St Augustine, Cranmer in the second of the two exhortations, 'To the Reading and Knowledge of holy Scripture', which open the *Book of Homilies*, denies that the Scriptures are too difficult for ordinary people.

For God receiveth the learned and unlearned, and casteth away none, but is indifferent to all. And the scripture is full, as well of low valleys, plain ways, and easy for man to use and walk in; as also of high hills and mountains, which few men can climb into.

(d) The authority of the ministry of the Gospel
The time has come to relate the terms, power and authority. In the synoptic gospels both the Greek words *dynamis* and *exousia* are used, sometimes synonymously (see Luke 4:36; 9:1; 10:19), and sometimes distinguishably. The distinction has been nicely put by C. K. Barrett, who states that authority (*exousia*) 'belongs to a stage of effectiveness which lies behind *dynamis*, which *dynamis* reveals, and on which *dynamis* depends'. This distinction is not peculiar to biblical Greek, and it corresponds to a similar distinction in English usage. *Dynamis* is, most commonly, miraculous power, the power of the Spirit (especially in Luke) and power outpoured at the end of time: the word does not

occur in the Johannine literature. *Exousia* is divine authority attributed to Jesus (Mark 2:1, cf. Matt. 9:8; 28:18 cf. John 5:27), or that of an officially authorised Rabbi (Mark 1:22, 27; 11:28); and authority is given by Jesus to the disciples to heal and cast out demons (Mark 3:15; 6:7). A similar pattern of identity and distinction emerges in the Pauline corpus. Paul claims both that God's power (*dynamis*) works in and through him (2 Cor. 13:3,4) and that he has been given divine authority (*exousia*) (2 Cor. 13:10). It is impossible, therefore, to base a theological theory of authority merely upon a study of the use of these Greek words.

There is an established distinction in modern philosophy between *de iure* power, and *de facto* power. *De iure* power rests upon the existence of a recognised legal code which can, provided the State possesses the necessary means, be enforced. *De facto* power may rest upon law, but need only entail the practical recognition of power. It is thus a much broader concept, and as such is hospitable to the notion of an intrinsic authority. The authority of an expert in art or music is based very largely on recognition; but that does not make him or her powerless. The idea of a person who possesses moral authority is, perhaps, wholly based upon recognition by others (that is, it may be nothing whatever to do with social status, education, or legal power); but, again, a morally authoritative person is far from being powerless. None of the Christian leaders or writers of the first century were in any position to have their decision enforced legally. Paul may have invoked civil power for personal protection, but that is another matter. (So far as I know, the first legally enforced Church decision was the expulsion of Paul of Samosata, Bishop of Antioch, by the Emperor Aurelian in 272 AD, four years after his condemnation for heresy.) They depended, in other words, wholly on *de facto* recognition of their power and this power (which they certainly claimed) may be likened appropriately to moral authority.

No writing is more expressive and poignant on this subject than Paul's letters to the Church in Corinth. Here the existence of quarrels involving Paul's status as an apostle makes constant reference to his authority unavoidable. The situation is made psychologically more complex by Paul's evident sensitivity to the charge of weakness (1 Cor. 2:3), which he eventually feels obliged vigorously to rebut (2 Cor. 10–13). Confronted by their disorder and disunity, Paul is totally and unambiguously confident that, as Christ's steward and servant (along with Apollos, 1 Cor. 3:5), he has the authority to put them right (1 Cor. 11:34). He is like a father to them (1 Cor. 4:15); he may have to chastise them (1 Cor. 4:21); he can send them a representative to speak and act for him (1 Cor. 4:17).

The disputes in Corinth show gradations of seriousness. Some can be solved by any wise man (1 Cor. 6:5); others are serious perversions of sound doctrine, and will entail divine punishment (1 Cor. 3:15); in one particularly serious sexual offence Paul commands the congregation to assemble (with him present in spirit), and in the power of Christ to excommunicate the offender (1 Cor. 5:3–5). This last, drastic exercise of authority (Paul expects the man to die) resides, it should be noted, with the whole congregation, assembled in effect to ratify a prior judgement delivered by Paul himself. Thus Paul both claims and exercises great power (he has actually performed the miracles (*dynameis*) demanded of a true apostle).

There are, however, two important qualifications, the first of which we have already noted above. The power of God is Jesus Christ crucified *in weakness*. This principle introduces a deep ambivalence in Paul towards the exercise of his unquestionably massive gifts of personality (supplemented, whatever he may say, by outstanding intellectual and rhetorical ability). He is, one might say, the first great Christian charismatic leader with a guilty conscience. The essential point is that he had critics who made him self-critical. The second qualification is equally important. Paul recognises that the Gospel he proclaims can only be proclaimed as *morally* authoritative.

> We neither practise cunning or distort the Word of God; only by declaring the truth openly do we recommend ourselves, and then it is to the common conscience of our fellow-men and in the sight of God . . . It is not ourselves we proclaim; we proclaim Jesus as Lord, and ourselves as your servants, for Jesus' sake. (2 Cor. 4:2–5)

The 'common conscience' referred to is the human capacity for moral judgement. The authority of the ministry is nothing apart from the authority of the open declaration of the truth. Whatever his credentials, if he, Paul, were to preach another Gospel, he was prepared to say that he ought to be held an outcast (Gal. 1:8). As liberating truth the Gospel may not be proclaimed by enslaving methods.

(e) Power in the Church

The large scale denominations which constitute the bulk of contemporary Christianity possess all the characteristics of human organisations, including inevitably, a distribution of power. Power struggles, pressure groups and all the attendant problems of decision-making are part of any church leader's personal experience. Has it ever been otherwise? Certainly Christian Churches have been smaller in size, and less bureaucratised. But even local congregations of no more than 40 persons have been known to split; the church in Corinth can hardly have been long in existence before experiencing the agony of internal division. It was John Henry Newman who observed that every great movement seemed to start with a prophet and end up with a policeman. This informally expressed thought has been significantly analysed in modern sociology, especially by Weber, in his discussion of 'the routinisation of charisma'. Of the (literally) charismatic quality of Paul's personal ministry there can be no historical doubt; and what seems to have happened within the early Church is not so much that charismatic enthusiasm evaporated to be replaced by formality of an inferior quality (namely church office), but rather that the charismatic qualities were embodied in a *latent* form in an institutional setting. From here they are always available as a source of revival, should they be necessary. The test of the permanent importance of a charismatic leader is his ability to invest the regular, orderly offices of a social organisation with some of his extraordinary qualities, so that they remain a resource under extreme conditions of social disorganisation.

It is in this light that we may view the obvious process of change between the Pauline epistles and later so-called Catholic epistles, (and indeed the later gospel of Matthew). It is Jesus who is, himself, irreplaceably 'the power of God'. It is he who gives authority to his apostles, who in their turn appoint representatives. Whether or not we speak of 'successors of the apostles' is less important than that we perceive that the power of Christ (Christ crucified!) has been lodged within the Church, and may, if the situation so requires it, break in directly to challenge and to cleanse.

In this context, it is highly pertinent to refer to the circumstance attending the emergence of the 'Anglican' Church. The Church of England acquired its authority in the sixteenth century by means of an Act of Parliament, and in the context of always complex and sometimes discreditable power politics. It had no definitive reformation era or leader. It produced no separate confession of faith. It neither abolished nor reconstituted what it understood to be the apostolic ministry. But it unquestionably saw itself as reformed according to the Gospel and the pattern of the primitive Church. It is, therefore, itself an expression of the latent power of the original charismatic moment, within the context of a traditional ministry. It does not deny the existence of power in the Church, as in any normal social organisation. As we shall see, it attempts clearly to identify where that power lies. But, if it is to understand itself aright, it must recognise that in its very life-blood lies the latent instinct for a return to the original charisma, and thereby the means for a searching critique of its own exercise of power.

The possibility of a tyrannous exercise of power within the church is already envisaged in the pages of 1 Peter (5:1–4). In conscious reflection of this passage the instruction of the archbishop to a newly consecrated bishop, on handing him a Bible, runs, in the *BCP* ordinal:

> Be to the flock of Christ a shepherd, not a wolf; feed them, devour them not. Hold up the weak, heal the sick, bind up the broken, bring again the outcasts, seek the lost. Be so merciful, that you be not too remiss; so minister discipline, that you forget not mercy, that when the Chief Shepherd shall appear you may receive the never-fading crown of glory.

The reminder could scarcely be stronger to the ultimate accountability of all exercise of power, or of the necessity for its use on behalf of the poor, or of the need for constant self-criticism in the balancing of compassion and rigour.

The following conclusions may be drawn from the evidence considered above:

(i)   The whole Christian faith is shot through with celebration of the mighty acts of God. The Church is itself the sphere of God's finally redemptive act in Jesus Christ, made available in the power of the Holy Spirit.

(ii) God's power is known, in the light of the cross to take the way of humble service and of suffering; and this is the only route to participation in the triumph of the resurrection.

(iii)   Hence, though Paul unambiguously claims both power and authority, he is aware that this is vitally qualified by the example of Christ and by the inherently moral quality of the appeal of the gospel.

(iv)   Power is invariably distributed in one way or another in church organisations; but the original 'charismatic' power can be 'routinised' in such a way as to make it latent for future emergencies.

The Anglican Experience of Authority

From the history of Anglicanism one can only select certain moments for special mention, two of which choose themselves, the era of the monuments of the Reformation and the era immediately influencing our own. The other two episodes referred to have been selected for their importance in shedding light on aspects of our contemporary problem of authority, namely the role of the laity and the question of theological criticism.

(a) Authority in the Anglican monuments (the Articles, the Ordinal and the BCP)

There is frequent and significant mention of authority in the Thirty-nine Articles. The overarching authority of the Scriptures is strongly emphasised (vi, xx, xxi). Two types of authority in the Church, living subject to the word of God, are affirmed, namely authority to decree rites and ceremonies in particular national Churches (xx, xxiv), and authority in controversies concerning the faith (xx, xxi). The authority of the ministry, lawfully called and sent, derives from Christ's own commission (xxii, xxvi). It is fully expected that the Church will exercise discipline in matters of morality, doctrine and ritual (xxvi, xxxiii, xxxiv).

The teaching of the Articles is strongly reinforced in the Ordinal, in which a frankly hierarchical pattern of authority and obedience is evident, bishop to archbishop, priest and deacon to bishop and other chief ministers. Authority to perform the duties of each office is specifically bestowed, and warning given to the seriousness of the responsibilities and duties incurred. Priests and bishops are required to promise that they will study Scripture and dispute erroneous opinions. Bishops, in particular, are expected to govern the Church, to interpret the Scriptures in disputes, and to exercise authority in a gentle and constructive manner. The overarching authority of the Scriptures is symbolised in the presentation of a New Testament or a Bible to each ordinand.

The *BCP* abundantly illustrates the pattern of authority by the roles it gives to the Minister in divine service and the administration of the sacraments, by the 'power of the keys' in absolution, by the openly disciplinary rubrics regarding admission to the Lord's Supper, and in the case of the bishop, the reservation to him of the power to confirm and ordain. Still more, the place occupied by the reading of Scripture, and especially the liturgical prominence given to the gospels reinforce the centrality of the testimony to the redemptive act of God in Christ in the life of the whole Church, clergy and people alike.

(b) Lay authority

The very same monuments of the Anglican Reformation unambiguously affirm the authority to the sovereign (Article xxxvii), attributing to him or her 'the chief government', but not a share in the ministry of word or sacraments. In the history of the Church of England, the parliamentary character of the monarchy and the powerful position of lay patrons has ensured continuous and effective involvement of lay persons in the governing of the Church. Outside England, for example in the United States, lay persons have taken a prominent part in Church government from the first. In view of the unambiguously hierarchical pattern of the ministry, it is somewhat surprising to discover that the laity by no means fit as subordinates on the lowest level as far as Anglican experience goes. The pattern is not a simple line of bishop – priest – deacon – lay person. Nor, on the other hand is even the English pattern that of sovereign (parliament) – bishop – priest – deacon. No single linear chain of command is adequate to the complexity and variety of the Anglican experience of lay involvement.

The reason for this manifestly lies in the character of the Anglican Reformation, which was conservative of the pattern of ordained ministerial order uncontroversially characteristic of the Church from the second century, but which retained the appeal to the apostolic Church of the New Testament, a Church manifestly less structured and demanding more by way of participation and involvement from each and every Christian than the post-Constantinian Churches came to do. It is in this latter connection that it is appropriate to speak of lay authority. As has been shown above, the power of the Gospel is part of the experience of the *whole* Church. To be the Church means to participate in the power of Christ, and of the Holy Spirit, in that fellowship which is his body. Even Paul, who exercises enormous personal authority in his congregation, understands his position in terms of the Gospel of the crucified Christ whom he proclaims and serves. Each Christian person in virtue of his or her understanding reception of the Gospel, and readiness to proclaim it, must be held to exercise authority in the Church.

The Anglican response to this feature of the New Testament is primarily seen in its insistence that the Scriptures and the liturgy be heard 'in such a language and order as is most easy and plain for the understanding both of the readers and hearers' (Cranmer, *Concerning the Service of the Church*). At the time of the Reformation (as now), there might be heard a very great diversity of opinions, lay and ordained, about the true doctrine of the Christian religion. To meet this situation the Anglican reformers provided simple, traditional summaries of Christian doctrine in the Apostles' and Nicene Creeds, the first of which was taught in the Catechism, and one or other repeated at every public service of worship; the open publication and public reading of the Scriptures ('he that readeth so standing and turning himself, as he may best be heard of all such as are present'); and an Article (vi) which denied the right of any person or group of persons, claiming no matter what official dignity, to prescribe as of necessity for salvation anything which might not be read in, nor proved by the same Scriptures.

It is misleading to summarise these procedures as 'the bestowal of the right of private judgement', as though the Prayer Book itself were not an attempt to express the mind of the undivided Church as an interpretative canon for understanding the Scriptures. But in a situation of great perplexity and wide divergence of theological conviction, it was unquestionably the case that individuals might well have to decide which of two theological opinions was correct; their lives might even depend upon it. Precisely in such a context, the Anglican reformers opted for the view, deriving from the New Testament as they under-

154

stood it, that the Gospel could be apprehended by learned and simple alike, and that it was part of the responsibility of the minister to equip the whole people of God with the means for judging aright. It was, and is, the making of this judgement which gives the laity an invaluable and inalienable authority in the Church of God. Whether it was done well, half-heartedly or not at all, the inherent potential of the Anglican liturgical order permitted the education of the whole people of God, as independent and critical of *any* generation of bishops, priests and deacons as the reformers had been of their own Church leaders. At its best, the training of the Church's critics has been an integral part of Anglican Church life.

(c) The reception of theological criticism

Despite the obvious connection between the theme of the previous section, and the outbreak of theological criticism in and after the European enlightenment, the 'critics' who have most troubled the Church have, for the most part, been clergy not laity. The reason for this is in part that theological education has, until comparatively recently, been a clerical monopoly. The critical theologians have, successfully or not, on the whole tried to represent to the Church the claims of an increasingly independent and autonomous (and thus, lay) 'world of learning'; the history of nineteenth-century Anglicanism shows how much distress and labour was involved in sifting true from false in these claims, in the realms of science and biblical criticism. Suddenly, however, Anglicans became aware of two major advantages in their position. On the one hand, they had already decided against the necessity of accepting as final the deliverances of the papal magisterium; and on the other, nothing in their formularies committed them to a doctrine of the verbal inspiration of Holy Scripture. The theory of a comprehensive Church, sufficiently committed to the 'essentials', and sufficiently flexible about other matters became attractive.

It is plain, however, that the limits of 'comprehensiveness' are no easier to define than the number of 'the essentials'. It soon enough became evident that biblical criticism did not leave the articles of the creed untouched. The unresolved ambiguity in the theological meaning of the fourth article of the Chicago–Lambeth Quadrilateral (on the apostolic ministry) was openly exposed by partisans and their critics. Public doubt began to be expressed whether Anglicanism stood for anything at all. The laity, far from desiring more criticism, might be heard to express the wish that the (clerical) theological critics would disappear.

The differentiated analysis of this situation is an urgent contemporary task. Throughout the Western world higher education and the influence of the mass media have given an entirely new power to any theologian who believes that he or she must challenge accepted opinion. Theological students, and much of the public, become aware of 'radical' authors and publications long before they know of orthodoxy and its defenders. The public promotion of conflict, on which the mass media in the Western democracies thrive, is as inescapable an element in the social context of those Churches, as are the constraints imposed by the hostile, central control of the media in Eastern block countries. Anglican experience is diverse, and no single analysis is remotely adequate to the complexity of each national context.

At the same time it seems to me, even from an examination of the biblical evidence, that the phenomenon of internal theological criticism and argument is intrinsic to the life of the Christian Church; and that it must learn to worship God and engage in Christian mission *at the same time* as it argues its way through difficult problems. Some of these problems are questions of political orientation or decision; others are matters of personal morality; others again are questions of intellectual integrity and the demands of evidence from the study of nature or history. Different cultures pose the questions in different ways. Christians everywhere find that the issues are serious and demanding, and the proposed solutions rarely other than controversial. Christian leaders are required both to give a lead, *and* not to mind contradiction. If the above argument about Anglicanism is correct, then Anglican leaders have a clear duty to be prepared to conduct their arguments openly, according to publicly available criteria, and to be protective of the rights of these critics who protest their loyalty to the commonly acknowledged courts of appeal.

(d) The theory of dispersed authority

The 1948 Lambeth Conference produced a report on the Anglican Communion which contained a statement of the Anglican principle of 'dispersed authority'. This statement has not, so far as I know, been superseded, and it seems doubtful to me whether it has in fact been bettered by any Anglican writer. Its background lies in the work of theologians, such as A. E. J. Rawlinson and W. Spens, who attempted to formulate a theory of authority in the light of criticism of Charles Gore, and especially after the violent suppression of the Catholic Modernists by Pope Pius X. Thus the statement commends 'a dispersed rather than a centralized authority' in whose multiple elements is recognised 'God's loving provision against the temptations to tyranny and the dangers of unchecked power'. The elements listed are Scripture, Tradition, Creeds, the Ministry of the Word and Sacraments, the witness of saints, and the *consensus fidelium*; an attempt is made to relate the elements to each other, and they are said to be fused and unified in the crucible of the public offering of worship.

It is not possible to analyse or discuss this statement in detail, and it is plainly open to criticism. But it is deserving of close study and reflection, as an attempt to give coherence to the not infrequently chaotic appearance of the Anglican experience of authority. The significance for the rest of Christendom of the concept of 'dispersed' authority has not diminished since 1948. In particular the ARCIC statement on authority, which refers to the 1948 and 1968 Lambeth conferences, reflects and responds to the post-Vatican II Roman Catholic adoption of a greater measure of dispersal. At the same time the impact of the liturgical movement in the Protestant Churches has given other denominations a more vital relationship with the unifying power of a traditional liturgical structure. Anglicans have, in my view, every reason to think that their concept and practice of a dispersed authority has a future, as well as a past.

Conclusion: Authority and Conflict

The military imagery of Old and New Testaments, from the early connotations of the expression 'Lord of hosts' to the description of the Christian warrior in Ephesians, reminds us that there is opposition to the rule of God and that the conflict is continuous and utterly serious. A major symbol in the traditional Christian doctrine of redemption is that of *Christus victor*, Christ triumphant over sin, death and the devil. In his or her baptism the Christian disciple enlists in Christ's service 'to fight under his banner . . . and to continue Christ's faithful soldier and servant' unto his or her life's end.

It is in the context of this ultimately decisive encounter that the whole Christian life is set. Wrong decisions, slackness or irresponsibility matter, because weakness in one part weakens the whole. The attractiveness of the concepts of obedience, discipline and a chain of command is rooted in this vision of Christian life as a military conflict. One of the earliest non-canonical writings, 1 Clement, derives the necessity of hierarchical order from precisely this image.

Nor is this a 'mere metaphor'. Evil in the world is, in the whole biblical tradition, a countervailing force against God. As I have tried to show above (a) the 'power of God' is not unchallengeable omnipotence. The Son of God endured the agony of God-forsakenness, and took to himself the lowest depth of human weakness. And in every century since that time, up to and including our own, men and women have suffered unto death for the sake, and in the service of their master. The Christian is engaged in that very struggle of good and evil which has been fought since the dawn of human consciousness, and in which the opposition is real, not imaginary, concrete not theoretical.

None the less conflicts are of very different kinds; and in this case there is every reason to think that the enemy is not invariably easy to recognise, and that the choice of weapons involves very difficult judgements. In resisting the obvious attraction of simple deductions from the military imagery, especially that of a single chain of command, Anglicans will have in mind the following considerations:

(i)   the 'captain of our salvation' is the elder brother of every member of the army;
(ii) the conflict involves every member, whose *personal* and *voluntary* allegiance to the captain is essential;
(iii) the conflict is not merely external, but *internal* to each and every member, who cannot be fully protected by others;
(iv) the conflict is fought in many different theatres of war, which must retain their own flexibility of response;
(v)   the armies are already disunited, and each member of the body needs to retain maximum sensitivity to the actions of other armies.

This last point is of particular relevance to the contemporary request for authoritative guidance. It is the Christian conscious of the disunified state of modern Christendom who calls out for an authoritative word, and this need cannot be met by a controverted statement from one part of it. Part of the peculiar dilemma of authority in the Anglican Communion derives from the Anglican commitment to, and experience of the ecumenical movement in this present century.

What then are Anglicans to make of the tradition in which they stand? How is this tradition to be developed so as to remain responsive to the ever-changing demands of different environments? The following conclusions seem to follow from the consideration both of Scripture and of the Anglican experience:

(i)   We acknowledge, and rejoice in the reality of divine power, the power of the Holy Spirit, in the Church. This is the dynamic (*dynamis*) from which all exercise of authority proceeds, and in virtue of which every member of the body takes his or her part in the conflict with evil.

(ii) This power may also be spoken of as the power of the Gospel of Christ, and it is given not to a privileged few, a hierarchy or intellectual élite, but to the whole Church. Every Christian, therefore, exercises the authority bestowed on him or her by his or her reception and realisation (in word and deed) of the Gospel.

(iii) This power is also mediated, humanly, visibly and audibly in the public preaching of the word and the administration of the sacraments, by persons called, chosen and commissioned for that function.

(iv) In both the above cases (ii) and (iii) divine and human power is inextricably intermixed. There is, therefore, an inherent and unavoidable potential for the abuse of claiming divine sanction for merely human judgements or behaviour. Neither supposed sanctity, nor official status is a protection.

(v)   Anglicans relate lay and clerical authority by simultaneously assigning a presidential role to the ordained person in divine worship, and by giving access to the criteria for all decisions in the Church by the public reading of the Scriptures interpreted in a traditional liturgical order; in short, by creating the conditions both for the actual exercise of power, and for its criticism.

(vi) The risk to both clergy and laity of misusing their authority is merely concealed, if it is pretended that power is not distributed in the Church. This would amount to massive self-deception.

Rather, the whole Church must ensure that the exercise of power is subject to the acknowledgement of voluntary constraints.

(vii) There are two principal constraints; first, that provided by the example of Jesus Christ, his service and humble obedience to death, and, secondly, the constraint of the appeal of the Gospel to the human moral will. Tyrannous or psychologically manipulative uses of power are to be identified, criticised and abandoned. It must be noted that their very recognition depends on a fallible, human judgement.

(viii) Anglicans remain true to their tradition, therefore, when they *simultaneously* insist on the exercise of real power by those genuinely entitled to claim it, and on the necessity of open criticism of the quality of the power so exercised. Both of these principles are derived from Scripture and are consistent with the traditions of the early Church.

(ix) Whether the power exercised in any place is thought to be tyrannous or manipulative will depend in part upon the intrinsic claims of the Christian Gospel to be a liberation of the human person for growth into a fully personal style of existence, and partly upon the patterns of authority acceptable in a particular culture. A dispersed, non-centralised structure, which both educates the whole Church in the vernacular, and gives institutional expression to the kinds of consultation familiar in a given society, has much to commend it.

I have avoided writing specifically about episcopacy, since my brief was a more comprehensive one. But at the same time I have inevitably reached certain conclusions. There would be no difficulty for Anglicans if critical historical study of the New Testament had unambiguously supported the statement in the *BCP* Ordinal that 'it is evident unto all men diligently reading holy Scripture and ancient Authors, that from the Apostles' time there have been these Orders of Ministers in Christ's Church; Bishops, Priests and Deacons'. The Preface to the Ordination Rites in the new American *BCP* accurately reflects the new critical situation by stating that the New Testament makes clear that there have been *different* ministries in the Church, and that since New Testament times the threefold order has been *characteristic* of the Church.

In a recent Faith and Order paper, the Greek Orthodox theologian

John Zizioulas argues brilliantly that it is the post-apostolic Church of the first three centuries to which we must return for the pattern of *episcopé* and of episcopacy, and not that of the apostolic age nor that of the fourth and subsequent centuries ('Episcopé and Episkopos in the Early Church', in *Episcope and Episcopate in Ecumenical Perspective, Faith and Order Paper 102.* The paper by Professor R. E. Brown, 'A brief survey of the New Testament Evidence on Episcopé and Episkopos' should also be noted). The appeal to the early, undivided Church is profoundly appropriate to the doctrinal principles of Anglicanism (e.g. 'The doctrine of the Church of England is grounded in the holy Scriptures, and in such teachings of the ancient Fathers and Councils of the Church as are agreeable to the said Scriptures', Canon A5, *The Canons of the Church of England*). But at the same time the evidence for the 'monarchical episcopate' falls a long way short of the kind of position for which at least some Anglicans have argued; and it is my belief that the kind of inner tension between office and charisma to which I have referred above (e) both reflects more authentically the inheritance of Scripture to the Church, and is more characteristically Anglican. Again I am persuaded that Anglicanism has a substantial contribution to make to the world-wide Church; but there is rather little evidence of any major research or writing in which this potential contribution is explored.

There is also a peculiar problem attaching to the actual exercise of *episcopé* in a disunited church. Since no Anglican bishop believes that he alone exercises the fullness of *episcopé* in any region in which other bishops or church leaders are active, he is bound to consult. If an Anglican bishop claims to be a bishop *in the Church of God*, as he does, he may not restrict the exercise of his *episcopé* to his own denomination. Uncoordinated oversight of the Church of God is simply not oversight. There is very good reason to believe that Anglican bishops ought to feel this problem with especial acuteness. Their use of the concept of 'collegiality' cannot, therefore, be borrowed unmodified from its use in Roman Catholicism. This theme also deserves much more careful scrutiny within Anglicanism than its somewhat casual use in the Lambeth documents of 1968 and 1978 suggests.

Nothing in my investigation of this topic has suggested to me any instant relief from the uncomfortable dilemma of authority in contemporary Anglicanism. Indeed it is my conviction, based on the evidence that I have attempted to discuss, that it is not the unsatisfactoriness of the Anglican Reformation nor contemporary Anglican weakness, but the actual nature of Christian obedience which gives rise to the challengeable character of the exercise of all authority in the Christian Church. I am also persuaded that it is very much more dangerous to pretend that power does not exist in the Church (or even to cloak that power by powerful use of the Pauline theme of 'weakness'), than it is openly to recognise it, and to insist on the need for criticism. But criticism is, of course, uncomfortable, and creates conflict. Criticism may be mistaken; it may be based on jealousy; it may lead to resentment. But it is, again, my conviction that the manifold and changing needs of, and challenges to the Christian Church require *both* the discriminating exercise of authority *and* the discriminating exercise of criticism if Christ's work is to be done in the world.

9

AUTHORITY IN THE CHURCH OF ENGLAND

First, I asked myself why there should be such public concern about *this* particular issue at *this* particular time. The reason, as ever, seems to be the conjunction of a variety of pressures and problems, not just one pressure.

For example, it is a feature of our times that the 20–year-old revolution carried out in the Church of Rome following the Second Vatican Council has seriously disturbed the world Christian ecology. By using that image I mean to imply the interdependence of Christian denominations. Anglicans, for example, derive support and sustenance for what they are as Anglicans at least in part from what Roman Catholics are on the one hand, and from what Baptists are, on the other. But if it is true, as Avery Dulles has recently argued in his book, *Catholicity*, that the Roman Catholic Church has internalised no less than ten standard Protestant criticisms of Catholicism, then the ecological balance is altered, and the question arises whether the separations out of which the Protestant movements arose are any longer necessary. All the major European reformers characterised their protest movements as provisional and regrettable necessities, and longed for a time when they would cease to be so. The question is, whether that time has now come?

Another reason for public concern about Anglican authority has to do with the security of one of its favourite appeals, the 'fundamental articles' apologia. From the sixteenth century onwards Anglicans have insisted that the theological basis of the Anglican Church is nothing less, and nothing more, than the faith of the primitive Church, summed up in the catholic creeds and expressed in various ways in the writings of the early Greek and Latin Fathers. Since the nineteenth century

163

there have been dissident Anglicans, like John Henry Newman, who thought that there could not be so *few* elements in Christian faith as that, or those who, like Hastings Rashdall, saw no reason why there should be so *many*. The theory of development may force Anglicans inclined to Newman's views to ask questions about Mariology and Papal Infallibility, and on the other the phenomenon of biblical criticism may prompt liberals to question the Virgin Birth and the Bodily Resurrection. In either case what is being scrutinised is the theory of fundamentals in which Anglicans have invested over 400 years of apologetic effort, but which is neither as simple as it sounds, nor as intellectually unchallengeable as is sometimes assumed.

Finally, the Church of England has a new mode of government. The General Synod, far from having had a period during which it could, so to speak, bed itself down, has been forced to debate and in some cases to decide a series of highly charged and complex problems, such as liturgical revision, matters of social and political ethics, schemes of ecumenical co-operation, and agreed statements on doctrinal issues. Changes in its relationship with Parliament have greatly complicated an already difficult period of adjustment. Despite this constitutional tie of most doubtful value, leading members of the Church of England who have been so swift to complain about the inadequacies of the Synod of Westminster ought surely to have had the humility to consider the more than 100 years' experience of synodical government which Anglicans in other parts of the world have had, for example in the USA, New Zealand, Ireland and South Africa. Be that as it may, the coincidence of pressures to make decisions and the comparative novelty of the procedures have certainly contributed to the special anxiety which attends the present moment.

But I have to say also that the rhetoric of crisis and of imminent catastrophe which one may now hear tends to deflect attention from a deeper and broader question. The theological issue we must address is nothing less than *authority in the Church of Christ herself*.

Anglicans understand themselves, in the words of Canon A.I., to 'belong to the true and apostolic Church of Christ'. And it is in virtue of our membership of *that* Church that we must ask the question, whether there has ever been a time when conflict has not characterised her life, and whether such conflicts have not always raised the question of final authority. It is something of a temptation to imagine that in other centuries and in other countries things were otherwise. But the books of the New Testament themselves would not have been written had there been peace in even the apostolic age.

Although contemporary New Testament criticism has sharpened our awareness of the complexity and diversity of the dissentions and schisms of the primitive communities, it is an extremely Anglican thing to do to point out the history of dispute. The first major *Apology of the Church of England*, published by Bishop Jewel of Salisbury in 1562, contains a long passage recounting the history of internal conflict starting with the Church in Corinth in the days of St Paul, and continuing into the late medieval times. Jewel cites *en route* the fifth-century Christian historian, Socrates, who remarked that Christians 'for their dissentions and sundry sects . . . were laughed and jested at openly of the people in their stages and common game plays'. Not that Jewel thought this a desirable state for the Church to be in:

> Of a truth, unity and concord doth best become religion; yet is not unity the sure and certain mark whereby to know the Church of God.[1]

The chronic recurrence of conflict in Christianity reinforces the suspicion that criteria for making decisions in the Church are not in themselves simple. So the issue of authority in the Church of Christ is not merely a matter of evolving a decision-making procedure which is final and unequivocal, as though the criteria for making decisions were already beyond dispute. Disputes of any seriousness and complexity are almost invariably also disputes about the criteria for settlement.

For example, Martin Luther's challenge to theological debate on the issue of the sale of indulgences was not in the first instance an attack on the authority of the Papacy. But it became such an issue, an issue of authority, when his opponents chose to deny that he had the right to argue theologically against what the Pope had already put into effect. From then on the dispute was *both* about the nature of Christian repentance *and* about authority in the Church, criteria and structures. Similarly in our own day there are many disputes which are *both* about theological issues *and* about criteria and structures. These are normal Christian disputes, and the rhetoric of crisis does us a disservice in deflecting our attention from the nature of Christian history. Those who sometimes speak as though reconciliation with the Papacy would be the only way of resolving the Anglican 'crisis of authority' forget that the criteria of authority are not locked up in the breast of one man. The growing capacity of Roman Catholic bishops and theologians openly to discuss matters which the Pope has purported to decide, such as the question of the control of conception, the marriage of priests, the ordination of women to the priesthood, and the treatment of practising homosexuals and of divorcees – this reminds us that there is an important function in controversy which is related to the whole course of Christian history and to the very embodiment of the Church of Christ in time.

But the strength and validity of a view of this kind will only become apparent if we examine with greater patience some fundamental aspects of the theology of authority.

1 God, the single divine source of all authority, takes the pathway among humanity of challengeability and service

Anglicans are accustomed, through their use of the Psalter, to 'ascribe power unto the Lord' (Ps. 29:2). But what kind of power? The very term 'Lord of hosts' passes, in the biblical period, through a series of changes of meaning, which continued in translations into the Greek *kurios pantocrator* (Lord almighty) and into the Latin *deus omnipotens*. Careless use of the idea of omnipotence conceals the fact that, in the Old Testament, the power of God is not the kind which obliterates the opposition by mere fiat. Rather, it is the sort of power which helps Israel in its confrontations, and which therefore has to admit the reality and strength of the opposition. From the start, then, the power of God is challengeable. The spiritual importance of this thought is apparent in the writings of both Jeremiah and Job. The relationship with God depicted in these works is one which permits a moment of controversy with God from within the heart of suffering and perplexity.

This view of the power of God is more strongly reinforced within the New Testament. For Jesus Christ takes with humanity the pathway of humility, of service and of weakness, as his route to the victory of the cross.

Here again is no obliteration of the powers of evil by mere fiat, but a patient persistence with the reality and strength of the opposition which is routed at the very moment of maximum helplessness.

The process of transformation of the very notion of divine power which this history entails is confirmed by the record of Jesus' explicit teaching on the nature of authority, when he denies the relevance of the example of dominative authority available in contemporary society: 'It shall not be so among you' (Luke 22:26). He commends, rather, the role and humility of a servant. Note, if you will, that Jesus does not deny the fact that authority in the community will require the exercise of power. But, he seems to imply, the responsibilities of the great and of leaders, when exercised in the manner of a servant, will inevitably involve suffering, here and now. The pathway of service, the route of challengeability, will be one of pain and of cost. The avoidance of pain, a human instinct of great profundity, is surely one of the motives guiding the Church's retreat from service in its exercise of authority, and the cause of its repeated and regrettable tendency to clothe itself in the mantle of unchallengeability.

2 God gives his gifts to the whole Church

One of the major reasons why service must characterise the Christian exercise of leadership is the fact that God has given gifts to the *whole* Church. His gifts are his empowerment of the body for its task of being the Church in the world. The Gospel is 'the power of God unto salvation, to everyone that believeth' (Rom. 1:16). But this Gospel is, precisely, the Gospel of the crucified and risen Lord. It is the whole Church, and 'every member of the same in his vocation and ministry', which engages in the apostolic mission of 'declaring the wonderful deeds of him who called [us] out of darkness into his marvellous light' (1 Pet. 2:9). Leadership in the Church is always leadership in her mission, in her realisation of her fundamental identity as the people of God, and necessarily involves attention to the particularity of the Holy Spirit's work in each one.

If every Christian has his or her own special 'vocation and ministry', then the authority which belongs to the act of proclaiming the Gospel of Christ inheres in each and every Christian person. There is a proper sovereignty which belongs to every member of God's own people which constitutes them corporately, as a *royal* priesthood. Christians share eschatologically in the victory of Christ, a victory over the world, the flesh and the devil in which they participate in virtue of their baptism.

Giving the whole people of God access to the Scriptures through the interpretative medium of the liturgy was the fundamental catechetical act of empowering the people, taken in the sixteenth century. It was the reformers' conviction that knowledge of the Scriptures was a necessary resource for the mission of the whole Church. The Christian life was such that an uninstructed or passive laity was unthinkable. And although Cranmer acknowledged that Scripture contained complexities, none the less he believed that its fundamental message was not too difficult even for the illiterate:

> For God receiveth the learned and the unlearned, and casteth away none, but is indifferent unto all. And the scripture is full, as well as of low valleys, plain ways, and easy for every man to use and walk in; as also of high hills and mountains, which few men can climb unto.[2]

And for the controversial times in which he lived, it was essential that the whole Church be sufficiently instructed to be able to discriminate between the claims of rival authorities, theological and ecclesiastical.

Here is a fundamental feature of the Anglican tradition which is anything but a matter of antiquarian interest. It involves the notion of a distribution of authority, which has received repeated endorsement to our own century. At the Lambeth Conference of 1948, a Committee of Bishops sought to epitomise this dispersal of authority in the following way:

> Authority, as inherited by the Anglican Communion from the undivided Church of the early centuries of the Christian era, is single in that it is derived from a single Divine source, and reflects within itself the richness and historicity of the Divine Revelation, the authority of the eternal Father, the incarnate Son, and the life-giving Spirit. It is distributed among Scripture, Tradition, Creeds, the Ministry of the Word and Sacraments, the witness of saints, and the *consensus fidelium*, which is the continuing experience of the Holy Spirit through His faithful people in the Church. It is thus a dispersed rather than a centralized authority having many elements which combine, interact with, and check

each other; these elements together contributing by a process of mutual support, mutual checking, and redressing of errors or exaggerations to the many-sided fullness of the authority which Christ has committed to His Church. Where this authority of Christ is to be found mediated not in one mode but in several we recognize in this multiplicity God's loving provision against the temptations to tyranny and the dangers of unchecked power.[3]

It is important to make two things clear about the theory of this now celebrated document. It would be erroneous to conclude from the phrase 'a dispersed rather than a centralized authority' that it has no conception of how the Church as a whole could proceed to make coherent decisions. On the contrary, it contains in the passage which follows a very strong affirmation of the episcopate, 'in synodical association with [the] clergy and laity', as the 'source and centre' of our order. Provinces, the normal decision-making unit in the Anglican Communion, contain, of course, many bishops, and provincial synods necessarily constitute a manifestation of centralised authority. By analogy, then, there would be nothing incongruous, on the basis of this common Anglican experience, in an international or universal decision-making body, provided it, too, reflected the 'synodical association' spoken of.

Secondly, the theology of authority which the document is striving to express does not constitute simply an Anglican theory, a rationalisation of existing differences over against 'papal tyranny' on the one hand, and 'mere congregationalism' on the other. Unless I am very much mistaken, this is the only kind of authority justifiable in the universal Church of Christ, and is one which we as Anglicans have every reason to explore, to expound and to defend, without a hint of that curiously smug self-deprecation which has so paralysed us in our public theological stances of late. Its essential feature is the recognition of the richness and historicity of the divine revelation. The distribution of God's gifts to the whole Church means that there are *voices* of authority, not one unambiguous, unequivocal *voice* of authority. It means that these voices of authority are the consequence of the call of God to every Christian believer to embody the saving Gospel in his or her own life, and to receive the empowering gift of his Holy Spirit to that end.

3 God calls a special ministry in his Church, whose limited powers are to be openly acknowledged

A special ministry entails the act of choosing particular people to exercise leadership or oversight. But these most ambiguous of words conceal a nest of difficulties and potential tensions. There are, after all, different kinds of leadership. The worship of the Church needs to be 'led'; so too does its necessary making of decisions. And one of the potential dangers for the Church is the development of incoherence between the oversight of an ordained ministry, and how it distributes its powers as an organisation. The office of the bishop has been traditionally and for very good reason the focus for these differing functions.

The growing size and complexity of the early Church imposed, as one would expect, certain sociological constraints upon it as an organisation. We can already see from the New Testament epistles the dangers which attended the development of a special ministry. In the first epistle of Peter, the author warns the *presbyteroi* or elders that shepherding the flock, now a paid occupation, must not be done with thought of financial gain. They are also alerted to the danger of a domineering style of exercising their powers. Thus arises what Professor Kingsley Barrett has called the 'paradox' of the ministry, which he formulates as follows:

> A church that rejects the gifts of leadership will greatly impoverish itself: a church that allows them to develop in a worldly way will destroy itself.[4]

Preventing the ministry from developing in 'a worldly way' will entail taking with the utmost seriousness Jesus' warning, 'But it shall not be so among you.' The whole notion of 'styles of leadership' or 'legitimation of authority' is informed by 'worldly' models available in given societies. We see this better in societies not our own, than in our own case. We observe for example, that some African bishops behave remarkably like some African tribal chiefs; or that some North American bishops behave like chief executives of successful business corporations. Our own bishops, perhaps, are expected to combine the charisma of a TV personality with the wisdom of a psychoanalyst and the skills of a chairperson of a charitable trust. If they subsequently develop qualities of superficial charm, phoney omniscience and a capacity for devious manipulation, we discover that their supposed 'gifts of leadership' have been allowed to develop 'in a worldly way'.

But what is to stop them so developing? All that we have argued for so far suggests that challengeability must be an important attribute of a Christian person who exercises authority. The document accepted by the Primates' Meeting in Washington DC in April 1981 draws out the meaning of *episcopé* in Anglicanism in the following way:

> In the continuing process of defining the *consensus fidelium*, Anglicans regard criticism and response as an essential element by which Authority is exercised and experienced and as playing a vital part in the work of the Holy Spirit in maintaining the Church in fidelity to the Apostolic Gospel.[5]

Here the statement explicitly accords status to the practice of 'hearing criticism'. It was when this particular feature of the document was described to me by one extremely prelatical bishop as 'a charter for the bloody-minded' that I knew it contained the truth. For it is precisely a characteristic of those who exercise power 'in a worldly way' to attempt to disguise it, and to protect themselves from criticism. In particular, the history of the Church knows the lengths to which authority will go in order to inhibit access to contrary views. The *consensus fidelium* can be prematurely contrived by the burning, banishing or banning of the opposition and their publications. The only way in which a leadership can prevent appeal to the *consensus* amounting to the phoney consultation of opinions already manipulated in advance is by an honest commitment to the education and nurture of the whole Church.

Anglicans, as we know, have committed themselves unequivocally to a hierarchical church order. The advantage of a hierarchy is that everyone knows officially where the power lies, and at whose door criticism should be laid. (All hierarchies develop unofficial power structures, as those familiar with Barchester Close will not need telling, but that is another story.) The problem for hierarchy in the Christian Church is the fact that it is simultaneously the focus of the exercise of power *and* of the dependence of the whole Church upon Jesus Christ, who is the source of her mission and the foundation of her unity. This problem is the source of that notorious difficulty in the phrase 'a centre of unity'. Bishops and their curates are, especially in the eucharistic celebration, 'the visible focus of the deep and all-embracing communion between Christ and the members of his body'.[6] But at the same time, they occupy in relation to their communities, positions of authority which are not beyond challenge, if my account is correct. They would have the right to *claim* to speak with authority to their congregations what they conscientiously believe to be in accordance with God's will for the Church and her mission, to minister – that is, necessarily, to interpret – the word of God in the name of Christ. In doing so they could not be expected to trim their utterances in order to avoid saying anything which would be subject to discussion, or even challenge and contradiction. On the contrary, Cranmer expected his bishops to be in the thick of controversy, teaching and exhorting with wholesome doctrine and withstanding and convincing gainsayers (from *The Consecration of Bishops*). To be both a focus of eucharistic unity and, even if unsought, a cause and focus of controversy, is no easy vocation. But both seem to me proper consequences of a true theology of authority; and if that were to involve the bishop in personal suffering, that consequence too seems to be part of the normal experience of a disciple of Christ and of the expected cost of the embodiment of the Church of Christ in time.

In the final section of this Paper, I want to draw out a few of the implications of this theology of authority for the Church of England as I see it at the present time.

(i) Whatever structures of decision-making the Church arrives at they will always embody a tension. This tension is between the fact that the criteria for making decisions about the life of the Church are open to all, and the investment of an inequality of power in a few leaders. Structures are variable, evolving and relative to time and place. For the sake of coherence, however, matters of jurisdiction cannot be wholly separated from church order, and for this reason Anglican structures have always found a special position of leadership for the episcopate. At certain times and in certain places bishops have had very considerable power; even so, my point about a necessary tension is still valid. No bishop ought to rule in such a way as to imply that to him alone is vouchsafed insight into the truth; that is the point of presenting him with a Bible, the very same book available to all, read publicly in the vulgar tongue for the sake of the illiterate. No one may be required, not even on episcopal authority, to believe as an article of faith 'whatsoever is not read therein, nor may be proved thereby' (Article VI).

The distribution of authority which this requirement implies has led Anglicans to develop decision-making structures which embody, or seek to embody, this principle of open access to the criteria. Hence the idea (in Anglican history not a new idea) of bishop-in-synodical-consultation. Clergy and laity too are part of a normal process of decision-making. The difficulty is that precisely the same tension at once arises. Those who are elected to consult synodically with the bishops enjoy an inequality of power. Their jurisdictional position has turned them into hierarchy, perhaps all the more dangerously because their position of inferiority in the hierarchy of orders conceals from them their actual status in the hierarchy of jurisdiction. They enjoy, it might be thought, a disguised power; and of them too it can be true, as of the most prelactical of episcopal hierarchs of past ages, that they can distort and manipulate the access of the whole Church to the criteria.

But the tension is still there, and must be recognised by all who occupy positions of authority. It can be put in the following form:

> The Christian Church is a Spirit-led community of equal brothers and sisters in the Lord; but in order to realise its radical potential in the context of a secular, stratified society it is obliged itself to become stratified.

Internal inequalities of power are only tolerable for the sake of challenge to the all-too-familiar inequalities of society, rich and poor, slave and free, Jew and Gentile, male and female. For those in a position of jurisdictional power to be oblivious of this tension will put in jeopardy the very notion of authority, which we examined.

(ii) All cultures, as we have suggested, offer to the Church models for the organisation of her decision-making procedures. Clement of Rome at the end of the first century delightfully and quite uncritically accepted the military chain of command as a norm, because, presumably, of the scriptural analogies between the Christian life and armed struggle. We do what the bishop tells us, he argues, simply because that is how we achieve coherence in fulfilling the battle aims of the Christian Church. In later times the Imperial Court provided further analogies for the papal curia, and in our own day, parliamentary procedures have shaped the General Synod's mode of life.

But all of these should stand under the scrutiny of the sentence, 'But it shall not be so among you.' The point of such an injunction is not that there is to hand an alternative, divinely-sanctioned blueprint for church government, which can simply be substituted for these models; nor even that all secular models are of equal desirability or appropriateness, provided they are open to a little gentle criticism. Rather *any* decision-making procedure is perceived as being likely to have secular analogies, not least in the minds of those who operate it, and by virtue of their influence is going to be open to abuse. Therefore, *any* decision-making structure must be open to scrutiny, and this ought to be as true of the workings of the Papacy as of the General Synod. There are many subtle corruptions in the exercise of power, and church history shows that no form of organisation is immune from them. The danger is all the more acute because of the claim, which the Church must make, that it is governed by the Holy Spirit.

(iii) Churches under pressure characteristically claim too much for their structures, or alternatively simplify the criteria for decision-making. Both of these are classic forms of legislation. The latter, the acute simplification of criteria, we can see in Calvin's Church of Geneva, which, he bravely announced, would be governed by the Scriptures alone. This was not the case, and events proved that it could not be the case. In due course Calvin conceded that the criterion of a Spirit-inspired Scripture could not be matched beyond dispute by Spirit-inspired interpreters of Scripture, and he acknowledged the need of humanly fallible scholars and councils of church leaders to decide in matters of controversy. This was a Church under pressure to explain the source of its authority; and we see the same phenomenon in the beleaguered Papacy of the nineteenth century. That, too, classically asserted an over-simple criterion, that of papal infallibility, which subsequent discussion has qualified extensively by insisting on the co-operation of bishops and on a *consensus fidelium*, the extent of whose ramifications grow ever more complex.

Unless I am very much mistaken the Church of England is also a Church under pressure, and one can certainly hear opinions advanced in favour of radically simplified canons and structures of authority. We have, however, a long history of *not* simplifying these matters. We could

174

do very much worse than ponder the highly differentiated account of authority given by Richard Hooker in the late sixteenth century. For him divine wisdom is imparted to humanity in diverse ways, not in one, and the interpretation of the sacred Scriptures requires the divine endowment of reason, in persons consulting, discussing and reasoning together in the community of the faithful.

(iv) *Any* authority without consent is tyranny. This applies as much to a synodical process, as to a direct form of episcopal government. It is of the nature of authority in religious matters, that if it does not acquire recognition, it undermines *de facto* such power as it may have *de iure*. For example, if it were to be in the hands of the bishop of a diocese to fire inefficient parish priests, no matter what his actual powers were, the bishop's decisions would be regarded with disdain if he were thought to be himself intemperate, unreliable and prone to partiality. Members of the General Synod have individually to consider the difficulty there is for a variable elected body, which is necessarily largely anonymous to church members, to establish and maintain a reputation for high spiritual and moral standards. Our Synod exists as an institution in a media context which demands passion, confrontation and spectacular display; every exhibition of folly is guaranteed an instant and dramatic magnification into the homes of hundreds of thousands.

If individual members of Synod behave badly and if Synod as a whole is volatile and unreliable it will simply forfeit that recognition by the Church at large which alone can bestow its moral and religious authority. But exactly the same argument applies to any *de iure* system of government in the Church, whether it be episcopal or congregational. And we may comfort ourselves with the following thought: A Church which has survived the Borgia Popes, so our Roman Catholic brothers and sisters tell us, must have received the assistance of the Holy Spirit. A *fortiori*, a Church governed by General Synod. Calvin, who was ready to admit that God did indeed use great councils of the Church for her guidance, believed none the less that even the best of them, such as the Council of Nicaea, were vitiated by exhibitions of human folly. This, he held, was providential. The Holy Spirit, he affirmed, 'so governed the otherwise godly and holy councils as to allow something human to happen to them, lest we should put too much confidence in human beings' (*Institutes* IV. ix. 11).

(v) One final matter needs mentioning, which is the Church of

England's attitude towards other Churches, when matters are decided which affect its relationships with them. The consideration of voices from *other* Churches could only be regarded, on the theory which I have been expounding, as part of the normal course of preparation for decision-making. Some Anglicans will think, on good historical grounds, that the separation from papal jurisdiction imposes a principal obligation to repair that breach ahead of all others. Other Anglicans, on no less good historical grounds, will think that the status of brotherhood and sisterhood which we enjoy with other parts of the *via media* reformation imposes the major claim. The classic nineteenth-century disputes between rival church parties have imparted to Anglicans a seesaw view of ecumenism, according to which a tilt in one direction implies a tilt away from another. Much of the ecclesiastical politics of ecumenism is conducted precisely on this assumption, and the well-developed bureaucratic party in the Church of England, with large numbers of harassed bishops as paid up members, sees itself in the business of balancing acts, balancing appointments, committees, statements, ecumenical gestures and so forth.

One of the least helpful features of this perhaps inevitable legacy of the theory of 'golden mean' is the habit of using relationships with other Churches as a *dis*suasive from pursuing a particular course of action. Of course these relationships matter. They *all* matter, and not just those closest to ourselves. We should make a habit of taking them clearly into account as voices to be heard and opinions to be weighed. But we have no business at all in Christendom if, as Anglicans, we have no confidence in our ability, under the guidance of the Holy Spirit, to think our way through the criteria of authority, to construct a suitable decision-making process, and to commend it to our brothers and sisters in Christ. To say that we have no authority to do X and Y is to make a radically unclear pronouncement; or rather, it is to trade on the sense in which no Christian Church has authority – to alter the Gospel delivered to it – in order to reinforce opposition to proposals which are manifestly (or at least arguably) within its jurisdiction. For to be what the Church of England claims to be, that is to 'belong to the true and apostolic Church of Christ' means to have authority to do what that Church can do. That is why I have argued in this essay not for a theology of authority in the Church of England, but in the Church of Christ. The problems for the Church of England are mostly those common to the whole Church, and we must learn to look not sideways to left and right, but forward to the future, confident that God can call even English Anglicans to set an example of what it means to be faithful and obedient to the vision of his kingdom.

NOTES

1. John Jewel, *Apology of the Church of England*, Part III, ed. J. E. Booty (Charlottesville, 1963), p. 47.
2. Thomas Cranmer, *First Book of Homilies* (1547), First Homily, Second Part: 'A Fruitful Exhortation to the Reading and Knowledge of Holy Scriptures'.
3. *The Lambeth Conference 1948* (London, 1948), Report No. IV, 'The Anglican Communion', pp. 84–5.
4. Kingsley Barrett, *Church, Ministry and Sacraments in the New Testament* (Exeter, 1985), p. 40.
5. 'Practical Implications of the Anglican View of Authority', in: Anglican Primates' Meeting, Washington, USA, April 1981, *Four Documents on Authority in the Anglican Communion* (London, 1981).
6. World Council of Churches, *Baptism, Eucharist and Ministry,* Faith and Order Paper III (Geneva, 1982), Ministry section 14, p. 22.

10

EPISCOPÉ AND POWER IN THE CHURCH

It is not our intention to find ways of reducing the bishop's power, but we desire and pray they may not coerce our consciences to sin.

(*Confessio Augustana* XXVIII, 77)

The treatment of the power of bishops in *CA* 28 turns on a distinction, long familiar in medieval Western theology, between the power of the Gospel and that of the temporal sword. But as George Lindbeck and Avery Dulles point out in their jointly authored essay on 'Bishops and the Ministry of the Gospel', the *Confessio Augustana* 'simply assumes that episcopacy should be retained'.[1] The question it faced was: given bishops, what should be their powers?

Modern Lutheran theology, however, after centuries of agreement that the structures of church government (or at least the titles given to church leaders) are a matter of indifference, now presents an apparently different face. Analysis of the Lutheran responses to the section on the ministry of the World Council of Churches' document, *Baptism, Eucharist and Ministry*, suggests that the relationship between the universal priesthood of all believers based on baptism and *any* form of inequality of power in the Church has become extremely problematic in Lutheranism.[2] The celebrated 'satis est' and 'nec necesse est' of *CA* 7 is notoriously capable of, and receives, widely differing interpretations. What I wish to offer here is an argument about the nature of the relationship between spiritual and ecclesiastical power, addressed to the fact that power is bound to be unequally distributed in the Church and most likely to be misused. It is an argument which assumes that sociological and theological methods of analysis ought to be distinguished but cannot be separated. The Church is, as Richard Hooker declared at the end of the sixteenth century, both a society and a society supernatural.[3] But, I propose to argue, there is a dialectic between the fundamental theological character of the Church and its necessary embodiment in specific and, of course, changing organisational arrangements. With the *Confessio Augustana* we may simply assume that there will be those who govern. The question is who, and how.

The Government of the Church as a Problem

In the work of a brilliant young seventeenth-century Anglican theologian, Edward Stillingfleet, there is a passage of sustained polemic against the institution of papal monarchy which runs along the following lines: Roman Catholics, he says, argue from the manifest excellence of the monarchy as a form of political institution to the manifest excellence of monarchy in church government. But the analogy is plainly defective. It must be remembered, he says, that we are speaking about the government of the Church which is spread throughout the world. How possibly could decisions taken in Rome be effective in Mexico or Japan? What is plainly needed, he argues, is decisions to be taken in those places where they can be put into practice at once. If one needs any political analogy for this procedure the more appropriate model is government by aristocracy.[4]

No one reading this passage could fail to be struck by two reflections. The first is that the cogency of Stillingfleet's argument, which derives from the extreme difficulty of communicating with Rome in the seventeenth century, is undermined by the astonishing ease of modern travel and the electronic transmission of words and images. The second thought is that the notion that aristocracy is itself politically attractive would only have occurred to certain particular people, living in certain countries at certain times, one of whom would have been a political conservative and defender of the national Church writing in England in 1664. A third reflection could be added to the effect that modern Anglicanism, which has somewhat modestly enhanced the role of the primates of the Communion's twenty-seven autonomous Provinces, has, in fact, implemented Stillingfleet's preferred model of government, justifying it in terms of 'collegial interdependence' rather than on any overt political analogy.[5]

The extent of the permeation of civil or political precedents or ways of thinking into what theologians may hope to be the unique mode of expression of authority in the Church is always easier to detect in societies or cultures other than our own. We may pray that 'the whole body of the Church' be 'governed and sanctified' by the Holy Spirit (Collect for Good Friday, 1662 *BCP*), but we constantly discover, sometimes to our distress, that this government does not preclude the (at least) partial fulfilment of secular role-expectations. Common sense suggests that this is what we would expect. Christians are not subject to the influences simply of the Church's teaching and socialisation. They carry their cultures around in their heads.[6] Cultures develop and legitimate modes of authority. Some styles of behaviour or ways of making decisions will necessarily seem to be justified simply on the basis of satisfactory common experience. If people are content with local arrangements for the distribution of political power they will find them, or their nearest analogues, natural and right in the Church. Stillingfleet, we note, was alert enough to detect argument by analogy and to challenge its precise applicability to the Church; but he was human – or at least English – enough to commend the Anglican model by reference to another political analogy.

The relationship of secular and ecclesial ideas about modes of government is, of course, part of a much wider issue of the relationship of Christ and culture, to which very considerable thought has been given since H. Richard Niebuhr's classic work of that name. In more recent years, under the heading of 'inculturation' or 'indigenisation' (a somewhat patronising terminology readily concealing normative assumptions), extensive consideration has been given to the processes involved in cross-cultural missionary activity. At least four stages have been distinguished. In the first, the period of primary colonial evangelistic activity, the culture of the 'Gospel' and that of the preachers of the Gospel has not been distinguished. In the second phase, the distinction is made and the Churches attempt to adopt local styles of music, dance, language, and imagery, and tentatively explore local models of authority. Then, in the third stage, ambiguities begin to emerge in the process of so-called indigenisation. The complexity and dynamic quality of local culture begins to become plain, especially if the country involved is subject to urbanisation and secularisation. Finally, a new critique of culture is undertaken which attempts to deepen its grasp on the distinctive model of human relationships to be found in the Gospel. A critique of social processes, whose nature and dynamic is now more fully understood, begins to be developed. The document from the 1988 Lambeth Conference which lays out this process adds the following comment:

> The business of freeing the Church from the 'Babylonish captivity' of colonial culture is multi-faceted and long-term; and it requires more than a merely guilty or sentimental politeness to what is thought to be 'indigenous' culture. It involves an imaginative sensitivity to the concrete social processes at work in specific contexts – to how nations and peoples are *actually* becoming themselves – and a serious listening to how people themselves perceive their hopes for fuller liberation from alien systems of domination.[7]

The presupposition behind the description of such a process is that it is possible to recognise an 'alien system of domination' in the light of mature and profound reflection upon the Gospel. It is important to see that the process, so described, is a critical one. It is not that the Gospel provides us with a series of instructions on the basis of which Christians can devise a completely satisfactory non-dominative system of church government. Rather the alien character of a system – which, until a crucial point, may have seemed to be a natural and appropriate way of arranging for the government of the Church – is disclosed as dominative in the light of the Gospel, either by immediate intuition or by a longer process of reflection such as has been described. In other words, the Gospel functions critically in a dialectical process rather than constructively by ideal realisation.

It is equally important, on the other hand, to realise that there was a political or cultural imperative in the original preaching of the Gospel. It was in part through political or quasi-political terminology that Christians expressed the sense of their own identity. To a certain extent the development of the episcopate stood for a new political reality in the ancient world, corresponding to the Church's consciousness of being a new people, or a new race, whose *politeuma* or commonwealth was in heaven (Phil. 3:20), at once strangers and sojourners in other people's cities, but also radically at home in God's world.[8] What we have identified as a dialectical process in relation to so called 'indigenisation' is kept in motion by an imperative deriving from the Gospel, by the knowledge that the God with whom Christians have to do is a God who establishes relationship with human beings of a particular, determinate kind. This relationship, which is spoken of in the New Testament as communion (*koinonia*), is the foundation of the relationships between persons, which it is the Church's mission to embody. How Christians arrange for the government of the Church, therefore, both is, and is not, a matter of indifference, but in contrasting senses. It is indifferent in the sense that no blueprint of church government is provided in the New Testament, which witnesses to the launching of the Christian movement into the dialectical process we have described. But at the same time it is not indifferent in the sense that the Church has the task of communicating a unique and distinctive pattern of relation between human beings which has its ground in the being and act of God himself. The problem of this Yes and No is what must occupy us in further detail.

Domineering Behaviour in the Church

I have spoken of the Christian movement being launched into a dialectical process. That, at least, is obvious on the pages of the New Testament documents, once we stop the habit of quarrying the text for legitimation of our own denominational arrangements. There is plainly an already serious problem about domineering behaviour within Christian communities. In Corinth, Paul had real difficulty in establishing his authority in the church, or churches, at least those of which he had been the founder and over which he claimed rights as a father. He was accused of being weak, and he reacted with direct divine legitimation backed by a rhetorical vigour which bordered on emotional blackmail. In its recollections about Jesus the Church preserved stories greatly to the discredit of at least some of his immediate disciples, who in the version recorded in Mark asked for special positions of rank in the eschatological kingdom (Mark 10:37) or who fell into jealous dispute about which was to be regarded as the greatest (Luke 22:24). The first letter of Peter makes clear that financial gain and love of power were already discernibly part of the motivation of those 'elders' who had pastoral responsibility for the community (5:2–3).

With such admissions of blatant abuse of authority we hardly need further evidence from the history of the early Church. But it is, perhaps, not so readily or honestly acknowledged as in the pages of the New Testament itself. One exception occurs in Book IV of Irenaeus's *Adversus Haereses*, where in instructing the Church to follow only the interpretation of the Scriptures provided in the Church by the presbyters who have the succession from the apostles, Irenaeus warns his readers against unauthorised schismatics or heretics who have set themselves up in opposition to the Church. He is, however, obliged to acknowledge that there are also those who are believed to be presbyters by many (their succession appears not to be in doubt), but who are proud and scornful and are 'puffed up with pride by the pride of holding the chief seat'. From all such persons one must keep aloof and resort only to those who guard apostolic doctrine and combine the order of priesthood (*ordine presbyterri*) with sound speech and blameless conduct.[9] Thus it appears that at an early stage in the history of the Church it was perceived that neither ordination in succession nor the profession of impeccable orthodoxy necessarily protected Church leaders from the moral abuses attendant on the exercise of power.

The fact that the New Testament communities themselves knew that the abuse of power was a possibility signifies one important truth, namely that domineering behaviour is not the prerogative of Churches which have formally structured themselves on a hierarchical pattern. The term 'hierarchy' is, of course, ambiguous. Taken literally it simply refers to rule or dominion in holy things; whereas sociological usage has focused on the ordering of rule in ranks or grades, one above another. But prescinding altogether from discussion of whether the communities reflected in the synoptic gospels and the first letter of Peter were or were not hierarchical in whatever sense, it is evident that those who are what sociologists may call 'higher participants' in an organisation have greater access to the exercise of power than 'lower participants'[10] and that this exercise of power is open to abuse and from the first has been abused in the Church.

In this connection it is worth making clear that Churches with what are reckoned to be hierarchies of order (for example, deacons, priests, and bishops in ascending sequence) may also have somewhat differently constructed formal or informal hierarchies of jurisdiction (for example, as in the Church of England, a lay sovereign – who has been for more than one notable reign a woman – lay members of Parliament, and lay persons of considerable power or influence in parishes).[11] Abuse of power is in principle as possible for higher lay participants as for ordained. Churches with large bureaucracies exhibit, moreover, the informal power networks characteristic of any organisation, the manipulation of which by clerks and secretaries, spouses and friends, is the common coin of ecclesiastical gossips and novelists, by no means all of whom have the stature of Anthony Trollope.

Merely to refer to these phenomena is sufficient to evoke recognition. And yet it appears that Christians have well-developed mechanisms for discounting their significance. It is a curious phenomenon that, despite the fact that domineering behaviour is ascribed to higher participants in the New Testament communities, Christian theology has been reluctant to give a clear account of the phenomenon of power in the Church. 'Power', it has to be admitted, is by no means a clear concept, and to that extent the failure is the less culpable. But the root of the malaise lies deeper. The concept of power itself is, as modern research has demonstrated, a negative one.[12] Raymond Aron has written: 'The words "power" and "Macht", in English and German, "pouvoir" or "puissance" in French, continue to be surrounded by a kind of sacred halo or, it may be preferable to say, imbued with mysterious overtones that have something terrifying about them.'[13] The association of the terms have to do, he points out, with Machiavelli, with *Machtpolitik*, with *die Damonie der Macht*, and with Lord Acton's dictum, 'Power corrupts, absolute power corrupts absolutely.' With such connotations as these, it is sometimes asserted or implied that the problem is not the abuse of power but the mere phenomenon of power. There are Christian theologians today who use the term 'power' to mean domination and for whom the only appropriate Christian option is a posture of powerlessness.[14]

When one bears in mind the sheer quantity of reflection on the phenomenon of power in organisations, undertaken in the last two decades, it is clear that one of the preconditions for this extraordinary development in Christian reflection is the wholesale abandonment of connection with contemporary sociology. But the Church's difficulties in the face of a demand for explanation for the presence of domineering behaviour in its leaders are of long standing. Two principle strategies have been developed: The first was to minimise the possibility of identifying the behaviour as domineering by maximising the entitlement of the officeholder to the possession and exercise of power. A straightforward theology of the charisma of office enabled ordained persons to claim that they spoke or acted, not on their own behalf or in their own name, but in virtue of the bestowal on them of the Holy Spirit and in the name of Christ. The biblical basis of this was the commissioning of the seventy in the gospel of Luke ('He who hears you hears me,' 10:16) and St Paul's claim to speak on the authority of Christ ('I am entrusted with a commission,' 1 Cor. 9:17). As we have seen, in the writings of Irenaeus it could be recognised that commissioning of ordination by no means protected the recipient from pride and moral error. But the ambiguity of the notion of entitlement attached to the point where the claim was greatest; from pride there could be no escape, even into the (paradoxical) claim to humility.

The second strategy was more subtle. This was the development of the conception of a ministry of service, specifically on the model of the ministry of Christ, deploying the 'myth' of *kenosis*. Again a biblical basis was to hand, especially in the synoptic and Johannine passages where Christ is spoken of as a servant. This strategy has existed in two main forms. So long as kenotic Christology was held not to involve the abandonment by the divine Son of God of his divine power and prerogatives (that is, so long as the Christology of the dogmatic Tome of Leo was approved), *kenosis* would not have the connotation of powerlessness. However, once nineteenth-century theology developed what we now call 'kenotic Christology' on the assumption of either the pouring out, *Entäusserung* (Thomasius), or, more radically, of the self-emptying, *Entleerung*, of the incarnate Lord,[15] then the way was clear for the root-and-branch denial that leadership in the Church could involve power of any kind.

Now it must be said that both of these strategies, despite their apparent biblical foundations, attract sociological suspicion. The first lends itself classically to analysis in terms of legitimation. One of the observable techniques of those who wish to exercise power over others is to clothe themselves (sometimes in ritually enacted performances) with the mantle of divine approval. The developing clash between the power of the Church's hierarchy and that of a theologically conceived secular imperium is the main historical example we possess for the escalation in legitimating claims. The ideology of extreme papal monarchy implied that the Pope was set over the Emperor, because the Pope alone had the power of eternal life or death, that is, literally the last word on an Emperor's destiny.[16] This power the Pope had in virtue of the gift of the keys of St Peter, a gift sufficiently ambiguous as to require acknowledgement in an unambiguous, but alas spurious, legend of the donation of Constantine. The point of divine legitimation is to exact compliance; its weakness is that, as a claim, it depends upon voluntary acknowledgement for its impact. But it was the last weapon in the armoury of an institution which was regularly threatened by force of actual weapons and whose influence could be and sometimes was swept aside by vulgar might. It was a threatened institution which equipped itself with the theological assertion of infallibility and ultimate control over human destiny. Having seen the processes of legitimation at work, we have become suspicious.

Suspicion no less certainly arises over the other strategy, that of the invocation of service and powerlessness. In fact power is not escaped by identifying it with force. The claim that one has no power is one which, in certain moral contexts, has considerable weight. For example, immigrants into the State of Israel discover that their status as the 'powerless' gives them influence with officialdom. Gandhi's politics of nonviolence achieved results in a moral climate which deplores the use of force on the nonresisting and unarmed. Were the theologians who endlessly celebrate servant-ministry less sociologically innocent they would know that the service conception of power is usually and especially favoured by the powerful and those employed in defending and promoting their power.[17] It also arouses the suspicion that an attempt is being made to conceal power. The invocation of service on the model of Christ is, in Christian contexts at least, also a form of legitimation.

I have spoken of these strategies as arousing suspicion, and the brevity of the discussion of the grounds for suspicion may provoke irritation. The reason for irritation is obvious enough. Those who exercise power frequently (though not invariably) have overt motives for doing so. My discussion raises what are best described as psychological considerations relating to the adequacy of the account of those motives. If Church leaders or officeholders say or do something decisive and affirm that they do so because they are empowered by the Holy Spirit, or because they wish to serve the Church, who is anyone to say that they are rather clothing themselves in the mantle of unchallengeability? What gives us the right to be suspicious of them? The answer can only be phrased in terms of general, not particular, considerations – for example, that we know that some of those in the past who have claimed divine support or high-minded motives have actually been in error or self-deceived and have even on occasion admitted as much subsequently. Motivation, we know, is complex, and the more important the question, or the more far-reaching the claim, the greater care which needs to be taken in its evaluation. Suspicion is appropriate, not because we know in advance that in all particular cases the least creditable motives are to be preferred to those which are honourable, but because we have a duty to take care. Suspicion does not, therefore, require the abandonment of the theological strategies we have mentioned; but is consistent with the idea of a dialectical process which we have already developed. Socio-logical observations on how people who are in possession of power frequently behave must be a partner in any careful analysis of the exercise of power in the Church.

The Theological Context of *Episcopé*

Anglicans or Episcopalians have the unenviable reputation in ecumenical circles for introducing episcopacy into discussion like a *deus ex machina* in an ecclesiological vacuum. There are reasons for this. They like to appeal to history; they do not wish to be tied down to one theological theory of the episcopate; their long history of permitting lay involvement in church government means that they cannot fully share the theologies of the episcopate advanced in Orthodox or Cath-olic circles.

But Anglicans or Episcopalians have not always appreciated why they are obliged to offer a theology of the episcopate to accompany its recommendation as a form of church government; the reason for this requirement can be very simply stated. Bishops are, for Anglicans, officeholders in the Church of God. There must, therefore, exist an understanding *of the Church* in the context of which the episcopate belongs. Although Anglicans have recently (that is, in the last 150 years) become reluctant to admit that they have, or ought to have, a theology

187

of the Church to bring to the ecumenical discussion table, it is ecclesiology which will make sense – or nonsense – of the office of a bishop. The same considerations hold good for any broader discussion of ministries of leadership and pastoral oversight, however they may be entitled or named, and irrespective of their view of a historic chain of ordinations. *Episcopé* in the Church must have an ecclesiological context.

The context in which it is intelligible, I wish to argue, is that of baptism. The reason for this view must be briefly sketched. The Christian community is the community of the baptised. Baptism defines who belongs to the church. There were baptisms of various kinds before the Christian movement came into existence; there were also groups which had a kind of relationship to Jesus' preaching, but which existed apart from what baptism signified to the later Church. But in general it is the case that we can speak confidently of the existence of the Church at the same time as we can confidently point to the practice of initiatory baptism.

Being baptised involves participating in the Church's foundational metaphor, that is, of passing from death to life by being ritually identified with Christ in his death, so as to rise again with Christ into newness of life. Being baptised means to receive the gift of the life-giving Spirit and thus to participate in the death-conquering new life which is the gift of the risen Christ to his Church. To be a 'member' of Christ implies that one has passed from the domain of death into that of life and has become a living limb or organ of a new reality. Baptism therefore establishes the sense of each individual person as having an irreplaceable part in an active system of persons-in-relation. This is that new personal identity which transcends the old identifying marks of humanity. Is one male or female, Jew or Gentile, in slavery or free? No, one is a new person in Christ. Nothing more fundamental can be said about anyone's life than that it has been lived as part of Christ's body. It is for this reason that *episcopé* in the Church must be understood first in relation to baptism.

In order to understand the relationship of baptism to ordination it is essential to distinguish between identity and role.[18] To be a 'member' of Christ is a matter of identity; to be a priest is a matter of role. It is for this reason that according to the theological definition of laity, however it may have to be used conventionally in other contexts, no priest ever ceases to be a lay person. No one ever gets 'beyond' baptism. The ordained do not become 'super-members' of Christ; on the contrary, as St Paul makes clear, in the body of Christ those parts which are commonly regarded as of least importance are given a special status.

The problem of how to conceive of ordination is, of course, an aspect of the doctrine of the Holy Spirit. Here the language of 'gift' needs to be deployed with discrimination, because human gifts (presents, money, attention) are all capable of being quantitatively increased. But the gift of the Spirit is not quantifiable. This gift is a divine self-giving without measure, pure superabundant grace; we note, in this context, the use of the analogy of excess which is designed to subvert our awareness of the human possibility of residual meanness of giving.[19] But God deals with all his people with superfluous generosity. Thus the idea of an increase in the Holy Spirit is, so to speak, an optical illusion; it is not the case that to certain persons is given more Holy Spirit than to others: rather, that in the lives of some there ceases to be such resistance or obstacle to the effectiveness of the Holy Spirit. For such increase of grace all Christians have both the need and the right to make daily intercession.

What then is the significance of the prayer for the bestowal of the Holy Spirit on those set aside for ordination? Ordination is the recognition by an act of special solemnity that a new role is being undertaken by a particular person which has consequences for every member of the Church. Solemnity at this moment is justified as in the case of the ritual observance of marriage or of the approach of death. Ordination is a life-transforming event, the outcome of deliberate decision by both people and candidate, is carefully prepared for, and involves intimate contact with most holy things, the preaching of the word and celebration of the sacraments. It would be inconceivable that the prayers of the Church at this moment of personal choice should not be given solemn, ritual focus.

Secondly, prayer for the gift of the Holy Spirit is an oblique acknowledgement of the special danger attaching to this particular role in the Church. We are speaking not now of the danger of contact with the holy, but rather of the more mundane temptations of pride which the public character of the office entails. Precisely because *episcopé* involves exposure to the possibility of abusing power, and thus to the risk of further obstacles to the realisation of the gift of the Spirit, it is wholly appropriate that the 'increase' of the gift of the Holy Spirit be sought at this moment.

Finally, inasmuch as a series of tasks are solemnly assigned to the officeholder, failure in which will have the most serious repercussions for the Church, the whole Church joins in common prayer to the Holy Spirit that what should be true of each baptised Christian will indeed be true of these baptised Christians, namely that they will truly be Christ to their neighbours. The service of ordination is a recognition of the public character of the life of the ordained in its assigned roles in liturgy and in preaching, undeniably a greater burden and responsibility, humanly speaking, than that of the non-ordained. In the prayer for the Holy Spirit there is an implicit recognition of the social anthropology of representation in religion, a phenomenon not peculiar to Christianity, nor one from whose potential, and difficulties, it is exempt. We shall discuss further the sense in which Christian theology both affirms and simultaneously subverts the representative character of Christian priesthood.

It is a corollary of the relation of *episcopé* to the theology of baptism that the Christian is able to be thoroughly realistic about the continued influence of death in the lives of individual members of the Church and in its institutional structures. The recovery in contemporary theology of the eschatology of the Church has enabled theologians of many denominations to recall ecclesiology from a triumphalism which seriously distorted the practice of *episcopé*. This recovery is the theological precondition for the admission of the idea of a dialectical process in relationship to the realities of power in the Church. It is not easy for those who hold power to perceive their own abuses of it. They have to be told, and the telling is not comfortable. Nor are those who cry foul invariably in the right. The influence of death and the politics of alien domination take many forms. Democratic institutions lend themselves to various specious distortions, as I shall argue, to which those sensitised to the more startling manifestations of authoritarianism are sometimes blind. The acknowledgement that we live in the midst of a dialectic enables the Church to hear the call to return to baptism, a call which is issued at every Eucharist.

Routinisation and the Contribution of Sociology

The contribution which sociology must be allowed to make to any consideration of the question of *episcopé* and power in the Church will largely be included with a discussion of Weber's formulation of the 'routinisation (*Veralltäglichung*) of charisma', one of the most successful sociological concepts ever to have been devised.[20] But before we examine this idea, a word is overdue about the terminology of 'power' and 'authority'. So far I have preferred to speak of power in the Church, and to accept the possibility that such power may be abused or used properly. There are also those who would sharply distinguish power from authority in relationship to the Church. They would do so on the grounds that the Christian faith sponsors the radical criticism of mundane views of power and that the resource it possesses, or with which it is endowed, is not power but authority.

The position which is being advanced in this essay is wholly consistent with the view that the Christian Church has a way of managing its institutional life which is sociologically utterly distinct, in the sense of being constructed solely from its own, spiritual resources. In all voluntary associations united to achieve common goals there takes place the distribution of powers such that one may distinguish higher participants from lower participants. In such voluntary organisations the source of the power is not force or physical constraint but whatever can be mobilised to sustain agreement. The Christian Churches, of course, have not always been voluntary organisations. There have taken place the forcible conversion and baptism of whole populations. Heretics have been physically persecuted and orthodoxy protected by censorship and far-from-idle threats. Of all these methods there has been criticism virtually since they were deployed, precisely because they undermine something precious to Christian faith, namely the sincere intention of the person to love God for himself. Insofar as the word 'power' has the connotation of 'force', or 'violence', it is appropriate for Christians to renounce it.

But is 'power' to be taken as the equivalent of 'force'? Modern sociology, which is fascinated by the complexity of the idea of power, has no one answer to that question. Writers on power are obliged to define in what sense they are using the term; and one of the difficulties of such definitions is that they fail to do justice to more than a part of the problem of power, as it is known in the ordinary speech conventions of modern societies. Furthermore, one of the suspicions with which one rises from the study of modern sociological literature is that religious people use the word 'authority' precisely because of its less negative connotations. It functions, in other words, to conceal behind bland vocabulary resources which in other contexts would be recognised as power.

The issue, like the literature, is vast, and all one can do here is to indicate the linguistic decisions which have been taken. The word 'power' I take to be a term of very broad meaning covering a spectrum of forms which generally are given other, more precise denominations.[21] Power in this sense includes violence, coercion, and force on the one hand, but also domination, manipulation, persuasion, and influence on the other. Power is a term indicative of resources available to human beings, the main types of which are economic, military, legal and ideological. It makes perfectly good sense, therefore, to speak of 'the power of ideas'.

On this account, therefore, authority in a religion is that form of power specifically appropriate to ideological power in a voluntary institution. When we speak of the 'authority of the priest', for example, this is to refer to a complex of powers needing further analysis. In part the authority consists in that person's intrinsic qualities (some of which, like humility, will be in part distinctive of Christianity, others of which will be attributes appropriate to any public leader); hence to 'speak with authority' will entail the recognition of those intrinsic qualities. But there are other aspects of the authority of the priest of greater ambiguity, for example the fact that the priest's legal status in a congregation may give him or her certain monopolistic rights in religious or even civil matters (such as marriages). Moreover the priest has, or may have, a number of sanctions at his or her disposal, such as the power of excommunication – or, in a more secular vein, the power of being in the position to spread information or disinformation about members of the congregation. If it is true that authority in a religion is a composite term in need of further analysis, the fact that such analysis may lead us into uncomfortable or embarrassing areas, where plainly secular power is an element of the picture, ought by no means deter us. Indeed, if the dialectical process we have depicted is actually to work, it is essential that our gaze does not waver at the point where we may be in danger of confusing the imperatives and power of the Gospel with alien, but convenient, supports. We do not escape from the realm of human resources by speaking of authority in the Church. There is much to be said for the use of the term 'power' in that it compels us to confront the probability that it will be abused.

Bishops and those who occupy positions of leadership and pastoral oversight in the Church have, then, powers of various kinds. Why should this have come to pass? Weber's explanation was that all religions, including Christianity, which start with charismatic leaders, have to go through a process of regularising leadership, so as to solve at least two problems: the preservation of the goals of the movement by focusing activity and the necessity of making financial provision for ensuring the movement's continuance. He listed a series of possible solutions of the problem of leadership after the original leaders' disappearance from the scene. Two of these feature in the New Testament, the choice by the charismatic leader of his successors and the election of new leaders with the agreement of the community.

In view of the prominence in modern New Testament scholarship of the thesis about so-called early Catholicism, it is important to stress that, in Weber's view at least, St Paul was already wrestling with problems which are recognisably those of routinisation. Paul himself should be regarded as 'charismatic' on Weber's definition and the leadership of the Pauline churches no doubt posed severe problems of routinisation.[22] But the Corinthian correspondence needs analysis in terms of routinisation and institutionalisation if we are to understand the nature of Paul's appeal to his commissioning by Christ himself, as well as the doubts which many apparently felt about its authenticity. Financial problems about his own maintenance are also clearly visible.

Routinisation, however, has other avenues, one of which is the development of ritual. Victor Turner has described with considerable insight the process whereby the life of a charismatic leader becomes the matter of a ritual process, and discipleship of the now long departed leader is preserved in the narration of a sacred text embodying and celebrating his significance.[23] This, we should note, is why the phenomenon of Christian baptism and the social reality of the Church are conterminous and why their theologies define each other. In particular, baptism constitutes a ritual which, on Turner's account, first separates the baptisand from his or her normal place in the structures of society, thrusts the baptisand out into a realm (which Turner calls the 'liminal' or 'threshold situation') characterised by the absence or negation of structure, finally to reaggregate the baptisand into society again, but changed and elevated by the ritual process. For Turner the threshold is a state of what he calls *communitas* or holy equality, characterised by the abolition or at least suspension of structural relationships. This is a greatly simplified account of Turner's highly sophisticated study of ritual processes which has already proved fruitful in more than one study of the Pauline practice and theology of baptism.[24]

I wish to comment on my own behalf on one paradoxical feature of the situation, namely the person and status of the baptiser. St Paul is vehement in his denial that the person of the baptiser is relevant to the identity of the Christian (1 Cor. 1:13ff). He does not even remember precisely whom he has baptised; the sole important matter was the Gospel faith underlying the baptism, a faith which should guarantee unanimity. The issue may, however, already have been that of baptismal pedigree from one or other leader, Apollos or Cephas. The baptiser appears to hold a privileged position in relation to the ritual by making the process happen. But at the same time, according to the liminal understanding of the ritual, all participants, the baptiser included, belong to one holy equality. Baptism, in other words, has the paradoxical capacity simultaneously to exalt the power of the baptiser and to undermine it.

This paradox deserves further exploration. The ritual affirms that there exists a world of human relationships other than the structured relationship of human societies, which erect and perpetuate divisions and hierarchies between different groups of people. This alternative world is, in Christian theology, a new humanity remade in Christ, claiming the whole world for the redeemed order. The community of the redeemed, therefore, has to manifest the new order of things. It is to stand for the reality which will be, to manifest the new being of the kingdom. But it is never possible totally to create an 'alternative culture'. The process of the subversion of existing societal structures is extraordinarily complex.[25] If the subversive intentions of the Christian community are to be realised, Christians themselves have to be mobilised to achieve this goal. But such acts of mobilisation impose their own organisational costs. Structures have to be created in order to focus Christianity's opposition to its competitors. Hence the paradox of the position of the baptiser, who at once is recognised as an authorised representative of the community but whose actions subvert the very structure which locates his or her role.

The importance of developing ideas concerning leadership and pastoral oversight in the Church in relation to baptism becomes at once apparent. The doctrine that baptism bestows upon the baptised the fullness of the gift of the Holy Spirit is the essential precondition for understanding the relationship of the ordained to the non-ordained. The roles in the Christian community of ordained and non-ordained may differ according to the stucture of an order necessary to the mission of the Church. But if we are to understand the provisionality of the structure within human societies, its openness to abuse, and the necessity for care in its justification, we shall have to take firm hold upon the doctrine of the Holy Spirit.

We shall not be surprised to discover that the same Spirit which is given to each and every Christian as a unique gift for the common good, is the very basis on which specific individuals claim either superior status in a hierarchy, or the superior rights of a spiritual élite. But the Spirit of God is the Spirit of love and the holy equality in virtue of which Christians are taught the difficult lesson of counting others better than themselves (Phil. 2:3). In the light of such a doctrine it becomes, or should become, institutionally impossible to identify the Spirit's guidance of the Church with the decisions of a hierarchy or élite.

A Comment on Authoritarian Liberalism

With this last consideration the essay begins to take on the tone of a standard piece of theological liberalism. Academic liberals in Western institutions of higher education have not, however, invariably perceived the self-interested character of attacks upon the standing of hierarchs and bureaucrats. They have failed to observe that by any appropriate criteria they too belong to the higher participants in church govern-ment, by means of the monopoly which they have established upon entry to the position of pastoral leadership in the Church. It is extra-ordinarily difficult to persuade scholars in the Church that their learn-ing and articulateness are resources which need as careful scrutiny as the more overt powers of hierarchs. But if it be the case that, despite

Kierkegaard's caustic observation of the failure of the New Testament to refer to professors of theology, intellectual skills are also gifts of the one Spirit, then the problem of how to count others better than themselves needs careful consideration by the Churches' scholars.

The authoritarian liberal is an increasingly familiar phenomenon in the modern Church. Liberals generally believe in increasing the participation in decision making to those who are to be affected by the decisions and are antagonistic to élites and cabals. Authoritarian liberals become exceptionally keen on such participation when *de facto* they control the processes whereby relevant information is minted and disseminated. Power is exercised not just by the arguments of the articulate, but also by their control of the agenda and their capacity to create a climate in which beliefs and desires are modified without overt attention being drawn to the process. Authoritarian liberals are generally experts at concealing the fact that they are as ready as any totalitarian of the past to manipulate the internal communications of the Church to ensure that the multitudes decide in favour of what they want to have confirmed.

Liberals also profess the principles of wide toleration of opinion, but are caught at the difficulty of tolerating opinions whose implementation would destroy the conditions of toleration for which they stand. The inevitable discovery of the limits of toleration persuades them of the need for vigilance, a vigilance which soon becomes the pretext for the return of authoritarianism, suitably disguised. Authoritarian liberals are expert at manipulation; they become spokespersons for selected minorities whose campaigns entail the promulgation of their own beliefs. In this way intellectual resistance to their systems of belief can be represented as the persecution of a minority, and thus intolerable, opinion. A whole series of campaigns on behalf of the genuinely persecuted or disadvantaged, whether Jews, blacks, women, homosexuals, or the mentally handicapped, have been harnessed to more or less naked expressions of the will-to-power among Christian liberals in higher education who have developed, in the process, fearsomely authoritarian traits.

But in the dialectic which I have depicted in this essay there is no guarantee that what are thought to be liberal institutional arrangements are more true and faithful resolutions of the problem of *episcopé* and power in the Church. It has to be realised that institutionalisation itself imposes costs upon the Church. A failure to appreciate this truth is responsible for the readiness of modern democrats to be suspicious enough of what are said to be – with all too little justification – representative assemblies. Liberalism itself can harden into a devious form of authoritarianism and will need to be subverted from within. The dialectic is not to be prematurely halted. The duty of a theologian is not to determine how the problem of the routinisation of charisma may finally be resolved, but to identify abuses; and that, I submit, is the sense of the passage from the *Confessio Augustana* with which we began.

NOTES

1. In G. W. Forell and J. F. McCue (eds.), *Confessing One Faith* (Minneapolis, 1982), p. 149.
2. Michael Seils, *Lutheran Convergence?* Lutheran World Federation Report 25 (Geneva, 1988), esp. chs. 5 and 7.
3. *Of the Laws of Ecclesiastical Polity,* Book I, xxv, 2.
4. *A Rational Account of the Grounds of Protestant Religion* (1664; new edition, Oxford, 1844), ii, pp. 277–80.
5. *The Truth Shall Make You Free: The Lambeth Conference 1988* (London, 1988); Resolution 18, 2a, p. 216.
6. See Wayne Meeks, *The First Urban Christians* (New Haven, Conn., 1983), p. 157; cf. pp. 112–13.
7. *The Truth Shall Make You Free,* para. 36, p. 90. The section on 'Christ and Culture,' pp. 87–92 is extensively based on the Inter-Anglican Theological and Doctrinal Commission's Report, *For the Sake of the Kingdom* (London, 1986), esp. chs. 6–10.
8. Compare *The Niagara Report,* The Report of the Anglican-Lutheran International Continuation Committee (London and Geneva, 1988), para. 46, p. 27.
9. Irenaeus, *Adversus Haereses* IV. 26. 3.
10. See Amitai Etzioni, *A Comparative Analysis of Complex Organizations* (New York, 1961), esp. 3–21.
11. See S. W. Sykes, 'Power in the Church of England', in James Provost and Knut Wolf (eds.), *Power in the Church (Concilium* 197) (Edinburgh, 1988), pp. 123–28.
12. Sik Hung Ng, *The Social Psychology of Power* (London, 1980), pp. 255–57.
13. 'Macht, power, puissance: prose démocratique ou poésie démoniaque', *European Journal of Sociology* 5, no. 1 (1964), 27. Article translated and reprinted in S. Lukes (ed.), *Power* (Oxford, 1986), pp. 253–77.
14. See for example the work of a Dutch Augustinian prior, Father Robert Adolfs, *The Grave of God: Has the Church a Future?* ed. and trans. D. N.

Smith (London, 1967), and its endorsement by D. M. MacKinnon in *The Stripping of the Altars* (London, 1969).

15. See M. Breidert, *Die kenotische Christologie des 19 Jahrhunderts* (Gütersloh, 1977).

16. Classically expressed in the eleventh century in a letter of Gregory VII: 'Every Christian king when he approaches his end asks the aid of a priest as a miserable suppliant that he may escape the prison of hell . . . To whom among them [kings or emperors] is given the power to bind and loose in Heaven and upon earth? From this it is apparent how greatly superior in power is the priestly dignity.' *The Correspondence of Pope Gregory VII*, trans. E. Emerton, Records of Civilization: Sources and Studies, 14 (New York, 1932), p. 171.

17. See S. Lukes, op. cit., p. 7.

18. The usual distinction which is introduced at this point in the discussion, that between ontological and functional understandings of the priesthood, is radically unclear. Often it is a disguised way of contrasting theological and sociological views of ordination, a contrast which, it must be said, has absolutely no fixed content. In the present passage both 'identity' and 'role' are conceived at once theologically *and* sociologically.

19. See, on the 'logic of overflow', D. W. Hardy and David F. Ford, *Jubilate: Theology in Praise* (London, 1984).

20. There is continuous discussion and refinement of Weber's original presentation, up to and including Anthony Gidden's 'theory of structuration'; see his *The Constitution of Society* (Cambridge, 1984), ch. 2.

21. See D. H. Wrong, *Power: Its Forms, Bases and Uses* (Oxford, 1979).

22. See Bengt Holmberg, *Paul and Power: The Structure of Authority in the Primitive Church as Reflected in the Pauline Epistles* (Philadelphia, 1980); and Reinhard Bendix, 'Umbildung des persönlichen Charismas. Eine Anwendung von Max Webers Charismabegriff auf das Frühchristentum', in W. Schluchter, (ed.), *Max Webers Sicht des antiken Christentums* (Frankfurt, 1985), pp. 404–42.

23. See esp. Turner, *Dramas, Fields and Metaphors: Symbolic Action in Human Society* (Ithaca, NY, 1974).

24. See esp. Meeks, op. cit. , ch. 5.

25. See, on the complexity of the process whereby the thrust against legitimation builds up harder legitimation, David Martin's sociological study of Christian theory and practice, *The Breaking of the Image* (London, 1980), ch. 10.

PART III

ANGLICAN DIRECTIONS

11

AN ANGLICAN THEOLOGY
OF EVANGELISM

'God loved the world so much that he gave his only Son' (John 3:16).
With that gift came the possibility of believing in the Son, in such a
life-transforming way that the author of John spoke of it – doubtless
from experience – as new birth, claiming that belief was a whole-
person inhabiting of the truth, amounting to the occupation of a
standpoint on absolutely everything, for which the only analogies are
adoption, in-grafting and marriage.

It is no easy process. The world – the resisting heart of unbelief – can
become the object of an exclusive and rival love. Is it then an accident
that God is said to love 'the world'? Or is this remarkable author
recognising the ambivalence of the world: it is loved by God, yet is a
threat to the children of God? On God's side there is an undeviating
and fundamental benevolence towards the human environment and
human kind; but that same world is not coerced by God's love and may
reject it.

The construal of the context for proclamation of the Gospel is a
primary task of the Church and, in the first instance, a theological one.
Our struggle is not against human foes but against authorities and
potentates; yet is it an accident that God in Romans 13 is said to have
created all existing authorities? Are not the very powers over which
Christ triumphs on the cross, made and beloved of God himself?

As we address the Church of England's response to and participation
in this Decade of Evangelism, elements of this Johannine realism begin
to speak powerfully to our situation. Realism and honesty compel
us to admit that despite an honoured tradition of Evangelicalism, we

*This essay appeared in two forms, one an introduction to a collection of essays
by John Booty and one in *Theology*. The present text draws on both.

201

have not been the most evangelically-minded of Churches, as has often been admitted. But I believe this present decade is an opportunity for us corporately to study and acknowledge the strengths and weaknesses of our own tradition with a view to deepening our grasp upon evangelism, and to do so without anxiety or over-cautious definition. We *know* that we are not going to launch ourselves into the deplorable antics of the Elmer Gantrys of this world; what we do not yet know is whether we have the courage and the resolve to rise to the real opportunities of the decade. In this process John Booty's rare combination of historical scholarship and active interpretative commitment is a vital resource.

I am struck by the way in which the dilemma of Churches with 'fine ecclesiastical pedigrees' has been formulated by Professor William Abraham in his impressively balanced work, *The Logic of Evangelism*. He notes with penetration their embarrassment with evangelism; how they lose interest in it in a welter of other activities; how they forget the fact that, and the ways in which, evangelism used to be carried out in their tradition; and how they develop a distaste for it and ridicule those who press for its rightful place. But the consequences are finally disastrous:

> Again and again evangelism has been driven to an underground group or even movement or ecclesiastical body. When this happens it is a tragedy for all concerned. The Church is no longer apostolic, for it has ceased to repeat the works of the apostles. Those driven underground or driven out are cut off from the full life and faith and they invariably end up reinventing the wheels of ancient ecclesiology or falling into superficial conceptions of faith or into outright nonsense or heresy. In the meantime the world fails to be encountered by the full signs of the coming Kingdom of God.[1]

But from what fundamental motive might Anglicans see evangelism as springing? For the cover of our symposium, *The Study of Anglicanism*, John Booty and I chose Marc Chagall's marvellous window in Chichester Cathedral illustrative of the text, 'Let everything that hath breath, praise the Lord.' In aspiration at least may not Anglicans think of themselves as a people of praise? 'Let all the world in every corner sing, my God and King,' wrote George Herbert, nurtured on the piety of the 1552 *Book of Common Prayer*.

Thou that hast giv'n so much to me
Give one thing more, a grateful heart . . .

Not thankful, when it pleaseth me;
As if thy blessings had spare days:
But such a heart, whose pulse may be
    Thy praise.

                          ('Gratefulness')

Would it not be consistent with the Anglican tradition to see our churches as offering on behalf of a specific part of the world which God loves the praise which it has largely forgotten how to express? In this surrogate role the Church would act on behalf of a whole population in much the same way as Herbert thought humanity should speak on behalf of the physical and animal creation, as the 'Secretary' of God's praise. Not that Herbert had any illusions about the zeal of the Church of his own day. Carelessness in God's service was something Herbert well understood. In 'Misery' he seriously considers resigning the task of praising God to the angels, so hopeless is humanity:

Lord, let the angels praise thy name.
Man is a foolish thing, a foolish thing,
    Folly and Sin play all his game.
His house still burns, and yet he still doth sing,
    Man is but grass
  He knows it, fill the glass. . . .

As dirty hands foul all they touch,
And those things most, which are most pure and fine:
    So our clay hearts, ev'n when we crouch
To sing thy praises, make them less divine.
    Yet either this,
Or none, thy portion is.

The alternative, 'Yet either this, or none, thy portion is,' still confronts our churches in the decade. I am deeply impressed with the way in which John Booty's work invites us to explore this theme. God's love for the world eliciting our praise is the fundamental motive for evangelism arising out of our tradition. It could not be claimed that this is in any way distinctive of Anglicanism as compared with other Christian traditions; that would simply be untrue. The case is, rather, that it is *consistent* with our tradition and thus with the way in which our Church has nurtured all its members over the years, in whatever part of that tradition they have been raised.

The varieties of contemporary English Anglicanism confront English bishops in all their dioceses, and to some extent the same is true in other parts of the Anglican Communion. It is all the more important, therefore, to argue, as John Booty does, from the accumulated stock of memories forming the natural language of Anglicans. We should want there to be family resemblance between the varieties of Anglicanism; we should want Anglicans to engage in mutual recognition of each other, and not to define themselves with the partisan exclusiveness that comes so easily in urban cultures. Many of our differences have roots in the past; all the more significant, therefore, is John Booty's method of considering our inheritance of faith in love and loyalty, as a way of bringing the Gospel of Christ to this generation, and of strengthening the bonds which hold us together.

It is apparent, then, when we consider the 1662 Prayer Book's services of Baptism, Eucharist, or Daily Office that the Church is being shaped and nourished as a people of praise. Gratitude for God's 'goodness and lovingkindness to us and to all' (General Thanksgiving) is the atmosphere in which our tradition has schooled Anglicans for over three centuries. None the less, it is no part of my argument to suggest that our liturgies already contain all that we need for the 'Decade of Evangelism'. My point is rather that we may engage in evangelism, and please God not just for a decade, on the basis of deeply-laid common traditions and instincts, without strain, pretence, or flimsy theological novelties.

But we have an obvious problem, and it is brought to us by the 1662 Prayer Book itself, which provided not just for a baptism of infants, but for baptisms of such as are of riper years, made necessary 'through the licentiousness of the late times crept in among us,' and 'useful for the baptising of natives in our plantations, and others converted to the faith' (preface to the 1662 *Book of Common Prayer*). The problem is that most of the rest of that Prayer Book treated baptism in infancy as the normative mode of entry into the Christian life. Baptism implied regeneration, and thereafter the problem was spiritual obtuseness. Thus, almost the entire energy of the ministry envisaged by the Prayer Book was poured into the pastoral problem of enabling the baptised people of God to understand and be moved by the wonder of God's graciousness, his 'manifold and great mercies'. 'See,' says the bishop to those about to be ordained priests,

> that you never cease your labour, your care and diligence, until you have done all that lieth in you, according to your bounden duty, to bring all such as are or shall be committed to your charge, unto that agreement in the faith and knowledge of God, and to that ripeness and perfectness of age in Christ.

Growing up into Christ (as described in the Ordinal's Epistle from Ephesians 4) is the goal of Prayer Book spirituality.

The basis of this spirituality is, I believe, Augustinian, and it shines through numerous collects which address themselves to the desires of the believer – 'pour unto our hearts such love toward thee,' 'graft in our hearts the love of thy name,' 'make us love that which thou dost commend,' 'nourish us in all goodness.' The 1662 Prayer Book confronted a people of very mixed spiritual capacity and insight, and invited and coaxed them to risk more of themselves in their response to the love and grace and mercy of God; it did so in much the same way as did St Augustine with the obtuse, recalcitrant, and half-converted congregations addressed in his sermons. What the 1662 Prayer Book envisaged may, in a certain way, be called 'slow conversion'. As a result it created a pattern of Christian life structured by the rhythm which John Booty identifies as that of contrition and praise, supported by a primarily pastoral ministry whose task it is to promote genuine contrition for sin and reconciliation, and then to lead the praise of the community. The same is true of all subsequent Anglican Prayer Books up to and including the Episcopal Church's *Book of Common Prayer* (1979) and the Church of England's *Alternative Service Book* (1980).

The evangelistic problem may be put very simply. It is that in many contexts not enough parents bring their children to baptism; and that many who do so do not then commit themselves to nourishment in the Church; and that the world has devised many powerful ways of pulling even those children who have persisted for some years into an alternative love. So we are confronted by the primary need for adult conversions, which is not what our Prayer Books have in mind.

But we are not helpless in this situation. Our attitudes to the tasks of evangelism neither need nor should entail policies or practices strange to – or remote from – the mind schooled upon our Prayer Books. There are, however, certain important provisos. The first proviso is that a praising community *is* an agent of evangelism. We shall have to set aside the intimidating thought that we are only ready for evangelism after we have taken this or that course of instruction. Lay education in the faith and increasing people's ability to be confident about the articulation of the faith is a continuous task of the Church, and it is *one* of the ways of being equipped for evangelism. But another is getting an existing Church to understand that praising God with heart and voice is also an essential aspect of evangelism.

Part of the challenge of the decade, I believe, is the empowering of the people of God in the congregations *as they are*, by setting before them something achievable related to the overall goals of the Church. So many of the connotations of the word 'evangelism' conjure up the unachievable and the inconceivable; they postpone tasks until after elaborate preparations have been undertaken; or they entail visits from exotic speakers who will not be present when the ordinary decisions of the congregation are being taken; or they involve fantasies about the impact of the existing worship of the Church upon new converts who have been through the spiritual equivalent of a trip to Mars. But to get a congregation to examine all that it is and does as a people of praise, and then to see that from the standpoint of a non-attender is both salutory and realistic and may lead to the setting of achievable goals. In such a way a community may itself become the major agent of evangelism.

The second proviso has to do with construing the context in which we try to proclaim the Gospel. We have to unmask the patent facts which confront us in the revolutions of our time, in sexual mores, entertainment, transport, and communications. The contraceptive pill, the car, the television set, and the computer are facts about a world which is deeply ambivalent. God loves this world, but there is a way in which it lures people away from the truth, and, as ever, wealth is there to harden the heart and deaden the perceptions. The people of God need to know the world in which they are living at some depth because it is inside our heads, not external to us; if we do not understand it, we shall become the unwitting agents of our own oppression.

I should like to underscore the importance of this. One of the legacies of some evangelical practice of the nineteenth and twentieth centuries is in the assumption that it is carried out by those who have made a firm distinction between the saved and the lost, to enable the former to target the latter. This is a deeply objectionable procedure and contradicts the standpoint I have developed in a number of ways. On the model of slow conversion those reared in our tradition will have come to understand that the world impinges mightily upon them too, and that God has some difficulty correcting them. As a people of contrition and praise, they will have come to experience a peace and joy which the world cannot give, and will want to share it with others.

Furthermore, if they have studied their Scriptures, they will realise that God alone knows the number of the saved, and denies to human beings the presumption of judgement. One of the advantages of the form in which the doctrine of predestination is treated in the Thirty-nine Articles (Art. XVII) is that God's counsel in the matter of salvation is 'secret to us'. The article does not teach a *particular* predestination of named individuals; there is simply the decree to save 'those chosen in Christ'.[2] The people of God are carriers of a blessing intended for the whole world. They will want to share this blessing with others from the motive of gratitude, not out of anxiety or a desire to dominate. A royal priesthood, a chosen race, a dedicated nation, God's own people, 'to proclaim the glorious deeds of him who called [them] out of darkness into his marvellous light' (1 Pet. 2:9) *is* an agent of evangelism.

It hardly needs to be mentioned, so obviously is it consistent with this formulation, that such a people praises God not only with its lips but in its life. As John Booty makes clear, the penitential practice envisaged in the Prayer Book involved forgiveness, social reconciliation, and restitution as a precondition of the partaking of Holy Communion. The object of prayer and aspiration for the state was that a whole people might be (simultaneously) preserved in wealth, peace, and godliness. The implications for education of the poor and for social reform are rightly indicated in John Booty's text. Yet, as we know, a self-congratulatory stance on the score of our social witness over the centuries is spectacularly inappropriate; and, thank God, we have not found it impossible from time to time to be penitent about our corporate failures as a Church. The point is a modest one, namely that Anglicans have always had a whole-life view of the tasks of a Church in its social context, and that the tradition does not require us to see any kind of competitive stress between evangelism and social witness. We do not need, even, to follow the WCC Bangkok Conference of 1973 in speaking of 'holistic evangelism'. It is the same motive, namely the praise of God, which compels, or should compel, the people of God into evangelism and into the confrontation of social disorder and oppression.

This is the necessary accompaniment of evangelism if the praises of the people of God are not to become an expression of the cheaply purchased satisfaction of the comfortable. As Professor Walter Brueggemann has reminded us in *Israel's Praise* (Philadelphia, 1988), praise disconnected from real liberation is in danger of degenerating into legitimation of a dominant terrestrial order. Psalm 102 states clearly the connection between liberation and praise:

> This shall be written for those that
>   come after: and the people which shall
>   be born shall praise the Lord.
> For he hath looked down from his sanctuary:
>   out of heaven did the Lord behold the earth;
> That he might hear the mournings of such
>   as are in captivity: and deliver the
>   children appointed unto death;
> That they may declare the Name of the
>   Lord in Sion: and his worship at Jerusalem.
>   (Ps. 102:18–21; *BCP* 1662 Psalter)

What, then, finally, *is* evangelism? At the end of Luke 4, Jesus is said to have retired to a remote spot after an exhausting day's preaching and healing. The crowds found him and begged him not to leave them.

But he said, 'I must give the good news of the Kingdom of God to the other towns also, for that is what I was sent to do.' (Luke 4:43)

On the basis of the Greek verbs, *euaggellizomai* and *apostellō*, we should not be very far wrong to précis that verse with the words, 'I must engage in evangelism, for that is my apostolic mission.' But the noun form, 'evangelism', is a little misleading, and not merely because it comes trailing clouds of unattractive or frankly disreputable modern history. It may confuse us into assuming that evangelism is one activity. If we were to use the word 'evangelising' we might be less misled. There are, in fact, no rational grounds for supposing that evangelism or evangelising amounts to a single task or enterprise. Professor Abraham puts the point well:

> Evangelism is necessarily a polymorphous activity. It is more like farming or educating than like raising one's arm or blowing a kiss. It is done in, with, and through a host of other activities that are intimately related to the specific circumstances in which the evangelist is working.[3]

What makes all these activities evangelism is, he argues, that they are governed by the goal of initiating people into the Kingdom of God. Evangelism has, on his analysis, a variety of dimensions, corporate, cognitive, moral, experiential, operational, and disciplinary. So it will necessarily involve a very large number of discrete tasks (which justifies the simile of farming), held together by what he calls the logic of the Kingdom of God, God's own activity within human history.

I endorse this standpoint. The people of God, who find themselves in our churches Sunday by Sunday, hear, if we are faithful to the good news, that before the foundation of the world they were chosen in Christ to be God's own adopted people, to be full of love, to be forgiven through the sacrificial death of Christ, and to have wisdom and insight lavished upon them, so that God's glory might be praised in the Church (Eph. 1). Evangelising is simply the consequence of wanting as many as possible to share as fully and as explicitly as possible in that belief and in all its consequences. We know that this is good news for the whole world, and that it entails a whole-person-inhabiting of the truth. We are not in the least surprised or discouraged by the fact that the 'world' which God loves is capable of deciding that other things are more interesting; and that this world is not simply external to us, but internal, undermining our own commitment, distracting our singleness of vision, and sowing discouragement. But a people of praise, schooled in the disciplines of penitence and constantly reminded of the great and tender mercy of God, is moved by God's love to lift up its heart, a heart whose very pulse is the praise of God. And if praise is the pulse of our heart, then members of the Anglican family of Churches, as they now are, are no more than a heartbeat away from every-member participation in the 'Decade of Evangelism'.

NOTES

1. William Abraham, *The Logic of Evangelism* (London, 1989) p. 179f.
2. O. O'Donovan, *On the Thirty-Nine Articles* (Paternoster, 1986); see p. 86 for a most valuable discussion.
3. Abraham, op. cit., p. 104.

12

THE GENIUS OF ANGLICANISM

I

The phrase 'the genius of Anglicanism' is scarcely imaginable upon the lips of John Keble (1792–1866), whom we honour in this essay, and not merely because, so far as we know, the term 'Anglicanism' is a neologism of the 1830s. Indeed Dr Rowell has offered me the opportunity of citing Newman's dictum that 'a man of genius cannot go about with his genius in his hand'.[1] We would perhaps be better employed examining the truth of Anglicanism's claims, or analysing its role and outlining its prospects.

Indeed we may suspect that the title presages the kind of enconium we associate with an obituary. In praising Caesar are we not a little engaged in burying him too? There is a moment in the life of institutions when their problematic character provokes a certain kind of anxiety, an attention which itself signals imminent demise. Yet I find that 'The Genius of the Church of England' was the title of two lectures given at the Archbishop of York's Clergy School in July 1945 by Bishop Rawlinson of Derby and Canon Charles Smyth of Cambridge, and published in 1947. Here are no last rites, but the continuation of a vigorous apologetic tradition begun in the sixteenth century by John Jewel; in this case adorned with twenty pages of footnotes by Charles Smyth on every conceivable subject, including the salvation of archdeacons and the role of professional football in preserving England's immunity to a proletarian revolution.

Perhaps the title is ironic. We are closer to the ironical with a passage from William James cited in G. F. S. Gray's admirable sketch of *The Anglican Communion*. Anglicanism, James wrote, is

So massive and all-pervasive, so authoritative and on the whole so decent, in spite of the iniquity and farcicality of the whole thing . . . Never were incompatibles so happily yoked together. Talk about the genius of Romanism. It is nothing to the genius of Anglicanism, for Catholicism still contains some haggard elements that ally it with the Palestinian desert, whereas Anglicanism remains obese and round and comfortable, and decent with this world's decencies, without one acute note in its whole life or history.[2]

Commentary of this kind on the 'yoking of incompatibles' has had an exceptionally long run. One loses count of the number of predictions of imminent collapse through internal incoherence, in the tradition of John Henry Newman's comment that Anglicanism was a paper, not a real, Church. Perhaps the following statement might also count as an example of the same basic genre:

> It would be more accurate to argue that the Anglican church, in the course of the long history of its reformations, incorporated into its basic documents an internal contradiction between Protestant and Catholic principles. There seems nothing to protect us from the conclusion that Anglicanism as it now exists is founded on an incoherent doctrine of the church; and that its attempts to resolve or conceal this gross internal antinomy has [sic] repeatedly led it into a series of chronic conflicts from which it barely escapes with any integrity.[3]

I fear that I cite myself. I thought this statement decently hidden in a group of essays published in Frankfurt, but it has returned in the altogether more exalted context of a Dominican study of Cardinal Ratzinger's theology,[4] and it will need a little glossing if its nuances are not going to be missed. The context is explicitly that of an *hypothesis* to the effect that Catholicism and Protestantism are mutually incompatible and antithetical ways of construing what it means to be the Catholic Church. That hypothesis I neither affirm nor deny. But in terms of that hypothesis Anglicanism, I argued, is bound to be seen as based on an internally incoherent doctrine of the Church. In this case the imperative driving Anglicans to interpret their Communion in a constructive doctrine of the Church should be all but overwhelming.

In fact nothing of the kind has yet occurred. There are two reasons for this. One is that Anglicans formulated in the course of their external and internal controversies the opinion that Anglicans have no distinctive doctrines; it follows, of course, that there can be no distinctive Anglican doctrine of the Church. Although this view is, I believe, manifestly and demonstrably incorrect,[5] its influence has effectively suppressed the theological enterprise which urgently needs to be developed.

The second reason for the failure to respond to the charge of incoherence is the absorption of so much time and effort, both leading up to and following the 1988 Lambeth Conference, in a largely fruitless effort to clarify the subject of authority in Anglicanism. It ought to have been obvious that it was impossible to arrive at theological or practical conclusions on authority *in* the Church without the help of a theology *of* the Church. But it has proved otherwise. And we have been painfully learning in the last decades, not least through ecumenical relationships, that we cannot borrow a doctrine of the Church from any other Communion of Christendom, and pass it off as Anglican with a few minor adjustments. The very refusal of Anglicanism to oblige its critics by withering or splintering to death may in due course drag us, however reluctantly, to the task of ecclesiological self-interpretation.

II

To this topic I shall return at the close of this chapter but in the first place it seems to me only proper to articulate the case against Anglicanism. Viewed, as it should be, not against the privileged backdrop of an English cathedral and university city, but from the standpoint of a bemused Italian or Greek or German, the plausibility structures collapse, and we are bound to ask how credible its claims are.

To focus, first, on the Church of England, the charges are so familiar as to require only a very brief exposition.

The numerical decline in baptised, confirmed and regular churchgoing members is very marked. It has reached the point where the Roman Catholic Church, which has far fewer baptised members, has now a larger number of Sunday-by-Sunday church attenders. This raises the question whether the Church of England has forfeited the right *de facto* to be regarded as the Church of the English people; whether its symbolic position in the person of the Sovereign, or the representation which it enjoys in Parliament, or the legislative role which Parliament occupies in its affairs any longer correspond to reality. Furthermore, it is asked whether the Church of England could ever survive as one denomination among many, shorn of the status and privileges which it so easily accepts, assumes, and then administers to non-Anglicans in culturally and socially condescending inclusion into the ranks of 'other Churches'.

The disputes which recurrently rack the counsels of the Church of England are not about minor details in the Christian faith, but concern its very heart and vitals. In 1947 Bishop Hensley Henson drew attention to two books by Anglican bishops, one by K. E. Kirk on *The Apostolic Ministry* (which he described as virtually Roman in 'type, temper and tendency') and the other by E. W. Barnes on the *Rise of Christianity* (which he designated 'not even, in any tolerable sense, Christian'); and he added, 'I do not think it possible that any Church can long cohere when such radical divergence on essentials is tolerated.'[6] Despite the fact that that was more than 40 years ago, it is not unreasonable to ask whether the situation today is not worse than before, whether the slow erosion of Christian belief and practice in England is not closely connected to the incoherence of a Church which disputes publicly about its essential or fundamental doctrines, and whether the removal of the cement provided by establishment would not precipitate the end of the Anglican experiment altogether.

The uncertainty and irresolution displayed by the decision-making organs of the Church of England on urgent modern problems, such as the possession of and threat to employ nuclear weapons, the eligibility of women for priestly and episcopal office, the status of the divorced in the marriage practice of the Church, and the attitude towards, and treatment of Christian homosexuals, are such as practically to disqualify it from the pretension to be a moral guide to the nation. The diverse and contradictory views of persons of weight and importance, and the vacillating and ambiguous pronouncements of its representatives, simply suggest that no one seriously expects the Church to teach on these matters, with authority. Instead it appears to be in constant retreat into long-winded complexity incapable of successful, popular communication. In this way it alienates the mass of the English populace, who have, in any case, long ceased to pay any attention. Has not the Church of England become a Church without a structure of authority capable of speaking with authority, and worse, a Church without vision, a Church which has ceased to believe that its corporate decisions could be guided by the Holy Spirit?

So much, so familiar; but there is more to say about the international Anglican Communion.

Precisely because of the past imperial association, international Anglicanism is now, it is said, in the throes of an identity crisis. No recent traveller to New Zealand, Australia, or Canada, for example, can fail to miss the element of sheer impatience with mother's apron strings which plays a distorting role in the quest for a genuinely local identity. Who, in the former Empire, wishes to be known as Anglican, once the meaning of the Latin phrase *ecclesia Anglicana* is explained? The Scottish and American Episcopal Churches, with their longer history of independence, know themselves under the non-imperial title 'Episcopalian', full of its own ambiguity. The sociologist, Dr Bill Pickering, has pertinently observed that 'many of the tensions in the contemporary Anglican communion seem analogous to those in the British Commonwealth.'[7] As the latter has lost its way, so has the former. There is no discernible agreement that the undeniably English (and Scottish) origins of the world-wide Communion have bestowed on it lasting spiritual benefits. In particular those Prayer Books (the English and the Scottish) which previously provided much of the family ethos to the whole Church are now undergoing extensive revision on a purely local basis, each autonomous Province holding itself to be competent to revise its liturgy without reference to any other. The result is inevitably an apparently ever-increasing pluralism, without discernible restraint or boundaries.

Closely connected to the same complaint is the limited global membership of the Anglican Communion. As Dr Pickering points out, it is difficult to give precise and at the same time meaningful statistics about any large religious group. But it appears that, despite the fact that there are Anglican Churches in over 160 countries, one country, England, has more than half the total Anglican membership, and eight out of every ten baptised Anglicans in 1985 were white. This is a fact which can be concealed in international Anglican assemblies because they are rightly sensitive about the dominance of white members. But the demographic reality of Anglicanism, as compared with Catholicism or Orthodoxy, is comparatively parochial. Can such a Communion really have a global future, in a world Christianity which is increasingly orientated towards the southern hemisphere?

The much canvassed problem of authoritative decision-making procedures at international level must also be mentioned. In comparison to the Catholic Church's centralised government Anglicanism has no legislatively competent authorities above the level of a Province or group of Provinces. Thus decisions about even such important matters as the authorisation of prayer books, or the passing of Canons relating to the ministry, are legally made in local churches. The consultative status of the Lambeth Conference makes unified response to the ecumenical documents exceptionally difficult, not least when one of those documents acknowledges the importance for the Church of a universal primacy. If Anglicanism is serious in envisaging the time when the whole Church will acknowledge such primacy, how can it at the same time suppose that its own informal and slow processes have any future? There are, moreover, in addition to the now hundred-year-old tradition of ten-yearly conferences, two new and relatively untried organs, the Committee of Primates and the Anglican Consultative Council, whose uncertain status and competence cast further doubt on the clarity of the Anglican grasp of its own processes. These focus on the ambiguity attaching to the theology of the episcopate which has never received authoritative, or even classical Anglican treatment. Are the bishops of the Anglican Communion apostles of the Churches, confident enough to magnify their office and humble enough not to exalt their own persons, or are they 'men in purple shirts', to cite an English episcopal cynic?

III

These are serious charges, and I suppose that in 1977, when I wrote *The Integrity of Anglicanism*, I had little idea that I was stoking a debate which has seen, in the last decade, an astonishingly large number of contributions. What I wish now to do is to respond to the case against Anglicanism which I have sketched, by trying to evaluate where things now stand with the arguments I presented in that book.

The Integrity of Anglicanism was written in the year immediately following the publication of *Christian Believing* (1976), a Report by the Doctrine Commission of the Church of England, whose membership included most of my theological teachers. The inner story of that Commission's work has yet to be told, but I am informed that it brought one of its distinguished members nearly to the point of resignation. A whole generation of Anglican scholars, including the Regius Professors of Divinity at both Oxford and Cambridge, plainly found the greatest difficulty in coming to a common mind about the significance of the creeds for the beliefs of the modern Christians. They glossed over this problem by asserting that whatever conclusions they had personally reached in matters of belief, none the less they operated a common pattern or method of thinking. In *The Integrity of Anglicanism* I quoted, and took issue with, the following passage:

> The vital requirement for Christians today is not to force them-selves to specifically agreed conclusions but to operate within the pattern – that is, to use in whatever way or proportion integrity allows the resources which the Christian community makes available.

But what was this pattern supposed to be? And what use was it to speak of 'the resources which the Christian community makes available', when one of the central elements of the discussion was the elimination of the creeds from worship?

The question, as many commentators made clear, was whether there were any limits in the Church to what might variously be called 'free enquiry' or 'unbelief'. My response to that was to argue that the Church of England as a whole had definite convictions and plainly insisted on a high degree of conformity to them. The definite convictions are those which inform its liturgical texts, and its insistence on conformity embodied in the canonical declaration made by every ordained person that he or she 'will use only the forms of service which are authorized or allowed by Canon'.[8] The Church itself, I argued, *has* a standpoint and the writings of its theologians will be characterised by that standpoint to the degree in which they subject it to painstaking scrutiny and interpretation, including, of course, the honest and truth-ful facing of many objections to it. Thus it is an error to deny that Anglican theology exists or should exist. There ought especially to be an Anglican theology of the Church. There is at least the beginnings of an Anglican standpoint on the dispersal of authority and the sheer inevitability of conflict in Christianity. The problem for Anglicans, I asserted throughout, was not that it had no standpoint, but that it had taken no trouble to study, criticise and reformulate it. There was a culpable intellectual failure here, the unintended consequence of F. D. Maurice's theory of Anglican comprehensiveness; a situation which only the restoration and recultivation of systematic theology (which I was then, by chance, professing) would mend.

There is much in the book which I do not regret. But there is also a certain amount of parade and folly for which I will doubtless have to suffer. An American woman meeting me for the first time said, 'I thought you would be older and crosser than you are.' There is a silly passage where I take considerable pains to discuss many possible but implausible meanings of some sentences from another work, and then elaborately excuse myself of pedantry. I was justly rewarded when the author of the said text pointed out that I had misquoted it.

One crucial issue which ought to have led to a good discussion, but did not, was the question of how I defined liberalism. 'Liberalism' continues, I think unforgivably, to be a battle cry in the polarised debates of modern Christians, Anglicans among them. My argument in *The Integrity of Anglicanism* to the effect that liberalism is not a substantive position, that one cannot be just a liberal, that one must be a Liberal Catholic, Evangelical or believer of another positive stance, elicited a certain, but rather inconclusive discussion.[9] The implication of that view is, of course, that anyone who wants to know whether or not I am a liberal, will be told that the question is incapable of any clear answer. The sooner it is realised that polarisation into liberals and conservatives is one of the main consequences of living in a modern and secular society, the sooner we shall free ourselves to examine calmly and in the light of history the many complex issues with which the Churches are all faced.

IV

We must now launch upon the attempt to answer the questions and objections I have made to modern Anglicanism.

English Anglican condescension is simply intolerable. Much of it, of course, is quite unconscious, and if you are an Anglican and have no idea to what I am referring, then you will have to seek help from your non-Anglican friends. It is the effortless superiority of the *beati possidentes*, those who occupy the high ground of English culture – or who used to. We own the cathedrals and ancient parish churches of this land, produced those literary masterpieces the *Book of Common Prayer* and the Authorised Version, claim for ourselves the rights of a pedigree of unbroken succession back to the Apostles, and crown the Sovereign of the land. We also, of course, helped to destroy Ireland and then forgot about it; persecuted and imprisoned Catholics and Non-conformists whilst congratulating ourselves on our comprehensive middle way; and in our own day when our Government invited vast numbers of Afro-Anglicans from the Caribbean, we failed to make them welcome and to foster their contribution to the Church's life.

The justification for any confession, of course, is not the guilt which accompanies it, but the amendment of life to which it leads, or should lead. The root of the difficulty lies in the story we tell about our past; or even the story we assume without being conscious of any narrative at all. There is a great deal that should give us pause for thought in our history. In the interests of truth and of honesty we should take into account the fact that the victors in any conflict always tend to write a history justifying their successes, in which the losers are presented as deserving to, or being bound to, fail. As Adolf von Harnack once said, 'Church historians become church politicians whether they like it or not.'

Even the very concept of 'Anglicanism' itself has a history. It was invented in the nineteenth century, possibly as an English adaptation of the (French) '*Gallicanisme*', an anti-papal tendency within French Catholicism. We are not surprised to find John Henry Newman in his High Church Anglican days as one of the first users, if not its inventor. But 'Anglicanism' is a term with no fixed content and it can be, and has been, used in a more or less blatantly one-sided way in the course of its history.

In either case the antidote has to be the study of Anglicanism, warts and all. It is not infrequently the case that Anglicans overseas take this more seriously than do English Anglicans. But it is a mistake to think that if one is English one has no need to study this history. A Church which has not examined its past, with the best methods of analysis and interpretation open to it, is liable to misinterpret its present situation. We live from our memories as well as our hopes, and our accustomed way of telling our own story needs to be purged of vanity and illusion.

The history of Anglicanism will show us, I believe, how dependent we are on our fellow Christians, on the Catholic Church and tradition for so much in our spirituality, on Lutherans and Calvinists for vital elements of our theology, on Congregationalism for so much of our modern thinking about the laity, on Methodist impulses wherever evangelical revival has been effective – and these are but a selection of possible ways of seeing our interdependence. It is important, I believe, now that we are quite clear about the importance of Anglican-Roman Catholic relations, not to be tempted to ignore or marginalise the Protestant Free Churches. We belong to one another in a complex ecological system, and there is a role for a national Church which is generous-minded and not condescending, and which is open-hearted and not imperialistic.

Is it scandalous that there should be open dispute between Anglicans about the fundamentals of the faith? Theologians and lay people have differing investments in the answer to this question. The theologian is absolutely right to point out that at no stage since the Reformation, when the idea of the fundamentals came into popular use, has it been possible for Protestants to agree what the fundamentals of the faith actually consist in. On the other hand the plain lay person has every right to demand that the public proclamation of the Christian faith be such as to be accessible to the theologically inexpert. Inevitably, then, there are different ways of answering this apparently simple question.

In my view, it belongs inherently to Anglican practice that the Scriptures of the Old and New Testament should be publicly read to the whole Church in the native language of the hearers, as part of the Church's normal worship. It is not, however, part of Anglicanism that the whole Scriptures should be considered to be infallible. Classic Anglicans of the Reformation and later eras did so believe and teach, but in the era of biblical criticism it was discovered that none of the Anglican confessional norms insisted upon verbal inspiration. If there are fundamentals which it is scandalous to challenge, they are not fundamental merely because they are taught in Scripture. Many Anglicans concluded that though there were fundamentals, no one could give an exhaustive list of what they were. This is a position which I consider to be fully defensible today, both theologically and practically. Anglican practice is to read the Scriptures, so that the whole people of God may hear the Gospel for themselves. They hear the Scriptures read, wrapped about by anthems and psalms articulating the praise of God, and crowned by the Creed. In this way is delivered to the Church the setting, the theme, the plot and the resolution of the narrative of God's way with his creation, in highly assimilable form.

But it is also true that every aspect of that narrative, beginning with the very word 'God' itself, is open to question and has been questioned and discussed by theologians within the Church from the very beginning. I would go still further and assert that it is impossible seriously to study the Old Testament without becoming aware that it reflects and contains the fruits of a centuries-long dialogue embracing the entire story of God's way with creation and humankind. Even in its much briefer time span the New Testament itself portrays a variety of theologies and modes of Christian discipleship, and frankly reveals (and, of course, deplores) the bitter acrimony with which the disputes were conducted. It is, in my view, the bitterness and inattention of the disputants which is scandalous to modern Anglicanism, as elsewhere. The disputes themselves are normal, and occur in every Christian Church known to me.

We need have no hesitation, of course, in asserting that some matters in Christian faith and practice are much more important than others. We can also be quite confident in saying that there is a boundary between beliefs which are solidly part of the faith and those which are incompatible with it. It is a mistake to think that disputes about precisely where the boundary lies in relation to any given belief, or aspect of belief, threatens confidence in the existence of any boundaries whatsoever. From time to time it may be the duty of a bishop or bishops collectively, to draw such a boundary because something fundamental is at stake. But it would seem to me normal and appropriate in the Christian Church for such judgements, and the arguments on which they are based, to be subject to further thought and appraisal.

We move immediately to the issue of Anglicanism's alleged uncertainty and irresolution. It has become the easiest of journalistic clichés to accuse the leaders of the Anglican Communion of sitting on the fence, fudging issues and woolly thinking. It is worth distinguishing pusillanimous behaviour, which simply lacks the courage to face a difficulty or the honesty to admit that one exists, with a fully justified refusal to fall into a neatly-set journalistic trap. 'We know you're a plain, honest-to-goodness, no nonsense kind of a teacher,' they said to Jesus once. 'What about this tax, then; should we pay it or not?' And the meaning of Jesus' famous reply, 'Pay to Caesar what is due to Caesar, and to God what is due to God' – an archetypal sound-bite – has been disputed ever since he uttered it. The refusal to give neat, categorical instructions on each and every issue is by no means a necessary sign of religious decay.

But it would be foolish to deny that the processes of decision-making which Anglicans have adopted in this century are public, slow and seem to lack authority. The question of authority we shall tackle next, but it ought to be asked by what processes is a Church in a culture such as our own supposed to consider complex and controversial topics. There are those Anglicans who have too easily forgotten with what intensity and agony the issue of the control of conception by artificial means was discussed in the first half of the century. There are some Roman Catholics who have forgotten the heated rows about biblical criticism. In these matters it is important to preserve historical perspective. There is no doubt, for example, that biblical criticism was pioneered in Protestant Germany, and that it was Protestants who endured the fiercest battles about the mere possibility of formulating theories which today are discussed on every side with equanimity. Individual critics committed, of course, folly after folly, and there were those who argued that the method of so dangerous and uncertain an enterprise was rooted in unfaith. But in a real sense both critics and their opponents endured the fight on behalf of the whole Church, and the result is that, with the exception of the sternest fundamentalists, it is nowadays thought that the mission of the Christian Church is impeded by holding that Moses did not himself write the Pentateuch, nor John, the Beloved Disciple, the fourth gospel.

Churches in modern cultures overhear one another's rows, and learn from them. The issue for Anglicanism is the truth, not the image; whether there is good Christian cause to argue about nuclear weapons, divorce, homosexuality and the rule restricting the priesthood and episcopate to males. My suggestion is that we be much less apologetic about being slow and careful, and public too, than we are. It does not follow that if we are criticised or mocked for this, we are in the wrong; nor even that if, in the debate, foolishness is on display with consequent disdain, we are not fulfilling a role in God's plan for his whole Church.

This brings me to my final charge concerning authority. Is Anglicanism a Church without a vision, one which has ceased even to pretend to believe that its decisions are guided by God's Holy Spirit? Having written on this subject in the last years an indecent amount, two things are now absolutely clear to me. The first is that Anglicans cannot claim exemption from the sociological rule which determines that authoritative texts require authoritative interpreters. Even so-called non-hierarchical Churches can be shown, on scrutiny, to have persons whose interpretative activity constitutes a centre of authority.[10] The issue for Anglicans is not whether, but who; and it is quite clear from the Thirty-nine Articles and the Ordinal that the Church has this authority, and that it pertains particularly to the episcopate.

In modern Anglicanism there has taken place, through the involvement of clergy and laity in synodical government, a practical experiment in expressing authority in a process, rather than in the issuing of definitive decrees. It is this experiment which has led to the expression of serious reservations. None the less the question whether synodical government necessarily leads to incoherence and confusion is perhaps too frequently decided on the basis of unexamined political or managerial analogies. 'Where, in the Anglican system', it is asked, 'does the buck stop?' It is not asked often enough whether Christian faith is the same thing as a party's political programme, or a company's industrial strategy.

This leads me to my second observation, which is that the problem of authority for Anglicans is not so much in the external organs of authority, whether that be synods or bishops' meetings, but in the hearts and minds of members of the Church. Authority in a voluntary society does not issue simply from claims, but from general recognition. Even Churches which have regularly claimed to be authoritative sometimes discover, as Roman Catholics do on the issue of the artificial control of conception, that recognition of authority is withdrawn. Authority in Anglicanism could not be conjured by fiat from resolutions or declarations. It has for too long entailed a process which includes the laity in one way or another; and if its latest experiment with structures has defects, the fundamental theology of the matter is, I believe, both clear and defensible.

It is rooted in a defensible, indeed plainly biblical theology, that God's gifts are given to the whole people of God, and that the gift of leadership is only bestowed within that context. The disputable element enters when a decision is taken to embody that doctrine in a specific structure. What that precise structure should be, however, is less important than the need for the theology to have a realistic sociological expression.

And behind that requirement lies a theology which includes what, I dare to think is, or ought to be, an Anglican theology of the Church (and here I should pause to add that it is not Anglican for the sake of its own distinctiveness, but for the sake of allowing other Christians who are not Anglicans to come to some understanding of why Anglicans persist in believing that God has things to accomplish in and through this Communion of Churches).

It belongs to the heart of this theology that we maintain that God's action in his world involves an affirmation *both* of created sociality *and* of that which is new, surprising and unique. This is true, in differing ways and proportions, of the incarnate Christ and of his Church. If we apply this insight to the Church, we arrive at a way of thinking and speaking which Richard Hooker put memorably when he said that the Church was both a society and a society supernatural.[11] This is an important insight. For if the essence of the supposed division and incompatibility between Catholicism and Protestantism consists respectively in the affirmation and the denial that God commits himself to the instrumentality of persons and objects in the salvation of the world, then Anglicanism may well find itself in an uncomfortable position. Anglicans will see no reason to hesitate in saying that the Church itself, its ministry and its sacraments, are a divine gift to our world; but also no reason to doubt that this gift is embodied in sociologically ambivalent ways in time, history and culture. This is not a hybrid construct of the Church, as though it could be thought of as fifty per cent heavenly and fifty per cent earthly; but a way of seeing the Church as at one and the same time embedded in created sociality and the agent of God's new creation.

When Anglicans reflect upon the history of the Church of England and of the Anglican Communion instinctively they find many things to regret and repent of, and some things which are more encouraging. This both–and at the heart of their corporate sense reflects, I would judge, the ecclesiology I have been sketching. Its natural mode is to allow debate, disagreement, and conflict as a normal part of its life. It will provide a structure for the God-given gift of insight and leadership and for understanding and consent; and that structure will be appropriate to differing patterns of authority in different cultures at various times.

In doing so, we are bound to accept what my predecessor in the See of Ely called 'a consequential untidiness'

> . . . given that the action were done in the integrity of obedience to the Christ – and we would trust that God's grace would hold us through our own conflicts and the attendant anomalies.[12]

This is in itself an authentic twentieth-century version of Richard Hooker's 'harmonious dissimilitude of those ways, whereby his Church upon earth is guided from age to age, throughout all generations of men'.[13] This, together with, please God, the gift of patience, is the true condition of the Church. Whether or in what measure it be the genius of Anglicanism to embody that condition is for others to judge; it is perhaps enough that we should bear our testimony to it.

NOTES

1. Letter to Stanislas Flanagan, 15. ii. 1868, quoted in J. D. Holmes, *The Theological Papers of John Henry Newman on Biblical Inspiration and on Infallibility* (Oxford, 1979), p. 158.
2. G. F. S. Gray, *The Anglican Communion* (1958). The quotation from William James is cited without reference on p. 165.
3. S. W. Sykes, 'Anglicanism and Protestantism' in *England and Germany, Studies in Theological Diplomacy*, ed. S. W. Sykes, (Frankfurt, 1982), p. 127.
4. Aidan Nichols, *The Theology of Joseph Ratzinger* (Edinburgh, 1988), p. 166.
5. See S. W. Sykes, 'Anglicanism and the Anglican Doctrine of the Church' in *Anglican Theological Review*, Supplementary Series No. 10 (March 1988), and J. Robert Wright (ed.), *Quadrilateral at One Hundred* (*ATR*, 1988); reprinted here pp. 101–21.
6. F. E. Braley (ed.), *Letters of Herbert Hensley Henson* (London, 1951), p. 204.
7. S. W. Sykes and J. Booty (eds.), *The Study of Anglicanism* (London, 1988), p. 368.
8. Canon C 15.
9. See M. Darrol Bryant (ed.), *The Future of Anglican Theology* Toronto Studies in Theology, Vol. 17 (New York, 1984); see especially the essays of A. J. Reimer and F. G. Kreiger.
10. The classic study is that of P. M. Harrison, who investigated the American Baptist Convention, *Authority and Power in the Free Church Tradition* (Princetown, 1959).

11. *Of the Laws of Ecclesiastical Polity*, I, xv, 2.
12. P. K. Walker, *Rediscovering the Middle Way* (London, 1988), p. 109.
13. *Of the Laws of Ecclesiastical Polity*, III, xi, 8.

Index

Some names and subjects are not indexed, or are indexed very selectively, because they are pervasive throughout the book. These include, for example, Anglicanism (most occurrences), Church of England (most occurrences), Anglican Communion (most occurrences) and Cranmer's liturgical work (indexed by title and not under Cranmer). Book titles are indexed under author, not separately by title, and only when the reference is to the book itself rather than to its content. Notes are selectively indexed. Page references in italics indicate illustrative matter.